D0986910

Government Contracts

Proposalmanship and Winning Strategies

Herman Holtz

Government Marketing Consultant, Silver Spring, Maryland

The battle for government contracts between large and small companies is often a case of David versus Goliath. The industrial giant flexes its corporate muscles, intending to overawe its apparently outmatched opponent — only to watch in confusion as the smaller company is awarded the contract.

The key to the victory? Proposalmanship — that is, the ability to "sell" the government on a proposal, much like any good salesman approaching a customer. What counts is not the sheer size or economic power of a company, but the expertise of its representatives at a modern art form — persuasive proposal writing.

After years of experience with preparing proposals, and extensive contact with those who read them, the author of *Government Contracts* can identify and discuss with authority the three basic elements of good proposalmanship: a writing style that "keeps the reader turning pages"; a lucid and thorough presentation; and intelligent salesmanship that makes the proposal convincing. Mr. Holtz's book reviews the workings of the government contract market, and provides specific "how-to" information, including those decisive strategies once only available to experienced professionals. Tracing the development of a proposal from idea to final submission, *Government Contracts* serves as a handbook for all corporate personnel who are involved with the hectic yet economically essential arena of government contract seeking.

Government Contracts
Proposalmanship and Winning Strategies

Government Contracts
Proposalmanship and Winning Strategies

Herman Holtz

Government Marketing Consultant
Silver Spring, Maryland

PLENUM PRESS · NEW YORK AND LONDON

Library of Congress Cataloging in Publication Data

Holtz, Herman.
  Government contracts.

  Includes index.
  1. Public contracts – United States. 2. Proposal writing in the social
sciences. I. Title.
HD3860.H64   650′.1   78-26522
ISBN 0-306-40114-2

© 1979 Plenum Press, New York
A Division of Plenum Publishing Corporation
227 West 17th Street, New York, N.Y. 10011

All rights reserved

No part of this book may be reproduced, stored in a retrieval system, or transmitted,
in any form or by any means, electronic, mechanical, photocopying, microfilming,
recording, or otherwise, without written permission from the Publisher

Printed in the United States of America

HD
3860
H64

Foreword

He who knows and knows that he knows is wise; follow him.

—ANCIENT PROVERB

During a long career of public service as a government procurement and contracting official, I am still surprised to find big, successful corporations making the same mistakes that neophytes in government contracting make. And this is particularly true in the matter of writing proposals, which are the crucial element in most major procurement awards.

It's true enough, as many suspect, that the big, well-known company has something of an edge over the smaller, lesser-known company competing for any given government contract—psychologically, at least: The typical government executives, whether contracting officials or program managers, tend to have a bit more faith in the ability of the large company to carry out the program successfully. All things being equal, then, the big company is more likely to get the nod.

However, because the large companies are well aware of that, many tend to become "fat, dumb, and happy"—they try to coast or rest on their laurels. That is, they get careless about making a strong enough case for themselves in writing their proposals. And when they lose, often to smaller companies, they are both puzzled and outraged. They have forgotten that all government procurement is a *competition*—usually both technical and cost competition—and that the "little guy" *can* win against the "big guy," if he tries hard enough. And especially if the bigger guy is a bit careless and does not put out his best effort.

Today, I happen to be chief of the Government Contracts Division of the Office of Business Development, Small Business Administration,

453691

working with minority contractors entered into the 8(a) program. Since most of these organizations are relatively inexperienced in government contracting, it is perhaps not too surprising that in many procurements, as few as one out of 10 proposals submitted are fully responsive to the government's stated needs. But in earlier years, when I was buying major systems for the Department of Defense, I also found such problems. One major defense contractor in Connecticut, for example, was sorely puzzled and even outraged that we did not "read into" his proposal what we knew about him. It was only reluctantly that he accepted—was forced to accept—the fact that he was credited only with what he specifically said in his proposal, and not with anything we added mentally to his proposal, as we reviewed and evaluated it.

There is no doubt that proposal writing is the key to success in negotiated procurements, which constitute, probably, as much as 85% of all government buying. And there is no doubt, either, that proposal writing has been elevated to almost an art form, at least in the contracting community. The large aerospace and electronics firms who pursue and win the really large contracts usually employ full-time proposal-writing staffs who specialize in the art. Obviously, the small firms cannot afford this luxury, nor are they writing new proposals constantly, as are many of the large firms. Yet, many small firms survive and prosper, and even grow into large firms, eventually, as a direct result of success in proposing and winning government contracts with a high degree of consistency.

Such success is due partly to hard work, of course, to "trying harder," in recognition of being in the number two position. But it is due primarily to something else, equally fundamental to success: *knowing how.* Many of these successful small contracting organizations which spring up suddenly are "spin offs"—firms founded by former employees of the successful large companies, based on the knowledge acquired in the service of the large company.

Now, in this long overdue work, Herman Holtz makes it possible to achieve this proposal-writing success in another way—through *his* successful experience and knowledge acquired in the service of larger companies.

As a government contracting official, I welcome this book because I look for it to result eventually in better proposals crossing my desk, and every contracting officer looks for that. In general, it is the contracting official's duty and hope to buy the best possible results in the shortest time at the lowest price. That is what he looks for in a proposal competition, and what he hopes he has bought when he selects a winner and makes an award. That is what you must keep in mind when you write your proposal. The government is not really different from the commercial customer in that respect: everyone wants to get the best value possible.

But remember, too, that government officials are humans and prone to human frailties of judgment. Don't expect us to read between the lines of your proposal or to be able to guess at your meanings. *Tell us* not only what you are offering and how much it costs, but show us why your offer is superior, why it will be a better buy for us, why we should select you as the winner.

I hope that this book will help you do that, and I know that Herman Holtz has the same hope, for I know personally of his great enthusiasm for propagating what he likes to refer to as "proposalmanship."

JOSEPH J. ZIMECKI

Washington, D.C.

Preface

How important are proposals in winning government contracts? Some professionals in government marketing believe that proposals are little more than formalities, at least where major contracts are involved, while many others believe that they are important, but not the most important aspect of government marketing. But here is what government officials say:

The chief contracting officer of one agency told me that as many as 90% of the proposals received in many contest awards are immediately rejected on first reading, with only 10% being considered technically acceptable.

An official at the Department of Energy confided that he rejects many proposals after reading only the first page, convinced immediately that there is no point in reading further.

An executive of the Occupational Safety and Health Administration (OSHA) told me that he has withdrawn or canceled procurements several times because he did not think that any of the proposals he received were acceptable.

In general, at least one-third of the proposals received in the typical procurement are "nonresponsive" and are, accordingly, rejected swiftly. In fact, again and again executives of government agencies responsible for evaluating proposals and selecting winners have expressed their frustration with proposal writers who "just don't seem to understand the problem."

The plain fact is that it is all but impossible to win with a poor proposal, no matter how effectively other marketing activities have been carried out, especially if there are better proposals submitted. On the other hand, many contracts are won by those submitting superior proposals, *with no other marketing activity whatsoever.*

Simply to avoid *rejection,* a proposal must demonstrate true and complete understanding of "the problem" or requirement to which the proposal responds and "responsiveness" to all specifications of the solicitation, and it must be reasonably "professional" in appearance and impact—literate, communicative, all forms properly executed, etc. Unfortunately, many proposals do not meet even this simple minimum, much less qualify as "superior."

To put this another way, as a minimum, the proposal should keep the reader reading—every page, from page 1 on, should cause the reader to *want to read the next page.* Once the reader stops turning pages, the contest is over as far as *that* proposal is concerned.

Simply stated then, *proposalmanship* is the art of inducing the proposal reader to keep turning pages, to find the proposal completely responsive to the need, and to find the proposal *persuasive.* For in the last analysis, the proposal is a sales presentation, and *proposalmanship* is sales persuasion or, as I like to put it, the art of persuasive writing.

Still, that is an oversimplification too, because proposalmanship—the art of *winning*—is also more than writing and presentation skills, important though they are. It is also strategy, clear thinking, analysis, planning, innovation, imagination. You must not only sell your proposed product or service but create a salable product or service. The customer is sophisticated; he won't buy snake oil, no matter how enticing your package.

In the world of proposal development, we have the two extremes: the technical/professional specialist who believes that all he has to do to win is to offer his great thoughts and awesomely impressive background, properly salted with words found only in the unabridged Webster's—and possibly some not even to be found there, because he himself has created many formidable coinages to reflect his state-of-the-art intellect; and the skillful wordsmith, who apparently believes that the age of gullibility has not passed and that he can sell anything with good enough Madison Avenue technique.

There is one other character you'll meet: the marketing man who believes firmly that the proposal is a formality and that it is his handshaking, good fellowship, sleuthing, and three-martini lunches with the client that always win the job.

To prove it, he can point to many mediocre proposals that have won contracts. What he will not face is that those mediocre proposals won because they were the best of a bad lot in each case—because the competition didn't do any better and made serious errors. And when a dark-horse candidate enters the lists with a truly superior proposal, such characters cannot explain why they lost. They're sure someone had a "fix in."

Every rule has exceptions. Some contracts *are* handed out on silver platters to favored contractors without giving others an opportunity to bid. The General Accounting Office has conducted studies and has demonstrated that this is true. And they have complained to Congress about it. (The GAO reports to Congress, as its watchdog, and does not report to the president, either directly or indirectly.)

Congress is now considering legislation—has already passed some, in fact—that will curtail even these few abuses. The Office of Management and Budget (OMB) is at work developing a data system that will shine the light of day more clearly on all awards of grants and contracts. And the OMB is also busy developing a standardized set of procurement regulations and procedures that will further curtail abuses of the system.

Still, the number of contracts awarded in this manner is relatively small, and the system is, overall, fair and offers opportunity to all. There are enough contract opportunities for which everyone has an equal chance.

The author has proved to his own satisfaction and to that of many contemporaries that the proposal is the most important element in the process and that dark horses can win consistently, with superior proposals.

This will be even truer in the future than it is today, as the government procurement totals continue to climb. Today no one can tell you with any certainty exactly how much the government does spend for goods and services. Certainly the figure for contracts alone is in the vicinity of $100 billion. Add to that the sums spent for grants and revenue-sharing programs, and it approaches $200 billion. (An OMB official recently estimated it at $170 billion but apparently did not include all the revenue-sharing programs.)

Government contracting has therefore become big business—among the biggest in the country. And a large portion of those contracts must be won through the submission of proposals. Large corporations who realize all or nearly all their income from government sales often maintain entire proposal-writing departments—staffs who do nothing but write proposals every day.

Small companies cannot afford that luxury. Typically, the chief executive in the small company, or some other senior executive, assigns proposal-writing chores to whoever is handy, is not too busy at the moment, and seems reasonably well qualified in the subject-matter area.

This is what leads to disaster all too often: the assignee, unhappily, may be the best-qualified individual to plan and manage the project sought and the worst possible assignee to write the proposal or to lead the proposal-writing team.

These are the people to whom this book is especially addressed. They are the people who need help the most in translating their skills and abilities into successful presentations.

The two forefingers that laboriously typed the manuscript for this book were attached to my very own two hands. The reality of the book, however, resulted from the patience, encouragement, and hard work of many others.

I am particularly indebted to Frank Columbus, of Plenum Publishing Corporation, who believed in me enough to gamble on my work, and who showed me nothing but kindness throughout the generation process. I am grateful to Plenum's hardworking and meticulous editor, Harvey Graveline, for the superb job he did in working the miracle of transforming my sheaves of paper into a true manuscript. My hat is off, too, to my attorney and good friend, Max Goldberg, who knows my weaknesses and insists on being my friend in spite of them.

I am compelled especially to bow to my business partner, friend, and loving wife, Sherrie, who really made it happen with her affectionate nagging, and who was responsible in the first place for the book ever having been born at all.

HERMAN R. HOLTZ

Washington, D.C.

Contents

PART I   THE WORLD'S BIGGEST CUSTOMER

1.   150,000 Customers 3
2.   The Facts—and Unfacts—of Government Marketing 8
3.   The Jungle 13
4.   Search for Opportunity: Prospecting the Jungle 35
5.   Get Help from the Government to Sell to the Government 54
6.   The Mechanisms of Government Procurement 61
7.   How to Prepare and Submit Your Bid 69
8.   How the Government Evaluates Proposals 83

PART II   PROPOSALMANSHIP: THE GRADUATE STUDY

9.   Introduction to Proposalmanship 91
10.   Step 1 in Proposalmanship: Analysis and Understanding 101
11.   Other Intelligence-Gathering 116
12.   Technical/Program Strategies 124
13.   Other Strategic Areas 139
14.   Proposal-Writing Considerations 181
15.   Proposal Formats and Packaging 218
16.   Production and Packaging the Proposal 244
17.   The Special Case of Architects and Engineers 249

18. Negotiations 252
19. A Few Final Words and Some Useful Information 257

APPENDIX

Other Useful Publications 259
Addresses and Other Key Information 260
All about Federal Supply Schedules 264
A Few of the Departments, Agencies, and Bureaus
    Encountered in Pursuit of Contracts 273
A Typical Work Statement and Instruction (for a Small
    Contract) 277

Glossary 281

Index 283

Part I

THE WORLD'S BIGGEST CUSTOMER

1

150,000 Customers

How would you like to answer the government's mail, at about $20.00 per answer? Run a government-financed travel bureau? Round up wild horses out West? Book go-go dancers into service clubs? Write TV and radio "spots" for public service announcements?

If you read the newspapers, you've heard about huge government contracts for high-speed fighter airplanes, rockets to the moon, missile systems, aircraft carriers, dam construction, and other multimillion (and occasionally multibillion) dollar projects and programs. But there are thousands upon thousands of government contracts let for such items as the above, and a myriad of other, more mundane services and goods: guarding buildings, operating computers, typing, printing bumper stickers, setting type, repairing buildings. There is hardly a product or service that the U.S. government does not buy, much of it regularly and in great quantities.

The U.S. government is undoubtedly the biggest customer in the world. In fact, the U.S. Government is not *a* customer; it's more like about 150,000 customers in some 34,000 government offices and facilities throughout the United States and possessions, as well as in many foreign countries. (In fact, there are more federal employees in California than there are in Washington, D.C.!)

How Big Is the Annual "Buy" of the Government?

No one—either in or out of the U.S. government—knows exactly how much the swarming government agencies spend each year for contracted supplies and services. In the government's own estimates (the

3

Office of Management and Budget (OMB) is still trying to get a fix on government spending in this area) the figure is currently about $100 billion. That's for contracts exclusive of grants, which are at least that high and are often used for the same purposes as contracts.

The figure is undoubtedly a low one. Many of the government's purchases are not technically classed as contracts but still represent contracted-for supplies and services. Thousands of "small purchases" (up to $10,000 each) are made through purchase orders, and some are bought with "imprest funds," a kind of petty cash fund. Taking these into account, as well as other methods used by government agencies for purchasing supplies and services, it is safe to say that the government spends not less than $100 billion annually for such purposes, and the figure is probably closer to $150 billion.

The Brookings Institution, in one of its studies,[1] came up with a figure of $124.4 billion for 1975, citing as its source the U.S. Department of Commerce *Survey of Current Business* for "Purchases of goods and services."[2] This figure takes into account some grant monies, apparently (although obviously not all grants) and some other monies that would not be contract expenditures, such as social security payments and welfare payments. At the same time, it obviously does not take into account much other money spent for goods and services but not qualifying technically as contract funds. This was in a year when the total federal budget was approximately $326 billion. The following year, with a total budget of approximately $366 billion, outlays for "goods and services" were estimated at $130 billion. If the ratio holds (35%–38% of the total budget spent for "goods and services"), the fiscal 1978 "goods and services" expenditure was about $170 billion.

The estimated federal budget for the current fiscal year (1979) is estimated at approximately $487.5 billion. (Congress has not completed all budget actions at this time, so the final figure is not yet known.) With the prior years used as a general guide, government expenditures for "goods and services" would then run approximately $185 billion in fiscal 1979! This makes our estimate of $170 billion appear entirely conservative, of course.

In any case, no matter what the final figure—and it certainly is not less than $100 billion and is almost certainly $170 billion at the least—one

[1]David J. Ott and Attiat F. Ott, *Federal Budget Policy* (Washington, D.C.: The Brookings Institution, 1977).
[2]Vol. 56 (July 1976), p. 41.

thing is certain: government contracting today is *big* business. And it's a business in which *everyone* can share, from the smallest to the largest business entity.

(One irony in the situation is that while competition for many government contracts is intense, there are many cases where the government is unable to get enough bidders and issues special appeals for bids!)

Whom Does the Government Buy From?

The answer to "Whom does the government buy from?" should be "Anybody and everybody." That is, the government is willing to buy from almost anybody and everybody who can satisfy the need and who is willing to make the effort to do business with the government.

Certainly, you have to be a large corporation to design and build a fighter airplane, a spaceship, or a missile system. But you do not have to be a large corporation to write a manual, answer mail, rewire a small building, or sell a few tons of sugar to a government agency. In fact, the government does a great deal of business with small companies and even with individuals. I have been one of them. After many years of selling to the government—winning government contracts for jobs as large as $9 million and small as a few thousand, as the employee of several companies, large and small—I started my own small business as a government contractor, putting my government marketing experience to work. I found out quickly that the principles worked at all levels: those techniques I had employed in behalf of large companies worked for me as a free-lance writer, contracting with government agencies.

I didn't even have a business address initially but worked at home. However, my first contract, with the Postal Service, included a furnished office and secretarial services in the government's own facility! And several subsequent contracts also required working "on site" and included complete office facilities.

I won those first few contracts without formal, competitive bidding: I simply walked around calling on people in government offices, offering my services until I found people who were interested—and they were always people who had problems.

People, whether in government or in any other business/professional calling, always have problems. Sometimes they call them needs, wants, or requirements. What they call them doesn't matter. What does matter is that they have problems of one sort or another and that they are always looking for help. They don't really want to hear what *you* want; they are interested in hearing what you *offer* that will help them solve their problems.

Later, when we get into the subject of bidding the larger and more important contracts, you'll find that this principle still applies. But it is easier to understand it on the one-to-one basis of walking around and winning contracts "across the counter."

My first client, when I started to become an independent government contractor, was a gentleman who was second in command to the director of the Postal Service Training and Development Institute.

The institute had been training postal managers in a variety of management topics for several years and had performed many studies of the training results. Now it was time to pull all those study results together to see how they added up and to demonstrate the worthiness of the training. I proposed a method for doing this, offering to document the study by designing a new document and doing so in a brief, informal proposal. I was awarded a purchase order for $4,990 to do the job.

A second contract came out of OSHA (Occupational Safety and Health Administration, Labor Department), as a result of a cold canvass of the organization. In this case, the agency had a new training program but no guidance document in how to organize, administer, and deliver the training. I proposed a method for doing this—the development of a training administrative manual, which would include an instructor's guide—and was rewarded with another small contract. Ultimately, having a great deal of additional work coming out of these and other contracts I won, I was able to open offices in downtown Washington, D.C. and to begin to grow a bit.

There are others who have done what I did—who operate as small, independent government contractors. *Anyone* can.

Where Do We Go from Here?

I hope that these few pages have whetted your appetite for what is a truly fantastic business opportunity, too long neglected by the small business person. The opportunities are beyond description, and there isn't enough good competition—*believe it or not.* Many of my contracts were actually for redoing, reworking, and/or otherwise salvaging poor jobs done by other—and larger—contractors. The government market is badly in need of energetic, sincere, and talented people. (It has far too many of the other kind.)

In the chapters to come, we're going to take a closer look at just what our government is (and is not), exactly how and what they (the government is "they," not "it") buy, and how anyone can succeed in selling to them, whether small or large.

Some information provided here will be "official," coming from government sources, and some—much—will come out of my own experience and the experience of others who have succeeded in this market.

The theories and philosophies you read will be largely my own, as will many of the recommended procedures and practices, and some will be borrowed from successful friends and associates in government marketing activities. But all will be based on actual experience—*successful* experience. And not just a few isolated cases, which might otherwise be dismissed as "flukes," but consistent, repetitive successes, which should demonstrate that the methods will work for anyone who will apply them faithfully.

2

The Facts—and Unfacts—of Government Marketing

If the first time you knew about it was when you saw it in the CBD, forget it; you haven't got a chance!

The "CBD" is the *Commerce Business Daily*, a five-day-a-week publication of the U.S. Department of Commerce, in which the government announces its bid opportunities. Anyone who markets seriously to the government subscribes to this publication and reads it daily. In it, you can learn what solicitations you can send for. (More about the CBD later.)

The quotation with which this chapter starts is an almost word-for-word statement you may expect to hear from many people who should know better—the people who bid regularly to the government. It would be no exaggeration to say that I have heard those exact words hundreds of times, often stated publicly in seminars for people learning the trade of selling to the government. Undoubtedly, those who utter those words believe them sincerely.

In a way, it is those words that are responsible for this book. After hearing them uttered in public to beginners who took them literally as "conventional wisdom," I was impelled to take some action to undo the harm those words have done. This book is one of the actions I took.

The implication behind these words is that you can't win government contracts without having done a great deal of personal marketing to the people who issued the solicitation reported in the CBD. That is, you must have almost a "fix in" to win. You can't simply play the game as it is supposed to be played: read the CBD, select items of interest, send for the solicitation packages, prepare your bid, and stand a chance of winning. So this statement says. Some even go to the verbal extreme of saying, "Anything you see listed in the CBD is already 'wired' for someone. Don't waste your time on it."

It's easy to see why novitiates in government marketing might believe this: they simply have no way of knowing better. It's easy enough to convince them that the entire thing is a rigged game, a dishonest system, a lip service to the law that requires that bid opportunities be published so that everyone has a chance. But why do those who should know better initiate and perpetuate these myths?

The ones who propagate such stories are those who do not win often enough. The myths are rationalizations—alibis for losing, excuses for *not being good enough* at the marketing skills necessary to win. Sour grapes. It's only losers who say these things. Winners have no need to say them. Or believe them.

In fact, the game is remarkably honest, far more honest than the procurement system of most governments. Certainly there's a shade of truth: there are cases where a little political influence has helped, and there are cases where a given bidder is favored over others and given something of an edge. But these are exceptions, and you will see later that they have to be: the system has several safeguards built in to prevent more than a modicum of such hanky-panky, and even that is minimized in its effect overall.

That is, even when a bidder has a favored position, for one reason or another, it usually can give him only a little edge and not a sure thing; "wired" bids can be unwired, and a number of case histories will prove this, later on.

Some other common beliefs are these:

- Only huge corporations can win government contracts.
- Profits on government work are virtually nil.
- The red-tape requirements are prohibitive.
- The government takes forever to pay its bills.
- Contracts go always to the lowest bidders.
- The government will tell you how to run your business.

All of these have a shade of truth, and only a shade. You have only to read the awards to individuals and small companies to expose the falsity of the first statement. Profits can be small—but they can be large, too. The red tape is really not bad at all. In fact, it quickly becomes a simple routine, with a bit of experience. The government is a bureaucracy and, as such, often screws up the paperwork, including invoices and pay-ments. It's not very hard to straighten out, when you know what you are doing. I've always managed to get paid in a reasonable time, often more rapidly than by private companies. The low bidder wins only certain types of contract by virtue of its low bid. And the government tells *everybody* how to run their businesses these days, whether they are under govern-ment contracts or not. In fact, the government has never told me how to run my business as a government contractor, but only how to do *their* job.

In many cases, the small business has a better chance than the big business, for at least two reasons:

1. Many government executives would rather give a small contract to a small firm because the job will be important to the small firm and get the full attention and dedication of their management, whereas a large firm often tends to put small contracts on the back burner and to assign sec-ond- and third-level (junior) people to the job.

2. Large corporations really can't handle small contracts well without losing money because it costs a large firm a great deal of money simply to get started. Moreover, when a large firm does choose to bid a small job, they put their second-string marketing team on the job, making them easier to beat.

There's still another good reason, related to reason 2 above: for small contracts, the small firm can often bid the job at a lower price than the large firm does. While the price alone is not the final determining factor in many cases, a low price certainly does enhance the chances of winning. Price is never unimportant. All too often, companies prosper in the gov-ernment market—win contracts consistently—without even knowing what they did that was right! That is, they often go on winning simply because their competitors are less competent than they, not because they are really good at what they are doing.

Quite often a government official responsible for selecting the win-ning proposal sighs because none of the proposals is really very good, and he selects whatever he believes to be the best of a bad lot, hoping that he can guide and manage the contractor to a good job, despite the poor proposal. And there are cases where the job is not terribly important and the government officer, finding that none of the proposals submitted meet with his favor, simply cancels the entire requirement, hoping that he can reissue the solicitation later and get a better set of proposals.

In such cases, "a big name" may help. Faced with a number of only fair-quality proposals, the government officer may be influenced and guided, finally, by the name and reputation of the company rather than by the proposal.

But in this kind of environment, a really good proposal is a breath of fresh air, and many a completely unknown bidder confounds the big-name competition by winning against the company who thought they had the bid all sewed up.

→ In addition to this, many contracts are set aside for small business, with big companies disqualified from bidding. This procedure is authorized by the Small Business Act (now undergoing revision in congressional committees), which is designed to aid small businesses in winning government contracts, as well as in succeeding generally in the business/industrial system.

One of the safeguards built in is the requirement that all proposals be evaluated objectively on actual point-scoring systems. In an almost-even contest, the scales might be tipped toward a favored bidder, but a poor proposal cannot win against a really good proposal, no matter who wrote it.

In addition, every bidder who does not win has the right to a "debriefing," in which the agency must go over his unsuccessful proposal with him (at his request) and explain where, how, and why it didn't quite make the grade against the one that did win.

→ And, in addition, there is the "protest" process, wherein an unsuccessful bidder may contest the decision to the GAO—the Government Accounting Office—and have the matter investigated and adjudicated. This possibility exerts a strong influence on contracting officers to be as fair as possible, since a protest will usually delay the award (and the start of the program) by many months. Moreover, it gives the contracting officer a great deal of extra work and makes him look bad in all cases, but especially when the GAO reverses the award.

Perhaps the most famous case of such a protest and reversal was that of Fairchild versus General Electric, when NASA awarded a $65 million contract to GE for a space satellite, and Fairchild protested. Fairchild's case was based primarily on the allegation that GE had not delivered its proposal by the deadline and that NASA accepted the proposal anyway. Moreover, claimed Fairchild, it had proved itself as technically competent as GE. After lengthy proceedings, Fairchild won its case. The award to GE was vacated, and Fairchild won the contract.

My own experience, over some 20 years, has been that the deficiencies in the system are due almost entirely to bureaucratic bungling, which is no surprise, probably, when one is dealing with one of the world's largest bureaucracies. Rarely, in my own experience and in my own viewpoint, have deficiencies been due to dishonesty or weaknesses in the system itself.[1]

The proofs are my own experiences not only in bidding for employers and for my own small company but in applying the principles in behalf of many client companies who have retained me to help them with their proposals. Many of those have won "surprise" victories against big-name competitors, through application of the principles, methods, and techniques to be revealed here as we go into greater depth in the various aspects of government marketing touched upon here.

[1]Shortly before this book was ready for press, revelations of dishonesty in the General Services Administration were revealed, with the opinion expressed by federal investigators that it would likely prove to be the greatest scandal, in terms of money involved, in United States history. Not all the problem is due to dishonesty, however, although there have obviously been payoffs for contracts; much of the scandal reveals bureaucratic bungling and general mismanagement. It is not the system *per se* which is at fault, but the management of the system which is responsible. And no amount of government reform, in my opinion, can do the job of policing the system properly. Only the contractors can do this, by refusing to accept such mismanagement, as Fairchild and other alert contractors have refused to accept being victimized by careless and incompetent bureaucrats.

3

The Jungle

The jungle is a hunting ground, where you find big game and small game among the vines and creepers and in the tall grass.

The bureaucratic jungle is over 3,000 miles long and 1,000 miles deep. It includes 12 departments, over 60 "independent agencies," and several dozen other official and quasi-official organs of government. Most are in the executive branch of the U.S. government, reporting to the president, but a few belong to the legislative branch (Congress) and a few to the judicial branch. Most rely on contractors, at least to some extent, to carry out their programs and discharge their statutory obligations. Some use contractors only occasionally; others use contractors regularly, in great abundance, and for great sums of money.

The length and depth are those of the United States, because these organs (or "agencies"), although they are headquartered in or near Washington, D.C., almost all have tentacles—regional offices, field offices, and district offices throughout the United States and its possessions: Guam, Puerto Rico, American Samoa, the Virgin Islands, and, in many cases, in numerous foreign countries.

Where the Bureaus Are Located

The government has divided the United States into 10 regions (see Figure 1). Most major agencies, such as departments, have a regional office in each of these, although some of the agencies have fewer than 10 regional offices. On the other hand, some agencies have many more than 10 offices scattered around the country.

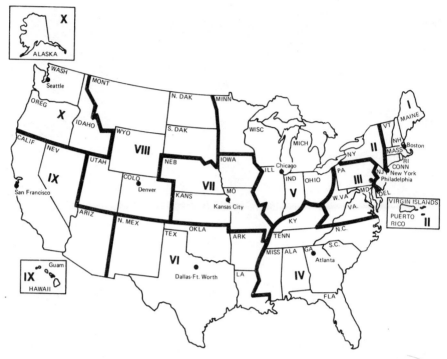

Figure 1. Standard federal regions.

Most of these offices can and do contract on their own, to at least some extent, as well as benefiting from contracts entered into by their headquarters offices. In fact, in some cases, a contract requires that the contractor be in proximity to the agency or office for which the work is to be done, where such proximity is a practical necessity.

In some cases, the U.S. government enters into contracts with American contractors in behalf of other countries. The kingdom of Saudi Arabia, for example, is engaged in a construction program that will cost the kingdom nearly $23 billion. The program is managed for Saudi Arabia by the U.S. Corps of Engineers, which is awarding contracts of many kinds (with Saudi Arabian approval, of course) to American contractors to carry out the program. Almost all of this $23 billion is being spent with American contractors, and it is Saudi Arabian money, although the contracts are with the Corps of Engineers.

Organizational Units and Subunits

The departments and the larger of the other government agencies are divided into many organizational components, some of them quite large themselves. The DOT (Department of Transportation), for example, includes the U.S. Coast Guard and the FAA (Federal Aviation Administration) among its many bureaus and offices. The OSHA (Occupational Safety and Health Administration) is part of the Department of Labor. The Public Health Service and the Office of Education are parts of HEW (the Department of Health, Education and Welfare). And the Public Health Service, in turn, includes the National Institutes of Health, the Food and Drug Administration, and many other agencies. Many of these subordinate agencies have their own sets of regional and field offices. The result is a welter almost too monstrously large and complex to grasp. In fact, it makes us suspect that our estimate of 150,000 customers is much too modest and that the U.S. government should be considered to be 150,000 *markets*.

Finding Your Way

There are guides available to aid in understanding this tropical growth of government,[1] but probably the best is the government's own *United States Government Manual.* It describes all government agencies and organizations, with organization drawings (although some of these are of organizations so huge that the chart has been reduced to illegibility), listings of key executives, descriptions of duties and responsibilities, and much other useful information. It's probably as good a map of the terrain as one can get, although some of the privately published guidance manuals also contain valuable information not found in the government's own manual.

The federal government has twelve departments (the Department of Energy is the newest one):

1. Agriculture (USDA)
2. Commerce (DOC)
3. Defense (DOD)
   Air Force (AF)
   Army
   Navy
   Defense agencies and joint service schools
4. Energy (DOE)
5. Health, Education and Welfare (HEW)
6. Housing and Urban Development (HUD)

[1]See Appendix.

7. Interior
8. Justice
9. Labor (DOL)
10. State
11. Transportation (DOT)
12. Treasury

Not all are known by initials or acronyms.

The General Accounting Office (GAO) belongs to Congress, serving a watchdog function over other government agencies. The Government Printing Office (GPO) and the Library of Congress also report to Congress.

Most other agencies, except those offices that belong to the judicial branch, report to the president. Those reporting directly, as part of the Executive Office of the President, include the Office of Management and Budget (OMB) and the Office of Economic Opportunity (OEO).

There are over 60 "independent agencies" that also report to the president as part of the executive branch. Those that are of interest to contractors include the following:

ACTION
Appalachian Regional Commission (ARC)
Civil Aeronautics Board (CAB)
Consumer Product Safety Commission (CPSC)
District of Columbia (DC)
Environmental Protection Agency (EPA)
Equal Employment Opportunity Commission (EEOC)
Farm Credit Administration
Federal Communications Commission (FCC)
Federal Maritime Commission
Federal Trade Commission (FTC)
General Services Administration (GSA)
Interstate Commerce Commission (ICC)
National Aeronautics and Space Administration (NASA)
Small Business Administration (SBA)
National Science Foundation (NSF)
Smithsonian Institution

Civil Service Commission (CSC)

Information Agency (USIA)

Postal Service (USPS)

Veterans Administration (VA)

There are also a number of quasi-official agencies, which include AMTRAK, the National Academy of Sciences, and the American National Red Cross.

The rationale of arranging the government bureaucracy in this manner is a political one rather than a practical one. Some of the independent agencies are quite large, larger than some of the departments. (Presumably an independent agency is either a small organization, a temporary one, or an ad hoc one, but this theory appears to have little to do with reality.) The large independent agencies, which represent substantial potential for business, include EPA, GSA, and NASA, but several others use contracted services frequently, although they are not large organizations by government standards.

Structures, Substructures, and Missions of Departments

Agriculture—USDA

"Ag" as it is often referred to, includes a wide variety of offices and bureaus for aid to rural areas and individuals, with loan programs, rural electrification, telephone-line installations, food inspections and standards, agricultural research, and other aids to individuals and organizations in rural America.

One major agency in USDA is the U.S. Forest Service, which has 10 regional offices plus many field stations. The Forest Service does a fairly large amount of contracting for various services and goods.

Commerce—DOC

The mission of Commerce is to "foster, serve, and promote the Nation's economic development and technological advancement." Its major subdivisions are the Economic Development Administration (EDA), the Maritime Administration, the Office of Minority Enterprise (OMBE, pronounced "ombee"), the National Bureau of Standards (NBS), the National Oceanic and Atmospheric Administration (NOAA, pronounced "noah"), the National Technical Information Service (NTIS), and the Patent Office. Considered something of a backwash in government agencies for many years, under its present Secretary, Juanita Kreps, DOC is gaining vigor rapidly, contracting regularly today to support many dynamic programs. OMBE, for example, funds 233 organizations throughout the country devoted to aiding minority enterprises. OMBE lets a large number of "technical assistance" contracts and grants each year and publishes a periodical devoted to the subject.

EDA conducts grant, loan, and loan-guarantee programs that will stimulate employment. It is the administrator for the two public-works grant programs ($6 billion; 10,000 projects) and regularly loans or guarantees loans in the private and public sectors for diverse needs—foreign-import damage to American industries, drought relief, and economic stimulation in depressed areas, for example.

Defense—DOD

Defense is, of course, a superagency, comprising the three military services, each of which is a department also. These agencies are the main market targets for a large number of corporations that sell little to anyone else, except perhaps for two other technological agencies, EPA and NASA.

At the same time, sales to the military agencies are not weapons and computers exclusively. The military organizations are virtual governments unto themselves, with their enormously diverse sets of needs, buying virtually every kind of goods and service that might be sold anywhere else in government markets. All have service schools, intelligence organizations, supply depots, offices specializing in research into human behavior, publication groups, laboratories, communications networks, headquarters organizations, and sundry other offices and functions.

However, the parent organization, Defense (headquartered in the Pentagon, of course), also has its own matching sets of offices and functions, including a centralized supply service, the Defense Supply Agency (DSA). The various military departments, including the U.S. Marine Corps (USMC), which is part of the U.S. Navy, buy both directly and through the DSA. Moreover, the military organizations buy through both their own centralized procurement and locally, at the individual military establishments. Even the military exchange system (retail stores on military bases, selling consumer goods) buys both centrally and locally. DOD has its own small-business program, which is an active one, making earnest efforts to assure small business of winning a fair share of contracts and subcontracts.

Health, Education and Welfare—HEW

HEW is also a superagency, rivaling DOD for size, budget, diversity, and contractual expenditures. It is or should be a major market target for anyone engaged in the fields of medical and social services and/or "human resource development," commonly referred to today as "HRD."

HEW is divided into four major divisions: the Education Division, which includes the Office of Education (OE) and the National Institute for Education (NIE); the Public Health Service (PHS), which includes the Food and Drug Administration (FDA), the National Institutes of Health (NIH), the Health Resources Administration (HRA), the Health Services Administration (HSA), the Center for Disease Control (CDC), the Social and Rehabilitation Service (SRS), and the Social Security Administration (SSA).

Some of these divisions are huge in themselves and break down into numerous major subdivisions. The National Institutes of Health, for example, include the National Cancer Institute (NCI), the National Heart and Lung Institute (NHLI), the National Institute of Mental Health (NIMH), the National Library of Medicine (NLM), and more than a half dozen others. And then each of these are further broken down into offices and bureaus.

It is HEW that has mounted and funded massive programs to study and try to combat alcoholism and drug addiction, often in cooperation with the Justice Department's Law Enforcement Assistance Administration (LEAA) and Drug Enforcement Administration (DEA). HEW also carries out numerous programs to promote the development of medical and social-service specialists, including some programs aimed at improving opportunities for minorities in related professional fields.

Housing and Urban Development—HUD

HUD is not a particularly fertile contract target. Its activities are largely concerned with the development of residential facilities, energy conservation in residential dwelling design, construction and mortgage loans, housing management, disaster assistance, and related functions.

Interior—DOI

Interior is, of course, one of the "oldtime" agencies, dating back to 1849. Its main mission and functions are easily inferred from the names of some of its subdivisions: Office of Oil and Gas, Office of Coal Research, Office of Water Resources Research, Fish and Wildlife Service, Sports Fisheries and Wildlife, National Park Service, Bureau of Mines, Geological Survey, Bureau of Indian Affairs (BIA), Bureau of Land Management (BLM), and Mining Enforcement and Safety Administration (MESA). The latter two advertise solicitations fairly often, although they usually involve relatively small contracts. In these days of concern over energy, however, Interior's functions regarding fossil fuels is becoming more important and more active. (Some of these will be or have already been transferred to the new Department of Energy.)

Justice

Today's Justice Department includes the Federal Bureau of Investigation (FBI), of course, as its best-known division, but has also the Law Enforcement Assistance Administration (LEAA) and the Drug Enforcement Administration (DEA), already referred to; the Bureau of Prisons; and the Immigration and Neutralization Service, among others. Principal business opportunities in Justice are with LEAA and DEA.

Labor—DOL

Labor is another large agency, and an excellent prospect for contracts. Among its many divisions, it numbers the Manpower Administration and the Occupational Safety and Health Administration (OSHA) each of which is actively issuing frequent solicitations for contract assistance.

Labor operates a number of training and apprenticeship programs, conducts studies, operates Job Corps centers, sets employment standards, adjudicates many labor disputes, and publishes statistics through its Bureau of Labor Statistics (BLS). The department's origins go back to 1913, making it a relative old-timer among departments.

State

While the State Department is large in size and old in history (established in 1789, with predecessor organizations), except for its Agency for International Development (AID), it is not a good contract prospect. And today even AID is not doing a great deal of contracting.

Transportation—DOT

Transportation is relatively new as a department, organized in 1966, but is made up largely of a conglomerate of older government bureaus, assembled into an entity now having departmental status. Its main subdivisions include the Coast Guard (USCG), the Federal Aviation Administration (FAA), the Federal Highway Administration (FHA), the Federal Railroad Administration (FRA), the Urban Mass Transportation Administration (UMTA), the National Highway Traffic Safety Administration (NHTSA), and others.

DOT has been a good market target, having funded many programs in mass transportation and in highway traffic safety, two of its most active areas. The Coast Guard (which used to be in the Treasury Department, for some reason) offers some contract opportunities, but not a great many. Although it operates somewhat like a military organization, it is condemned, like the Marine Corps, to depending heavily on hand-me-downs from other sources, using worn and weary equipment that has outlived its usefulness to the military. FAA offers a few contract opportunities, but, again, not on a grand scale.

Treasury

Treasury, as almost everyone knows, includes the Internal Revenue Service (IRS) and the Customs Bureau. Contract opportunities do arise, from time to time, but Treasury is not a major target for companies doing business with the government.

Energy—DOE

The Department of Energy is newly formed and business possibilities are best judged in the context of the older organizations that make it up. DOE was assembled, as DOT was, from other organizations already in existence. Its two principal components are the Energy Research and Development Administration (ERDA) and the Federal Energy Administration (FEA). To these were added other energy-related groups, such as the Federal Power Commission and bureaus from other departments.

Both ERDA and FEA offered many contract opportunities and will almost undoubtedly continue to do so. ERDA is primarily a technological (state-of-the-art) organization, responsible for technological improvements in energy utilization and development of new energy sources, such as wind energy and solar energy. FEA, on the other hand, was concerned primarily with the conservation of existing energy and energy utilization, oil imports, education of consumers in energy conservation, and the like. The new DOE is starting life with 20,000 employees and a $10.4 billion annual budget, and it will undoubtedly offer a great many opportunities for contracts.

Other Agencies and Opportunities

Consumer Product Safety Commission—CPSC

CPSC is, as its name tells you, concerned with consumer product safety. Its mission is to detect hazards in consumer products and to take counteractions, including banning, development of standards, and education of the public in product safety. It has been a fairly prolific source of contracts, some of them rather substantial in size.

Environmental Protection Agency—EPA

EPA has, of course, made a major impact on life in the United States, especially with regard to automobiles. EPA has three major divisions, concerned with air pollution, water pollution, and solid waste, but it also has major programs with regard to radiation hazards and pesticide hazards.

EPA has been a primary target for many government contractors and has spent substantial sums of money for contract goods and services. EPA operates several major installations, each of which is a potential business target.

General Services Administration—GSA

GSA is relatively new (established in 1949) and has become a major business source (procures about $5 billion per year) because of its basic nature as a management and supply function for the civil government. Its major divisions include the Federal Supply Service (FSS), the Public Building Service (PBS), the Automated Data and Telecommunications Service, and the National Archives and Records Service. The PBS is a major target for architects and engineers and for construction contractors, while the FSS is a huge market for suppliers of all kinds of commodities and proprietary goods, stockpiling over 4 million items in several supply centers, and currently spending about $3 billion per year.

National Aeronautics and Space Administration—NASA

NASA is, of course, a well-known agency of a highly technological nature that is established in a number of large physical facilities. One of its facilities, Goddard Space Flight Center, near Washington, D.C., is reputed to have the largest single population of computers in the world— well over 200. Obviously, NASA makes many purchases and issues contracts in connection with computers. NASA also buys a great deal of equipment, much of it through engineering research and development contracts, and many other services and supplies.

National Science Foundation—NSF

NSF is well known to the scientific and academic communities as the sponsor/funder/buyer of scientific research, much of it in basic science, as distinct from applied science. While the foundation does issue some contracts, it is a better source for grants for scientific research and occasionally will issue grants to for-profit organizations, although grants are primarily used to fund work by nonprofit corporations and institutions.

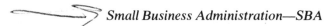 ### Small Business Administration—SBA

SBA has a mission that is fairly narrow and sharply focused on training, education, counseling, guidance, and financial assistance to small businesses. SBA establishes the standards by which distinctions are made between small and large business in each industry, works with other agencies to set aside certain procurement for competition among small businesses only, acts as counselor/surrogate for some small businesses having difficulties with government contracts, and operates the special 8(a) program, which is so named because clause 8(a) of the Small Business Act authorizes the program. It offers special assistance to minority enterprises in winning government contracts through the mechanism of having the agency award the contract to SBA, which then *subcontracts* the job to the 8(a) (minority) firm selected. Most SBA contracts are therefore awarded to minority firms, although there are some opportunities offered to firms at large to do business directly with SBA.

Postal Service—USPS

USPS is today a government corporation rather than a department, as it once was. Nevertheless, it is part of the government, although it follows its own procurement policies. These sometimes differ slightly from those used in other agencies, but they must still conform to the requirements of procurement regulations and public law.

When USPS was organized, it became a highly active buyer of contracted goods and services, establishing training facilities, bulk mail plants, and other new undertakings. But because of its deficit operations, it has slowed down considerably as a customer.

A major procurement activity of USPS is in the construction and renovation of post office facilities, automotive supplies and vehicles (USPS is second only to the U.S. Army as an owner of vehicles), and the transportation of mail. Other than for these essential services, which are inherent in its day-to-day operation, USPS is not today a particularly good target for contracts.

Contracts from other agencies are spasmodic, usually for one-of-a-kind and only occasionally needed goods and services. These are not to be disregarded—they do occasionally offer an excellent business opportunity—but are not dependable sources on a year-in, year-out basis.

On the other hand, no agency really is that dependable. As programs change, organizations change, moods in Congress and appropriations change, and procurement patterns—government markets—change drastically. The successful government marketer will be conscious of this and will always be alert for changes.

What Is a "Market"?

Some people use the word *market* in one way, some in another. To some, there is "an electronics market." Others may consider "the military market" or the "navy market."

Understanding government markets, no matter how you define the term, can be tricky. Any agency might and probably will buy certain goods and services, regardless of its main functions as an agency. Computer-related goods and services, for example, are one common denominator, as are training, education (in most government agencies, "training" is what you provide for employees and to prepare others for employment, whereas "education" is what you provide for the general public, as in product-safety awareness), publications, and other common needs. On the other hand, many needs are peculiar to given agencies, and your "market" for these is restricted to those agencies, as far as government business is concerned. But even here, the marketing problem is far from simple, and success at marketing to the various agencies depends to a large extent on your understanding of government, its agencies, how and why they were conceived and established, and what they are charged by law with accomplishing.

· All government agencies have their own missions and statutory obligations. In many cases, these account for the apparent redundancy and overlapping of functions, although there are lines of demarcation clearly implied in most cases. (But in some cases, the lines are not sharply defined, and jurisdictional disputes result.)

For example, SBA (the Small Business Administration) is charged with aid to and support of small businesses. One of their major programs is aiding small business with loans and loan guarantees.

——> However, the EDA (Economic Development Administration of the U.S. Department of Commerce) also makes loans and loan guarantees to businesses, an apparent duplication. The difference is this: SBA makes loan/loan guarantees to aid small business in getting started and in surviving. EDA makes loan/loan guarantees to create or save jobs that are threatened. While a firm might go to either agency for help, the application and justification would have to be different in each case. To apply to SBA, the firm would have to qualify as small business under SBA-established standards for that industry and otherwise demonstrate eligibility under SBA regulations (the Small Business Act), whereas an application to EDA would require no qualification as small business but would require proof that jobs would be created or saved as a result of the loan or loan guarantee.

The Occupational Safety and Health Administration (OSHA) is concerned with environmental pollution and health hazards *in the workplace*, that is, where it affects the health of the worker. EPA (the Environmental Protection Agency) is concerned with environmental pollution *outside the workplace*, that is, where it affects the health of the population as a whole.

The Consumer Product Safety Commission is charged with safety in consumer products only, and *product* is the $64,000 word here. For several years, we have known that aluminum house wiring presents a fire hazard—not because aluminum is itself a fire hazard, but because it presents certain special difficulties in use, in the manner in which it must be connected to receptacles and switches. This has created a problem of jurisdiction—of law, in fact. The law authorizes—requires—the commission to establish standards for product safety and to take action when specific products are found to be unsafe. But the commission has been struck down in its efforts to do anything about aluminum wiring because it is not the product—aluminum—that is unsafe; it is the manner of its connection. That places it outside the jurisdiction of the act authorizing the commission's activities.

At one point, the commission seriously considered regarding the entire home as the "product" in order to legalize actions regarding aluminum house wiring, but that too was struck down, and the issue is still unresolved. Only an act of Congress will resolve the problem apparently.

It is necessary to understand each agency and its statutory obligations to do business with it effectively. That helps you to understand the problems of the agency, and the ability to help them solve their problems is an open sesame to the contract offers. It is important, however, to know where and how to tread in the labyrinth of laws, regulations, and policies.

For example, one office charged with value engineering for its agency was quite unhappy with the official manual on the subject and wanted me to prepare a better one. But getting a new *official* manual approved, especially where one already exists, is most difficult and time-consuming. To get around the problem, I suggested that we call the new manual a training guide to the subject, which could exist side by side with the official manual and be used in its place. The suggestion was adopted, and I wrote the new manual. A rose by any other name. . . .

Jealousy and competition exist between and among the many agencies. One for whom I was writing a sizable home-study program learned that another was about to launch an effort in the same direction. To discourage this effort, my customer advised the other agency that we had almost completed such a program and urged me on to greater speed to present the other agency a fait accompli before they could get up to speed on their project.

Some agencies—Labor, for example—have centralized procurement; all contracts go through a central contracting office for the entire agency. Others have decentralized procurement, and numerous contracting offices may be found throughout the agency and its facilities.

Contracting officers are individuals. Some are strong and dominate procurement in the agency. Others are easygoing and give "program" people a great deal of self-determination in what and how they buy. (Or perhaps some program executives are much tougher than their contracting officers!) Contracting officers, along with agency heads, set procurement policy, which is sometimes more stringent than the law requires and sometimes skirts the law carefully. For this reason, some agencies grant a great many sole-source contracts, while others have such stringent standards for justification of sole-source awards that few contracts are ever awarded without open competition. Some contracting officers will fight hard for any bidder whose price is low, while others will yield readily to the preferences of the program executives who evaluate the proposals.

If the bureaucratic structure is a jungle of tropical growth, the laws, regulations, and policies regarding procurement are an even greater jungle, affording agencies a multiplicity of trails and paths to pursue in reaching their contracting goals. There is little standardization in procurement policies and practices because somewhere a regulation may be found that authorizes almost anything the agency wants to do!

——> The basic rules are set out by the *Federal Procurement Regulations* (FPR), which most civilian agencies follow. The armed forces have a set of regulations which are somewhat similar to the FPR: ASPR (pronounced "asper")—the *Armed Services Procurement Regulations*—which incorporate many special provisions of value to the military procurements. And NASA, not to be outdone, has its own set of procurement regulations, based on the foregoing two.

——> The Office of Federal Procurement Policy is developing the Federal Acquisition Regulations (FAR), which are intended to replace the existing sets of regulations and provide a single, standardized set for the first time in modern history. The process is a five-level one, which examines each clause of the FPR and ASPR, and classifies it as "discard," at one extreme, and "incorporate as written," at the other extreme, with three levels of modification and rewriting between the extremes, plus the addition of entirely new clauses, in some cases.

Perhaps the best news of all about this is that each member of the project staff has been required to undergo at least one week's training in writing clearly, and the new regulations should reflect this.

The new regulations should go into effect sometime late in fiscal 1979, perhaps even before the end of calendar 1979.

This regulation will not clear up all the problems of non-uniformity. Agencies will still have many alternatives from which to choose in making procurements. But it should eliminate at least some of the disputes in interpretation and make it easier for the layman to understand the language of the regulations.

To illustrate again the lack of uniformity, most companies doing business with the government have established a special pool of indirect expenses called *G & A*—general and administrative costs. This originated because military contracting practice dictated that a company's marketing and sales expenses could not be repaid, in cost-reimbursement contracts, as part of the company's overhead but would be reimbursable as a "general and administrative" cost. Yet, at least one company, in my own experience, has never had a G & A expense pool in their accounting system because they did most of their business with a military organization that did not pursue that stated policy.

This makes marketing to the government more an art than a science. It involves a large pool of knowledge, a great deal of flexibility, and a generous measure of resourcefulness to cope successfully with all the situations you encounter.

Market Analyses and Target Setting

The government markets can be classified in many different ways:

- Size: big-buck markets versus small-buck markets
- Products versus services
- Types and classes of products
- Types and classes of service

Those are some broad, first-cut classifications. Each may be subclassified in several ways and interclassified—any of the latter three classifications, for example, may be subclassified as big-buck versus small-buck markets.

Some contractors specialize, either in type of product or service offered or in agencies addressed. Some defense contractors, for example, concentrate primarily on the U.S. Navy. Others are strictly in the missile business, while still others are strictly into communications equipment. One contractor may offer R & D (research and development) with no production capabilities, while others may concentrate on production.

One small contractor near Annapolis, Maryland, specializes in designing and building battery chargers for the U.S. Air Force, although he diversifies to a small extent in the manufacture of relays and choppers. But his main revenue derives from the sale of spare parts for the battery chargers he provides the U.S. Air Force every year.

Sometimes it is the contracting policies of customers that dictate the posture a firm takes. Whereas most military organizations issue prime contracts, the U.S. Navy generally tends to be its own prime contractor. This requires a bit of explanation.

A large contract today almost inevitably means that the contractor is going to have to let a number of small subcontracts. When RCA won the BMEWS (Ballistic Missile Early Warning System) contract, it was the first time a billion-dollar prime contract had been let. Big as RCA is, they could not do the entire job themselves. In fact, they subcontracted approximately two-thirds of the program to something in excess of 300 subcontractors.

However, whatever a prime contractor subcontracts, the responsibility overall falls on the prime contractor. This means that he must handle all the administrative and coordinating functions, manage all the subcontracts, and perform all the system-level functions of preparing system manuals, reports, budgeting, scheduling, etc. It's a huge administrative job in itself, and most agencies prefer to have some private corporation handle it all through awarding them a prime contract.

The U.S. Navy likes to be its own prime contractor, awarding a multiplicity of contracts for its major procurements. However, it is not prepared to do all the management and administration required and therefore lets one or more contracts to have those functions handled also by private for-profit firms. At least one firm in the Washington, D.C., area subsists largely on such contracts.

Target setting is therefore based partially on what you want to sell and partially on what the market opportunities are. That is, you may form and structure what you offer to what the opportunities are, as many companies do.

Custom-Hardware Markets

The military services are, as noted already and as is widely known, the major targets for hardware R & D. NASA was a major market too, prior to the successful Apollo program, and is still a substantial market. DOE is a good market for hardware and hardware R & D related to energy, and EPA is a fair market for hardware related to its goals. These are the primary markets for state-of-the-art technology, although other targets appear occasionally.

Custom-Services Markets

The custom-services markets have been growing among government agencies for years and continue to do so. HEW and its many subordinate organizations fund many kinds of service projects:

Training development	Surveys
Studies	Publications

Social research	Conference/symposium
Medical research	management

These are in demand in connection with many programs of: child care, care of the aged, improvement of the status of the underprivileged ("the socially and economically disadvantaged"), alcoholism and drug abuse, the education and training of professionals and subprofessionals in the various fields, and dozens of related programs.

Labor contracts for many services for its many programs to train the disadvantaged and the unemployed generally to make them employable.

The military organizations contract for many service programs that parallel programs undertaken by civil agencies.

Almost any agency, military or civil, is likely to contract for "management" services, which often include the development of computer programs, training, and related publications.

Underlying Causes for Procurements

Ordinarily, there are two reasons for inspiring an agency to solicit contracts rather than undertaking the job with federal employees:

1. Specialized knowledge, skills, and/or facilities, not available in the agency, are required for the job.
2. The agency simply does not have enough personnel to do the job in-house.

→ Frequently, both causes are responsible: the agency does not have enough staff, nor does it have all the skills and facilities.

With agencies having long-term missions requiring highly specialized skills and long-term, large-scale programs, frequent or continuous contracting is a way of life, and a steady stream of contracts issues forth from some agencies, such as the military, HEW, Labor, NASA, and to perhaps a somewhat lesser extent, EPA and a few others. This is what enables some companies to specialize in terms of one or two agencies, as well as in terms of types of products and/or services.

Among the other agencies, the contractual issuance is spasmodic, sometimes constituting a stream, for a time, then drying up for a time. (Some agencies issue almost all their contracts near the end of the fiscal year, then issue few throughout the rest of the year.) Some agencies have only occasional contracts, rarely having money or programs that make contracts necessary. Some, given a new program, will contract more-or-less regularly for a year or even several years and then dry up. The Postal Service is one example of this.

Sometimes a brand-new agency is formed, such as OEO (Office of Economic Opportunity) and the government corporation, the Pension Benefit Guaranty Corporation. In the case of OEO, there ensued several years of almost frantic contracting—almost everything was contracted out, and the programs were substantially large. In the case of the Pension Benefit Guaranty Corporation, it took nearly two years before it began to contract, and then the results were hardly worth waiting for.

Commodities and Supply Contracts

The government, in all agencies, uses vast quantities of ordinary, commercial supplies and commodities: furniture, both home and office types; foodstuffs; paints; lubricants; tools; office machines; office supplies; printing; books; clothing; and a host of other commodity items of all sorts.

There are three centralized procurement functions among government agencies: the Federal Supply Service of GSA, which acts as supplier of commodities to all agencies who wish to use their services; the Defense Supply Agency, which performs a similar function for the military organizations; and the Postal Service supply center at Topeka, Kansas, which buys centrally for the Postal Service. For the most part, these supplies are defined in painstaking detail by federal specifications, both civilian and military, and are purchased in that manner, almost always by strictly low-bid standards. However, many ordinary commercial goods are bought that way too: the government has not written a specification for *everything*, but primarily for those items that they buy regularly and in large quantities.

Even so, these services are convenience services for the various agencies, and the agencies are not compelled to "buy" from government supply sources, but may—and do—buy independently. And, in some cases, buying locally is the only sensible answer to the supply problems. For example, a military base can hardly avoid buying milk and pastries from local sources.

The GPO and Printing Services

The Government Printing Office, which operates more than one printing plant, is probably the largest printing establishment in the world.

Yet, GPO probably contracts out far more printing than it does in-house! Certainly, it contracts out a huge volume (about 70% of its current $500 million annual figure). Under the law, no agency is permitted to have its own printing done by a contractor unless it persuades GPO to issue a waiver authorizing the contract. Except for such infrequent cases, all printing must be sent to GPO. GPO, however, cannot handle it all and subcontracts a huge volume of printing almost every day of the week. Many printers, large and small, depend on GPO for the bulk of their work.

But printing is not all that GPO contracts for. It contracts also for typesetting and for certain other services. For example, GPO prints or has printed government periodicals, of which there are many. In some cases, GPO is also responsible for maintaining the subscription lists and mailing the copies out. But again, GPO usually contracts such services out. Some GPO printing contracts are on a single-job, one-time basis, while others are on annual contract, for an entire year's service.

GPO printing bids are highly competitive, almost always based on award to the low bidder. However, for some specialty printers who have special equipment, such as the manufacturer of snap-out forms, the competition is not great, and the bidder may price accordingly. Too, GPO generally allows a generous amount of time for each job, allowing the contractor to use GPO work as filler for slack periods. Some printers snort at GPO work as being unprofitable, but many others find it quite satisfying and do work for GPO gratefully, year after year. GPO bid opportunities are plentiful, available almost every business day of the week, the year round.

Targets of Opportunity

We noted that many agencies do not contract on a regular basis, but only irregularly. When HUD wishes to update its computer system, it may issue a contract, even a sizable one, to procure services but may not have such a contract opportunity to offer again for years. GAO, which does not contract very often for anything, recently solicited proposals for management consulting services to help develop a better, faster system for handling award protests. SBA has decided to computerize its directories of small business firms, resulting in a sizable contract.

Such a multiplicity of agencies and subdivisions of agencies constitutes, overall, a dependable source of business. If one scans the spectrum of all agencies' contract solicitations regularly, hardly a week will pass without several opportunities to respond to a solicitation, although one might never do work for the same agency on two consecutive contracts. Many companies subsist in this manner, rarely getting comfortably nested with any single agency but usually able to win enough contracts for survival.

This approach requires alert and able marketing, in both market surveillance and market response. This is where proposalmanship becomes most important as the key to business survival.

Interagency Projects

There are numerous occasions when a contract with an agency is being paid for, wholly or partially, by another agency. For example, SBA issues contracts—actually subcontracts—for jobs contracted to it by other agencies. And in the case of their new project to establish a computer directory of small business firms, at least part of the cost is being borne by several other agencies who will participate in and benefit directly from the results of the project.

The DOE predecessor, ERDA, contracted much work in wind-energy conversion systems to NASA, because NASA had the physical facilities, the technical staff, and the time (after the post-Apollo slowdown in NASA programs) to devote to the program. NASA, in turn, contracted or subcontracted many of the tasks to industry.

An experiment in use of multimedia educational technology was carried out at the Annapolis Naval Academy several years ago, using funds furnished by the Office of Education.

Government market analysis is therefore far from a simple undertaking. It's an enormously complex and, in essence, unstructured market, particularly in services. And many small- to medium-sized companies have sprung up in response to the opportunities thus presented, which reflect the formlessness of the government custom-services markets.

Management Services/Management Consultants

These latter companies are generally regarded as management consultants, offering management services. Some, such as the Mitre Corporation and Systems Development Corporation, tend to be linked to or based on computer system technology, some have sprung from a base as certified public accountants, some from a base as psychologists and training or human-behavioral specialists, and some from no discernible original identity.

However, such companies tend to be oriented to and staffed heavily with academic professionals, with a concentration of advanced (graduate) degrees among them. They fire at will at all targets of opportunity, now undertaking a training development, now a survey, now an energy study, now a housing study. They work across the spectrum of all agencies, civilian and military, able to write credible proposals and win a wide variety of professional/technical/management projects.

Their strengths are based only partially on their track record in past projects; they stem primarily from the credentials of their high-level staff professionals and the sophistication of their proposals.

In many cases, government programs have created the need for technical/professional specialties, and the government is often the only customer or the only substantial market for the skills and experience represented. Modern programs, especially but not exclusively those of HEW, have created a need for many conferences and symposia and have stimulated the growth of associations, so that today we have individuals and firms specializing in conference arrangement and management.

Many agencies undertake a great many studies and surveys, and that too has become a major activity for many firms and their staffs.

Custom training-development, given an enormous initial velocity by OEO in the mid-1960s, is still moving strongly, with government agencies the prime customers. (Private firms are reluctant to spend the large sums needed for custom development of training programs.)

And, of course, social workers and medical workers are in increasingly short supply to man the many programs, both federal and local, that are funded with federal money.

This has been a rough sketch of the incredible government market today, swarming with small companies and large ones, with suppliers of everyday commodities and of high-technology products, and with providers of workaday services and highly sophisticated skills. Before we consider seriously how to win contracts in these markets, we have to take a look at how to prospect these markets and find the bid opportunities.

4

Search for Opportunity: Prospecting the Jungle

The law requires free competition in government procurement. This is to keep the game honest: everyone gets the opportunity to win government business, and the government gets the advantages of competitive prices.

To encourage competition and provide opportunity for all businesses, the government makes its requirements known in a number of ways. And, except for those cases where an agency can justify arbitrary selection of a supplier, as required by law, all procurement must be submitted to the competitive process.

The Commerce Business Daily

The chief medium through which government agencies make their wants and bid opportunities known to the world at large is the *Commerce Business Daily*, published every official business day of the year by the Department of Commerce (see Figure 2). In the CBD, as it is familiarly referred to, are to be found all the requirements expected to exceed $10,000, as well as announcements of all contract awards in excess of $25,000, and several miscellaneous items, such as notices of surplus sales and foreign market opportunities.

The CBD costs $80.00 a year, mailed second class. As a periodical, it is supposed, under postal regulations, to be "preferential mail" and receive the same treatment as first-class mail. Unfortunately, that service has gone the way of mail service generally, and the CBD is regularly arriving as much as a week late.

FRIDAY, JUNE 23, 1978

Commerce Business Daily

U. S. DEPARTMENT OF COMMERCE
Juanita M. Kreps, Secretary

A daily list of U.S. Government procurement invitations, contract awards, subcontracting leads, sales of surplus property and foreign business opportunities

U. S. GOVERNMENT PROCUREMENTS

Services

A Experimental, Developmental, Test and Research Work (includes both basic and applied research).

★ **A - - NON-GAUSSIAN EFFECTS IN DYNAMIC SYSTEM ESTIMATION PROBLEMS.** Negotiations are to be conducted with Systems Control, Inc., 1801 Page Mill Road, Palo Alto, CA 94304. See Note 46.

★ **A - - OPTICAL CLIMATOLOGY.** Negotiations are to be conducted with McDonnell Douglas Astronautics Company, St. Louis, MO 63166. See note 46

★ **A - - CONTACT STRESS ANALYSIS OF CERAMIC-TO-METAL INTERFACES.** Negotiations are to be conducted with AiResearch Manufacturing Co of Arizona, 111 South 34th Street, Phoeniz, AZ 85010. See Note 46.

★ **A - - THIN FILM DISPLAY RESEARCH.** Negotiations are to be conducted with Panel Displays, Inc., P.O. Box 660, Marina Del Rey, CA 90291. See Note 46.

★ **A - - ANALYSIS AND ASSESSMENT OF ATTACK SUBMARINE MISSION REQUIREMENTS.** Negotiations are to be conducted with Operations Research, Inc., 1400 Spring Street, Silver Spring, MD 20910. See Note 46.

★ **A - - STUDY NUMERICAL METHODS FOR OCEAN FORECASTING AND OBJECTIVE ANALYSIS.** Negotiations are to be conducted with Science Applications, Inc., 8400 Westpark Dr. , McLean, VA 22101. See Note 46.

★ **A - - FURTHER RESEARCH ON THE MECHANISM OF SUPER-RATE AND PLATEAU BURNING OF DOUBLE BASE PROPELLANTS.** Negotiations are to be conducted with Space Sciences, Inc., 135 West Maple Ave., Monrovia, CA 91016. See Note 46.

★ **A - - ADDITIONAL RESEARCH ON GAIN AND ABSORPTION PROCESSES IN THE MERCURY-CADMIUM EXCIMER.** Negotiations are to be conducted with Northrop Corporation, 3401 West Broadway, Hawthorne, CA 90250. See Note 46.

★ **A - - FURTHER RESEARCH ON HYDROACOUSTIC AND SEISMIC SIGNAL PROCESSING.** Negotiations are to be conducted with Underwater Systems, Inc., 8121 Georgia Avenue, Silver Spring, MD 20910. See Note 46.

★ **A - - POLYMERIZATION OF FLUORINATED ACETYLENES.** Negotiations are to be conducted with Fluorochem, Inc., 6233 N. Irwindale Ave., Azusa, CA 91702. See Note 46. (171)

Office of Naval Research, 800 North Quincy St., Arlington, VA 22217

★**A - - STUDY TO IMPROVE FM COMMUNICATIONS FOR ARMY AIRCRAFT** RFP DAAB07-78-R-1613. An award is being made to Communications Components Corporation.

★**A - - LASER SOURCE DETECTOR TEST SET** R&D, RFP DAAB07-78-R-1604. An award is being made to Laser Analytics Inc.

★**A - - MILLIMETER WAVE TRAVELING WAVE TUBE (TWT)** 1 item, Award is being made to Hughes Aircraft Company, Electron Dynamic Division, PO Box 2999, Torrance CA 90509, for additional power requirements, controls, and engineering effort by modification to Contract DAAB07-78-C-2914. See Notes 27, 46.

★**A - - HANDHELD ELECTRONICS AUTHENTICATION DEVICE** (HEAD) IAW Electronics R&D Command Development Specification DS-EH-0243B(A), The work will be on a sole source basis with Magnavox Co., Fort Wayne Division, Fort Wayne, Indiana; modifying on-going Contract DAAB07-77-C-0174. See note 46, 73.

★**A - - LARGE SINGLE ELEMENT** 10.6um PV Detector. A nine month effort is required which is a continuation of Contract DAAB07-76-C-0803, to Santa Barbara Research Center, Goleta CA under RFP DAAB07-78-Q-1594. See note 46. (171)

U.S. Army Communications and Electronics Material Readiness Command, Fort Monmouth NJ 07703

A - - SELECTION OF CALIFORNIA RESERVOIRS AMENABLE TO MICELLAR-POLYMER FLOODING A one year study. To assure a solid engineering base is available for extending the Enhanced Oil Recovery Technology, data will be collected from past and on-going field and laboratory efforts primarily directed toward California sandstone reservoirs. Such data may include chemical and reservoir fluid compatibilities, detrimental rock/chemical interaction, excessive chemical absorption, mobility control, injectivity, produced emulsions and sand control. Requests for Proposals are anticipated to be available O/a 30 Jul 78. Requests for copies of this solicitation, accompanied by two self-addressed mailing labels. Such requests should be received by DOE-BERC not later than 10 days from the date of listing of this synopsis in the Commerce Business Daily. Telephone requests will not be honored. A copy of the RFP will be available for perusal in the reference library at the below address. (171)

U. S. Department of Energy, Bartlesville Energy Research Center, PO Box 1398, Bartlesville OK 74003, Ref: REP ET-78-R-03-1896, Attn: B. Jones

★ **A - - WIND TUNNEL TESTING OF PRELIMINARY DESIGN HELIOSTATS.** Negotiations are being conducted with Martin Marietta Corp., Denver, Colorado 80201. See note 46.

★ **A - - DEVELOPMENT AND PREPARATION OF PROJECT PLANS, AND COST/BENEFIT ANALYSIS.** Negotiations are being conducted with Aerospace Corp., P.O. Box 92957, Los Angeles, CA 90009. See note 46.

★ **A - - PREPARATION AND EVALUATIONS OF ELECTROCATALYSTS FOR PHOSPHORIC ACID FUEL CELLS** Negotiations are being conducted with Stonehart Associates, Inc. 34 Five Fields Road, Madison, CT 06643. See note 46.

★ **A - - AMMONIA VAPORIZATION STUDIES RELATED TO OTEC.** Negotiations are being conducted with GEOSCIENCE LTD, Solana Beach, CA 92075. This is a continuation of a program already undertaken by the above firm. See note 46. (171)

U.S. Department of Energy, 1333 Broadway, Oakland, CA 64612

A - - COLLECTING RESERVOIR DATA, SELECTING TARGET RESERVOIRS, AND DRILLING TEST WELLS FOR CARBON DIOXIDE MISCIBLE FLOODING The purpose of the contract will be to build a solid engineering foundation upon which field pilot tests may be conducted for the purpose of extending the technology base in carbon dioxide miscible flooding, a cost sharing type of contract is anticipated. However, a CPFF arrangement for selected tasks will be considered. Interested parties should request a copy of RFP EW-78-R-05-8341; Firms that have already requested the RFP as a result of the synopsis in PSA-7069, 5 May 78, should not submit another request for the RFP. Copies of the RFP will be sent only to requests complying with note 67.(171)

U. S. Department of Energy, Oak Ridge Operations Office, Attn: M. Krisberg, Contract Division, PO E, Oak Ridge TN 37830

★ **A - - DEVELOP AND IMPLEMENT A PROGRAM PLANNING/MANAGEMENT INFORMATION SYSTEM FOR THE S-3 WEAPON SYSTEM IMPROVMENT PROGRAM.** Negotiations with Arinc Research Corp., 2551 Riva Road, Annapolis, MD 21401. See note 46—NAVAIR Synopsis 262-78.

★ **A - - RESEARCH STUDY ON THE USE OF POLARIZATION DISCRIMINATION TECHNIQUES FOR RADAR DETECTION OF SEA TARGETS.** Negotiations with Teledyne Micronetics, 7155 Mission Gorge Road, P.O. Box 20396, San Diego, CA 92120. See note 46—NAVAIR Synopsis 261-78. (171)

Naval Air Systems Command Headquarters (A02E1), Washington, DC 20361

★**A - - KWAJALEIN MISSILE RANGE DATA CENTER** A twelve month requirement for maintenance services for automatic data processing equipment consisting of CDC 7600/6400 and related peripherals and EAM, software support services and operational services at the Kwajalein Missile Range, Marshall Islands, Pacific Trust Territory—RFQ DASG60-78-Q-01611—will be issued on 20 Jun 78—Firms interested in subcontract opportunities should contact Control Data Corporation, Attn: Mr. John Paterson, 8100 S. 34th Ave., Minneapolis MI 55044. See note 40.(171)

Ballistic Missile Defense Sys Comd, Contracts OFC, Attn: Mr. W. J. Edwards/205/895-4420, PO Box 1500, Huntsville AL 35807.

A - - DEMONSTRATION OF VAPOR CONTROL TECHNOLOGY FOR GASOLINE LOADING OF BARGES. The Contractor will be required to evaluate and assess the economics, performance, safety and general suitability of several candidate vapor control systems, and to install and operate a pilot version of one of the candidate systems at a marine terminal. Interested parties may receive copies of the RFP No. DU-78-A223 by submitting written requests to EPA within ten days after the date of this advertisement. (171)

Environmental Protection Agency, Contracts Management Division (MD-33), Office of Administration, Attn: NCCM-L, Research Triangle Park, NC 27711

★ **A - - EVALUATION OF CARBON-14 CONTROL TECHNOLOGY AND COST FOR LIGHT WATER REACTOR FACILITIES.** Negotiation of a purchase order with Nuclear Consulting Services, Columbus, Ohio 43229. See Note 46.

★ **A - - ANALYSIS OF HUMAN ACTIVITY PROFILE**Negotiation of a contract (WA 78-C437) with Wyle Research, 128 Maryland Street, El Segundo, California 90245. See Note 46. (171)

Environmental Protection Agency, Headquarters Contract Operations, Procurement Section C, (PM-214-C), Crystal Mall #2, Washington, D C 20460

★ **A - - FABRICATE AND TEST 25MM AND 30MM HIGH EXPLOSIVE DUAL PURPOSE (H.E.D.P.) PROJECTILES** to determine the effects of spin (range) on penetration performance. Negotiations with H.P. White Laboratory, Bel Air, Maryland to formalize an unsolicited proposal from that source. RFQ DAAK10-78-Q-0205 H. Franks, Tel 201/328-6577.

★ **A - - NEUTRON RADIOGRAPHIC EVALUATION OF LIQUID PROPELLANTS.** Negotiations on this requirement will be conducted with Oregon State University, Corvallis, Oregon 97331. RFQ DAAK10-78-Q-0200. See Note 40. J. Kirkbride, Tel 201/328-6563. (171)

U.S. Army Armament R&D Command, Dover, NJ 07801

★**A - - COMBAT DATA EVALUATION OF TACTICAL ELECTRONIC SYSTEMS** Collect and evaluate data on damage to electronic systems under combat conditions in term of conventional weapon effects and to include some estimate of system functional loss from component damage and data reliability—RFQ DAAK11-78-Q-0183 to be released o/a 30 Jun 78 with closing date o/a 31 Jul 78—See notes 49, 64, 80. (171)

Chemical /Ballistics Procurement Division, Attn: DRDAR-PBR/T. Douglass, Bldg E4455, Aberdeen Proving Ground (EA), MD 21010.

A - - CONDUCT RESEARCH ON THE SOCIAL COSTS TO THE NATION OF SEASONALITY AND CYCLICALITY IN THE CONSTRUCTION INDUSTRY for the labor management services Administration (LMSA) of the U. S. Department of Labor. Prospective offerors may request RFP L/A 78-43 within 10 days from the date of this notice. Only written requests will be honored. (171)

U. S. Department of Labor, Office of Administrative Services Division of Procurement Rm S1514, 200 Constitution Avenue, NW, Washington DC 20210.

★ **A - - HIGH POWER AMPLIFIER MODIFICATION TO ENABLE USE WITH TWT AND AN INSTANTANEOUS BANDWIDTH INCREASE.** Anticipate negotiations with Raytheon Co. 141 Spring Street, Lexington, MA. See Note 46.

★ **A - - NAVIGATIONAL TECHNOLOGY SATELLITE PROGRAM STUDY.** Anticipate placement of a contract with D and D Associates Inc. See Note 46. (171)

Supply Officer, Naval Research Laboratory, Washington, D C 20375

★ **A - - SEARCH AND ASSESSMENT OF NEW AND ADVANCED TECHNOLOGIES** RFQ DASG60-78-Q-0167 to be negotiated with LaJolla Institute, 1250 Prospect St., LaJolla, CA 92038—See note 40.

★ **A - - "OPTICAL CONCEPTS DEFINITION ANALYSIS"**—to be completed not later than 31 Mar 79, RFQ DASG60-78-Q-0165—Negotiations will be conducted with Teledyne Brown Engineering, Cummings Research Park, Huntsville, AL 35807. (171)

Ballistic Missile Defense Systems Command, Contracts Office, BMDSC-CRS, P.O. Box 1500, Huntsville, AL 35807

Content

Page
SUBSCRIPTION INFORMATION, SEE COL. 3 20
Description of Legends, Col. 2 20
Procurements of Services and Supplies .... 1 to 19
Research & Development Sources Scught .... 19 & 20
Contract Awards 20
Surplus Property Sales 20

Figure 2. A sample front page of the *Commerce Business Daily.*

The Commerce Department urges you to spend $105.00 a year, in return for which they promise to mail the CBD by first-class mail. Perhaps that will help, but it seems doubtful, given mail performance of recent years.

The sample page shown (Figure 2) illustrates some typical notices. The notices are published under more than 100 classifications, divided into the two classes of "Services" and "Supplies." Most, but not all, services are procured via RFPs (Requests for Proposal). Most, but not all, supplies are procured via IFBs (Information for Bid).

RFPs are used when the work is custom work and the agency wishes the freedom to judge a bidder's proposed program and qualifications on its merits, regardless of price, and to be able to select other than the lowest bidder when it appears to be in the best interests of the government. Under the IFB, the bidder submits prices only, and the low bidder is awarded the job with only rare exception.

The rationale is, of course, that the only difference between one supplier of sugar, nails, or IBM typewriters will be price, whereas there may be a world of difference between one custom-designed radar set and another, and accepting the low bid may well result in a disaster rather than a good contract.

The CBD is a mainstay of government marketers despite its shortcomings, one of which is that many notices appear too close to the bid deadline to be of practical value. And this drawback is made even more serious by the slowness of delivery services, so that all too often the notice is academic. Still, a serious bidder can find enough items to pursue among the several hundred printed every day under the many categories.

How to Read the CBD

Much of what is printed in the CBD is a jargon of terms peculiar to government contracting: *indef qty, COB, IFB, RFQ, RFP, BOA, Sol, o/a,* and many others. It takes some practice simply to learn to read the items as though they were in everyday English.

Here is an example of an item:

---

34 Metalworking Machinery.

---

34 - - GRINDING MACHINE—Carabide saw blades. Items required are brand name or equal to Foley Mfg. Co.'s Model 310-33 or Model 357 w/attachments & supplies. NSN: 3415-01-M10-5712. End Use: Shop equipment, 2 each. F.O.B. Destination to various depots in conus—PP&P shall conform to C/L. 100% option. IFB DAAA09-78-B-6687—Issue Date o/a 26 May 78, with opening date 30 days from issue. Phone inquiries, 309/794-4664 or 4166. See Note 57. (142)

US Army Armament Materiel Readiness Command, ATTN: DRSAR-PCP, Rock Island, IL 61299

Translated, it says this:

Two grinding machines, as described, are to be purchased. They must be either Foley Manufacturing Co.'s Model 310–33 or Model 357 with attachments, but may be another if equal to these and meeting specifications of NSN 3415–01–M10

–5712. Contractor will prepay shipping charges to various destinations in conti-
nental United States. Write to address below and request solicit IFB DAAA09–78
–B–6687, which will be available about May 26, 1978, with bids due approximately
30 days following. You may call the listed telephone numbers for more information, if you have questions.

That is what the item *says*. However, unless you have some familiar-
ity with government procurement forms and practices, you still may not
have the full meaning. One thing you should know is that the solicitation
is an IFB, which means that the contract will go to the lowest bidder, and
that the bids will be opened publicly and read aloud. Anyone may attend.
The exact date, time, and place of the bid opening will be given in the bid
set.

Note 57 is one of a pageful of notes published in the CBD each
Monday. If you look this one up, you will find that it simply urges speed in
responding. This is rather typical of a one-time, definite-quantity
procurement.

Here are three more items. The first is a Request for Quotations
(RFQ). An RFQ is not really a procurement solicitation but is just what it
says—a request for quotations, with the quotation binding on neither
party, as the fine print on the RFQ form will tell you. Should the government decide to act on one of the quotations submitted, a purchase order
will be issued. Usually, but not always, the RFQ is used for procurements
expected to run not more than $10,000.

---

71 Furniture.

---

71 -- METAL STORAGE CABINET 7125-00-893-5580-W/Sliding Glass
Doors-o/a DIM. 24'' D, 72'' H, 48'' W, 4 Adj. Shelves-18 ea for delivery to
Norfolk, VA-Request for Quotes No. 8PN-E-M6245-1—Opening Date 12 Jun
78. (143)
**General Services Administration, Region 8, Business Service
Center, Building 41, Denver Federal Center, Denver, CO 80225**

---

❶ **71 -- CABINETS, STORAGE,** NSN 7125-00-357-5337, IAW Mil Spec
MIL-C-40009C dtd 16 Mar 71, 595 ea. Destns various—IFB DLA400-78-B-
2402—Bid Opening 26 Jun 78. Technical information Mr. Wilkinson, 804/275-
3608. See notes 70, 72 and 80. (142)
**Defense General Supply Center, Richmond, VA 23297
Tel 804/275-3350**

---

71 -- PLASTIC CATALOG CARD CABINETS and Magazine Rack, NSC
NONE, IAW description cited in IFB—185 ea—Destns. Various—IFB DLA400-
78-B-2504—Bid Opening 23 Jun 78. Technical informaton, Mrs. Eudailey,
804/275-3263. See notes 72, 73 and 80. (142)
**Defense General Supply Center, Richmond, VA 23297
Tel 804/275-3350**

The second item is a competitive, sealed bid—an IFB type of solicitation, with shipments to various destinations. The notice does not specify

"FOB" (Free on Board) or government B/L (Bills of Lading) furnished, so you'll have to read the bid sets to find out whether you pay the freight (FOB) or whether the government pays by furnishing the bills of lading for the shipments. You'll want to be sure to determine which is the case, if the bid set fails to specify.

Note the special symbol beside the second item—the "1" in a small circle, printed in reverse. If you look this up, you'll find that this means that the procurement is a set-aside for small business, and large corporations are thereby barred from bidding. The item, therefore, is for 595 storage cabinets to be bought and shipped to various destinations.

The third item is similar to the second one, a sealed-bid, competitive procurement, with shipments to various destinations.

Most commodity items, whether they are required to match government specifications or be of standard commercial quality, are bought this way, and by far most frequently via the IFB rather than the RFQ. On the other hand, if you study the items reproduced in the sample front page of the CBD (Figure 2), you will note that most of them list an RFP number. This means that the bidders will have to submit formal proposals, since *RFP* means "Request for Proposal," and be judged on other factors in addition to price.

You may note that some items specify that "negotiations will be conducted with" some firm named. These are sole-source or selected-source procurements, and they are usually for services of a highly technological nature, calling for specialized experience. Even in these cases, the selected firm usually must prepare a proposal, however, to establish a base for negotiations.

The items are listed under the categories shown in Table 1. And even with this large number of categories, there is a "Miscellaneous" one for both services and supplies to accommodate any requirement that does not appear to fit one of the standard ones.

Table 1. Goods and Services Listed in the Commerce Business Daily

Services

A	Experimental, Developmental, Test, and Research Work	N	Installation of Equipment
H	Expert and Consultant Services	O	Funeral and Chaplain Services
J	Maintenance and Repair of Equipment	P	Salvage Services
K	Modification, Alteration, and Rebuilding of Equipment	Q	Medical Services
L	Technical Representative Services	R	Architect–Engineer Service
M	Operation and Maintenance of Government-Owned Facility	S	Housekeeping Services
		T	Photographic, Mapping, Printing, and Publication Services
		U	Training Services

Continued

Table 1. (Continued)

Services

V	Transportation Services
W	Lease or Rental, except Transportation Equipment
X	Miscellaneous (Services)
Y	Construction (Various)
Z	Maintenance, Repair, and Alteration of Real Property

Supplies, Equipment, and Materiel

10 Weapons
11 Nuclear Ordnance
12 Fire Control Equipment
13 Ammunition and Explosives
14 Guided Missiles
15 Aircraft and Airframe Structural Components
16 Aircraft Components and Accessories
17 Aircraft Launching, Landing, and Ground Handling Equipment
18 Space Vehicles
19 Ships, Small Craft, Pontoons, and Floating Docks
20 Ship and Marine Equipment
22 Railway Equipment
23 Motor Vehicles, Trailers, and Cycles
24 Tractors
25 Vehicular Equipment Components
26 Tires and Tubes
28 Engines, Turbines, and Components
29 Engine Accessories
30 Mechanical Power Transmission Equipment
31 Bearing
32 Woodworking Machinery and Equipment
34 Metalworking Machinery
35 Service and Trade Equipment
36 Special Industry Machinery
37 Agricultural Machinery and Equipment
38 Construction, Mining, Excavating, and Highway Maintenance Equipment
39 Materials-Handling Equipment
40 Rope, Cable, Chain, and Fittings
41 Refrigeration and Air-Conditioning Equipment
42 Fire-Fighting, Rescue, and Safety Equipment
43 Pumps and Compressors
44 Furnace, Steam Plant, and Drying Equipment; Nuclear Reactors

45 Plumbing, Heating, and Sanitation Equipment
46 Water Purification and Sewage Treatment Equipment
47 Pipe, Tubing, Hose, and Fittings
48 Valves
49 Maintenance and Repair Shop Equipment
51 Hand Tools
52 Measuring Tools
53 Hardware and Abrasives
54 Prefabricated Structures and Scaffolding
55 Lumber, Millwork, Plywood, and Veneer
56 Construction and Building Materials
58 Communications Equipment
59 Electrical and Electronic Equipment Components
61 Electric Wire; Power and Distribution Equipment
62 Lighting Fixtures and Lamps
63 Alarm and Signal Systems
65 Medical, Dental, and Veterinary Equipment and Supplies
66 Instruments and Laboratory Equipment
67 Photographic Equipment
68 Chemicals and Chemical Products
69 Training Aids and Devices
70 General Purpose ADP Equipment, Software, Supplies, and Support Equipment
71 Furniture
72 Household and Commercial Furnishings and Appliances
73 Food Preparation and Serving Equipment
74 Office Machines, Visible Record Equipment, and Data-Processing Equipment
75 Office Supplies and Devices

Table 1. (Continued)

Supplies, Equipment, and Materiel

76 Books, Maps, and Other Publications	85 Toiletries
78 Recreational and Athletic Equipment	87 Agricultural Supplies
79 Cleaning Equipment and Supplies	89 Subsistence
80 Brushes, Paints, Sealers, and Supplies	91 Fuels, Lubricants, Oils, and Waxes
81 Containers, Packaging, and Packing Supplies	93 Nonmetallic Fabricated Materials
	94 Nonmetallic Crude Materials
83 Textiles, Leather, Furs, Apparel, and Shoe Findings; Tents and Flags	95 Metal Bars, Sheets, and Shapes
	96 Ores, Minerals, and Their Primary Products
84 Clothing, Individual Equipment, and Insignia	99 Miscellaneous

Using the CBD

We've talked about reading the CBD—interpreting the jargon and abbreviations and understanding the nature of the various bidding situations described by the items. But *reading* the CBD is not the same as *using* the CBD.

For one thing, there is the matter of selecting the classifications you will read (see Table 1). If you are a supplier of metalworking machinery, category 34 is your natural target. However, such other categories as 35, 36, and perhaps even 20 may be useful for you to read: they may very well list bid opportunities of value.

Rarely does a contractor find himself restricted to only one category, for a variety of reasons. A technical writer would expect to find most relevant bid opportunities under category T, but would, in fact, then miss opportunities listed under categories A, H, U, and X, and perhaps even under R. This is because many jobs are difficult to classify, but it is also because mistakes are made and sometimes poor judgment is exercised.

---

81 Containers, Packaging, and Packing Supplies.

---

81 - - PRESSBOARD FOLDERS for PHS Indian Hospital in Wagner, Rapid City, Rosebud, and Sisseton, South Dakota; also for Ft. Totten, North Dakota, and Winnebago, Nebraska—IFB 2887-3-8-78 opens 3 Mar 78—Requests for copies of the IFB will be honored if received within 15 calendar days after issuance on February 13, 1978, Attn: Contracting Officer.

DHEW, U.S. Public Health Service, Aberdeen Area Indian Health Service, Federal Building, Aberdeen, SD 57401

Here is an example of a misclassified item. Pressboard folders are stationery items—office supplies—and should normally be listed as such, rather than as packaging materials. Obviously, few suppliers of crates, cartons, and shipping containers handle pressboard folders, and few stationers would look here for bid opportunities.

You will note, too, that category 69 is for "Training Aids and De-vices." That refers to models, training equipment, and other hardware or physical aids rather than to software—manuals, lesson plans, films, slides, etc. However, such software is occasionally listed in this category, and writers or producers of training software would do well to monitor this classification.

Category 74 is for data-processing equipment and generally lists only data-processing hardware. However, computer software is sometimes listed here. So an alert and conscientious monitoring of the CBD will turn up many unexpected opportunities, and the most attractive feature of these is that many others will have missed the item, thereby sharply reducing the competition.

"Research and Development Sources Sought"

The CBD also lists long-lead advance notices frequently, advising the reader of anticipated future procurements, under the heading "Research and Development Sources Sought." A typical item is reproduced here, along with the explanatory heading. The purpose of these notices is, usually, to develop a bidders' list of qualified firms in anticipation of issuing solicitations.

RESEARCH AND DEVELOPMENT
SOURCES SOUGHT

In order that potential sources may learn of research and development pro-grams, advance notice of the Government's interest in a specific research field is published here. Firms having the research and development capabilities de-scribed are invited to submit complete information to the purchasing office list-ed. Information should include: the total number of employees and professional qualifications of scientists, engineers, and personal specially qualified in the R&D area outlined, and description of general and special facilities, an outline of previous projects including specific work previously performed or being per-formed in the listed R&D area; statement regarding industrial security clearance previously granted; and other available descriptive literature. Note that these are not requests for proposals. Respondents will not be notified of the results of the evaluation of the information submitted, but the sources deemed fully qualified will be considered when requests for proposals are solicited. Closing date for submission of responses is 14 days from publication of the notice, un-less otherwise specified.

AERODYNAMIC ANALYSIS OF AIRCRAFT FIRES. Exploratory Develop-ment Area PMRN 79-67. Determine the effects of aerodynamic parameters on the initiation and perpetuation of aircraft fuel fires and to develop an anlytical modeling technique that will enable the aircraft fuel fire phenomena to be stud-ied in existing test facilities. Major program tasks will entail a survey of appli-cable test and combat data, the generation of an analytical model, the develop-ment of a set of scaling parameters, a study of the adequacy of acailable test facilities and the design of a model verification experimental test program. The results of this effort will be documented in a final report detailing all aspects of the program. See Note 11, 31, and the first paragraph of 68. Firms responding to this announcement should indicate whether they are or are not a minority enterprise. Closing date for submission of responses is 20 days from publication of this notice. Sponsor -, Attn: AFFDL/FES, T. Sabick, Phone 513/255-6303.

BIPOLAR TRANSISTOR DEVELOPMENT. (Research) Area PMRE 79-86. Analytic and experimental capabilities relative to the development of microwave power transistors in the 8-10 GHz frequency range are sought to conduct an exploratory development program for improved performance and reproducibility of these devices. Qualifications shall be presented with respect to processing technology capabilities such as electron beam lithography, ion implantation and epitaxial techniques as applicable to microwave transistors. Demonstrated capability in the area of fabrication and packaging of microwave transistors in this frequency range is required. See Notes 11, 31 and the first paragraph of 68. "Firms responding to this announcement should indicate whether they are or are not a minority business enterprise." Closing date for submission of response is 20 days from publication of this notice. Sponsor: AFAL/DHM, Neil DiGiacomo, (513) 255-4024.

STRUCTURAL ADHESIVES. Exploratory Development Area PMRR 79(20). Further develop the dielectric cure monitoring technique for adhesive bonded metallic and composite joints using film type aerospace structural adhesives. Monitoring of the curing adhesive shall indicate the attainment of the optimum cure to produce joints of maximized strength and durability. Improvements shall be made in the technique reliability and signal quality of the dielectric probes embedded in the bondline. Determine the affect of adhesive components on the monitoring response of several generic formulations of aerospace structural adhesives, such as elastomeric modifiers, metallic fillers, etc., and the percentage content of these in the adhesive. Investigate the effect of process parameters such as heatup rate, hold time, etc., on the signal response and joint quality. Relate monitor response to chemorheological effects of adhesives and surface preparations involved in the various joints. Investigate the long time structural durability of bonded joints containing embedded probes under various environments. Respondents must have documented experience in dielectric cure monitoring, fabrication and evaluation of adhesive bonded joints, both organizationally and in terms of current personnel. Facility requirements include monitoring equipment, heated platen press, autoclave, structural durability test fixtures and apparatus for compositional analysis of uncured film adhesives. See notes 11, 31 and the first paragraph of 68. Firms responding to this announcement should indicate whether they are or are not a minority business enterprise. Closing date for submission of response is 20 days from publication of this notice. Sponsor: AFML/MBC, E. Arvay, 513/255-2201.

INVESTIGATE METHODS TO IMPROVE THE EFFICIENCY AND PRODUCTIVITY OF RESEARCH AND DEVELOPMENT ENGINEERS AND THEIR DIRECT SUPPORT STAFF through the use of advanced office automation system techniques, to design such a system for RADC usage and to perform feasibility experimentation to demonstrate achieved success. Investigation will include compilation of subjective data regarding personnel, training requirements and paperwork processing procedures. Experimentation will require contractor provision of machine time, workstations, output devices, system engineering and programming to support the contractor-proposed automated office environment. Qualified sources must demonstrate extensive knowledge and capabilities in large-system office automation and data base management.

Rome Air Development Center (PKRL), Attn: Capt Hunter, Tel 315/330-2317. Griffiss AFB NY 13441

The explanation provided tells the story. The agency listed requests that interested parties submit information presenting the respondent's qualifications to undertake the program and expressing desire to be included on the bidders' list. Usually there is a time limit of 10, 20, or 30 days (from date of notice) for the response, and only those responding and considered to be qualified will be invited to submit bids later.

These items are usually in technological areas, frequently addressing some specific problem or requirement the advertiser anticipates, but may be in any of the many areas of industry and science. For example, the items listed here are in electronics, fire fighting, aviation, adhesives, and industrial engineering.

The way to respond to such items is with a letter expressing interest and enclosing a statement of the respondent's capabilities. Company brochures may be enclosed, if available and relevant.

"Miscellaneous"

The "Miscellaneous" categories make interesting reading, as well as furnishing many unexpected opportunities for business. Almost any kind of item may spring up here, for almost any kind of federal agency. The "Miscellaneous" category in the "Services" portion of the CBD is where you can find requirements for go-go dancers, wild-horse roundups, refereeing services, and many other unexpected and novel projects.

Between the two "Miscellaneous" categories, if you read them regularly, you will soon learn the truth of the allegation that there is virtually no goods or service that cannot be sold to the government.

X Miscellaneous.

X - - OPERATION OF PHYSICAL MAP DISTRIBUTION PROCESS—The Department of Housing and Urban Development (HUD) prime contractor E.D.S. Federal Corporation requires the services of an experienced physical distributor with adequate facilities. The objective of the physical map distribution process is to distribute HUD-produced Flood Hazard Boundary Maps ("FHBMs") and Flood Insurance Rate Maps ("FIRMs") for use by qualified agents, brokers, and lending institutions who participate in the National Flood Insurance Program. The process will be composed of receiving maps from HUD, receiving map orders via teleprocessing channels, fulfilling the map orders and shipping the maps to qualified requestors within definitive time schedules; and installing and maintaining a map distribution system for production of shipping labels, reference files for the stock of maps in inventory and prior and current recipients and production of reports required by the program. There will be a transition period prior to inception of the contract in which the successful bidder will be required to participate. It is suggested that experienced and qualified organizations interested in subcontracting opportunities in connection with this procurement submit their request in writing to the prime contractor direct. In that the solicitation package will contain considerable volume of information and documentation, it has been determined that a $50. deposit is required and must accompany the request before the solicitation package will be shipped to the requestor. If a requestor of the IFB submits a bid, the $50. deposit will then be refunded. Requests will not be accepted after 21 Jul 78, at 5:00 P.M. Telephone request will not be honored. Solicitation IFB #1. (173)

National Flood Insurance Program, P.O. Box 34294, Bethesda, MD 20034; Att: Contract Administrator

---

X - - SUPPORT OF THE ACTIVITIES OF THE U.S. NATIONAL COMMITTEES' PARTICIPATION IN THE MEMBERSHIP IN THE INTERNATIONAL COUNCIL FOR BUILDING RESEARCH STUDIES AND DOCUMENTATION Proposed award of a single source contract to the National Academy of Sciences, Washington, D.C. To effectively perform, the Contractor shall provide a liaison mechanism for the International Council for Building, Research, Studies and Documentation (CIB) and the exchange of building research data and information between U.S. public and private organizations and CIB. The Government knows only of this single source who can perform the required service. Inquiries concerning the proposed award should be made within 10 days from the publication date of this notice.

DHEW Contracts Branch, Division of Materiel Management, ASC, Attn: Mrs. Stephenson, Room 3B-26, Parklawn Building, 5600 Fishers Lane, Rockville MD 20857

Selling Proprietaries to Government Agencies

A question that constantly arises in my mail and over the telephone concerns how to sell someone's special, proprietary item or service. For example, a recent call was from a lady in nearby Silver Spring, Maryland, who runs a home business with her husband, manufacturing some sort of presentation folio. She told me that it was an unusually effective tool for making presentations, and she wondered if there were some prospect for selling it to the government. My answer was an enthusiastic "Yes." I can think of no organization that makes more presentations within their system—and to others outside the system—than the U.S. government. Agencies are constantly called upon to make presentations to each other, to heads of departments, to congressional committees, and to outside parties, such as industry groups and general community groups—the U.S. public. Certainly there should be a great deal of interest, if the product is what the lady claimed for it: a better way.

One direct attack on this problem is to take it to the General Services Administration, Federal Supply Service, and offer it as a better product. If it takes their fancy, they might well buy a sample stock and try it out. You might offer to furnish samples at your own expense, if you choose to. The same procedure may be followed with the Defense Supply Agency, of course. You may also be able to have a Federal Stock Number furnished for your item, if it is received well enough and the government wishes to stock it regularly.

None of this precludes you from offering it directly to each and every government agency, either, since they do not have to go to their centralized supply sources for their purchases.

BIDDER'S MAILING LIST APPLICATION	INITIAL APPLICATION	FORM APPROVED OMB NO.
	REVISION	**29–R0069**

Fill in all spaces. Insert "NA" in blocks not applicable. Type or print all entries. See reverse for instructions.

TO (*Enter name and address of Federal agency to which form is submitted. Include ZIP Code*)	DATE

1. APPLICANT'S NAME AND ADDRESS (*Include county and ZIP Code*)	2. ADDRESS (*Include county and ZIP Code*) TO WHICH SOLICITATIONS ARE TO BE MAILED (*If different from item 1*)

3.   TYPE OF ORGANIZATION (*Check one*)   **4. HOW LONG IN PRESENT BUSINESS**

INDIVIDUAL		PARTNERSHIP	NON-PROFIT ORGANIZATION	
CORPORATION, INCORPORATED UNDER THE LAWS OF THE STATE OF				

5.   NAMES OF OFFICERS, OWNERS, OR PARTNERS

PRESIDENT	VICE PRESIDENT	SECRETARY
TREASURER	OWNERS OR PARTNERS	

6. AFFILIATES OF APPLICANT (*Names, locations and nature of affiliation. See definition on reverse*)

7.   PERSONS AUTHORIZED TO SIGN BIDS, OFFERS, AND CONTRACTS IN YOUR NAME (*Indicate if agent*)

NAME	OFFICIAL CAPACITY	TEL. NO. (*Incl. area code*)

8. IDENTIFY EQUIPMENT, SUPPLIES, MATERIALS, AND/OR SERVICES ON WHICH YOU DESIRE TO BID (*See attached Federal agency's supplemental listing and instructions, if any*)

9.   TYPE OF OWNERSHIP (*See definitions on reverse*)

MINORITY BUSINESS ENTERPRISE	OTHER THAN MINORITY BUSINESS ENTERPRISE

10.   TYPE OF BUSINESS (*See definitions on reverse*)

MANUFACTURER OR PRODUCER	REGULAR DEALER (*Type 1*)	REGULAR DEALER (*Type 2*)
SERVICE ESTABLISHMENT	CONSTRUCTION CONCERN	RESEARCH AND DEVELOPMENT FIRM

     ☐ SURPLUS DEALER (*Check this box if you are also a dealer in surplus goods*)

11.   SIZE OF BUSINESS (*See definitions on reverse*)

SMALL BUSINESS CONCERN*	OTHER THAN SMALL BUSINESS CONCERN	
If you are a small business concern, fill in (a) and (b):	(a) AVERAGE NUMBER OF EMPLOYEES (*Including affiliates*) FOR FOUR PRECEDING CALENDAR QUARTERS	(b) AVERAGE ANNUAL SALES OR RECEIPTS FOR PRECEDING THREE FISCAL YEARS

12. FLOOR SPACE (*Square feet*)		**13.** NET WORTH	
MANUFACTURING	WAREHOUSE	DATE	AMOUNT

14.   SECURITY CLEARANCE (*If applicable, check highest clearance authorized*)

FOR	TOP SECRET	SECRET	CONFIDENTIAL	NAMES OF AGENCIES WHICH GRANTED SECURITY CLEARANCES (*Include dates*)
KEY PERSONNEL				
PLANT ONLY				

THIS SPACE FOR USE BY THE GOVERNMENT	CERTIFICATION
	I certify that information supplied herein (*Including all pages attached*) is correct and that neither the applicant nor any person (*Or concern*) in any connection with the applicant as a principal or officer, so far as is known, is now debarred or otherwise declared ineligible by any agency of the Federal Government from bidding for furnishing materials, supplies, or services to the Government or any agency thereof.
	SIGNATURE
	NAME AND TITLE OF PERSON AUTHORIZED TO SIGN (*Type or print*)

129–105   **STANDARD FORM 129** (REV. 2–77)
Prescribed by GSA, FPR (41 CFR) 1–16.802

Figure 3A. Standard Form 129 used to apply for inclusion in regular bidders' lists.

Studying the CBD regularly is one way of identifying the agencies most likely to be interested in your service or product. If we take the case of the presentation folio, for example, it's an item of general enough interest to make any and all agencies potential customers. At the same time, some agencies make presentations more frequently than do others.

INFORMATION AND INSTRUCTIONS

Persons or concerns wishing to be added to a particular agency's bidder's mailing list for supplies or services shall file this properly completed and certified Bidder's Mailing List Application, together with such other lists as may be attached to this application form, with each procurement office of the Federal agency with which they desire to do business. If a Federal agency has attached a Supplemental Commodity List with instructions, complete the application as instructed. Otherwise, identify in item 8 the equipment, supplies and/or services on which you desire to bid. The application shall be submitted and signed by the principal as distinguished from an agent, however constituted.

After placement on the bidder's mailing list of an agency, a supplier's failure to respond (*submission of bid, or notice in writing, that you are unable to bid on that particular transaction but wish to remain on the active bidder's mailing list for that particular item*) to Invitations for Bids will be understood by the agency to indicate lack of interest and concurrence in the removal of the supplier's name from the purchasing activity's bidder's mailing list for the items concerned.

DEFINITION RELATiNG TO TYPE OF OWNERSHIP
(See item 9)

Minority business enterprise. A minority business enterprise is defined as a "business, at least 50 percent of which is owned by minority group members or, in case of publicly owned businesses, at least 51 percent of the stock of which is owned by minority group members." For the purpose of this definition, minority group members are Negroes, Spanish-speaking American persons, American-Orientals, American-Indians, American-Eskimos, and American-Aleuts.

TYPE OF BUSINESS DEFINITIONS
(See item 10)

a. Manufacturer or producer—means a person (or concern) owning, operating, or maintaining a store, warehouse, or other establishment that produces, on the premises, the materials, supplies, articles, or equipment of the general character of those listed in item 8, or in the Federal Agency's Supplemental Commodity List, if attached.

b. Regular dealer (Type 1)—means a person (or concern) who owns, operates, or maintains a store, warehouse, or other establishment in which the materials, supplies, articles, or equipment of the general character listed in item 8 or in the Federal Agency's Supplemental Commodity List, if attached, are bought, kept in stock, and sold to the public in the usual course of business.

c. Regular dealer (Type 2)—in the case of supplies of particular kinds (*at present, petroleum, lumber and timber products, machine tools, raw cotton, green coffee, hay, grain, feed, or straw, agricultural liming materials, tea, raw or unmanufactured cotton linters*). **Regular dealer**—means a person (or concern) satisfying the requirements of the regulations (Code of Federal Regulations, Title 41, 50–201.101(b)) as amended from time to time, prescribed by the Secretary of Labor under the Walsh-Healey Public Contracts Act (Title 41 U.S. Code 35–45). For coal dealers see Code of Federal Regulations, Title 41, 50–201.604(a).

d. Service establishment—means a concern (or person) which owns, operates, or maintains any type of business which is principally engaged in the furnishing of nonpersonal services, such as (*but not limited to*) repairing, cleaning, redecorating, or rental of personal property, including the furnishing of necessary repair parts or other supplies as part of the services performed.

e. Construction concern—means a concern (or person) engaged in construction, alteration or repair (including dredging, excavating, and painting) of buildings, structures, and other real property.

DEFINITIONS RELATING TO SIZE OF BUSINESS
(See item 11)

a. Small business concern—A small business concern for the purpose of Government procurement is a concern, including its affiliates, which is independently owned and operated, is not dominant in the field of operation in which it is bidding on Government contracts and can further qualify under the criteria concerning number of employees, average annual receipts, or other criteria, as prescribed by the Small Business Administration. (See Code of Federal Regulations, Title 13, Part 121, as amended, which contains detailed industry definitions and related procedures.)

b. Affiliates—Business concerns are affiliates of each other when either directly or indirectly (i) one concern controls or has the power to control the other, or (ii) a third party controls or has the power to control both. In determining whether concerns are independently owned and operated and whether or not affiliation exists, consideration is given to all appropriate factors including common ownership, common management, and contractual relationship. (*See items 6 and 11.*)

c. Number of employees—In connection with the determination of small business status, "number of employees" means the average employment of any concern, including the employees of its domestic and foreign affiliates, based on the number of persons employed on a full-time, part-time, temporary, or other basis during each of the pay periods of the preceding 12 months. If a concern has not been in existence for 12 months, "number of employees" means the average employment of such concern and its affiliates during the period that such concern has been in existence based on the number of persons employed during each of the pay periods of the period that such concern has been in business. (*See item 11.*)

● **COMMERCE BUSINESS DAILY**—The Commerce Business Daily, published by the Department of Commerce, contains information concerning proposed procurements, sales, and contract awards. For further information concerning this publication, contact your local Commerce Field Office.

129-105   ☆ U.S.GPO:1977-0-241-530/3521   STANDARD FORM 129 BACK (REV. 2–77)

Figure 3B. Standard Form 129 (reverse) instructions.

Agencies directly involved with consumer interests, for instance, are likely to make many presentations to congressional committees and to nongovernment groups. Such agencies would include the Consumer Product Safety Commission, the National Cancer Institute, and the Department of Energy.

Getting on Bidders' Lists

Every procurement office in government maintains bidders' lists, usually a number of them, organized according to interests. One list might be of computer-software developers, another of technical writers, another of office equipment suppliers, etc.

The mechanics for getting on these lists is the use of government Standard Form 129, *Bidder's Mailing List Application* (see Figure 3). Filing this with each procurement office is supposed to ensure getting you on the appropriate bidders' lists, so that you will automatically receive all solicitations of interest to you.

This is effective to only a limited extent, for several reasons. In many cases it simply doesn't work: you file the form but never receive a bid set unless you write and ask specifically for that bid set. Another reason is that you are relying on the agency's ability to match your Form 129 application with each given requirement, and the agency often is unable to do this accurately or effectively; that is, they are unable to judge which bid sets are likely to interest you. (The solicitation rarely matches the SF 129 information exactly.) And another reason is that the agency may already have a long list in your category, and agencies rarely send out more than 50 bid sets unless prospective bidders make specific requests in excess of that number.

Even when filing the standard form does work—and it usually does with the Federal Supply Service more than it does with agencies buying custom services—if the bidders' list on file is a long one, you will be "rotated." You'll get a bid set when your turn comes up, which may be only every third or fourth solicitation. At the same time, the contracting office will invariably request that you file Form 129 when you request that your name be put on the regular bidders' list.

When it does work—when you do get bid sets, after filing a 129—you must protect your position by responding to every bid set you get. If you choose not to bid, you send the procurement office a "no bid," that is, a brief message stating that you are not bidding that particular requirement but wish to be kept on the list for other requirements. If you fail to make any response to a number of bid sets, your name will be dropped (understandably).

One method that helps is to make your first bid after finding the announcement and requesting the bid set. Once a procurement office actually receives a bid from you, and you have a 129 on file, the office tends to send you future bid sets—if you continue to respond with bids or no-bid advices.

Bid Rooms

Agencies that issue frequent bid sets often maintain bid rooms as part of the procurement function. Here you will find all current bid sets posted on bulletin boards. You may scan them and request copies of any that interest you.

Procurement offices that do not maintain bid rooms with bulletin boards usually have all current bid sets in a binder of some sort, which is available for your reading.

Other Methods of Learning of Bid Opportunities

There are many government publications (see the Appendix), some of which will alert you to bid opportunities, immediate or long-range. *The Federal Register,* for example, reports daily on congressional actions and is often a good advance indicator of future programs and contracting opportunities.

Many agencies have publications of their own, some available free of charge from their public affairs offices, others requiring paid subscriptions. Reading these furnishes clues to future programs and requirements quite often.

Unsolicited Proposals

Unsolicited proposals are productive for many contractors. These are proposals offering goods or services, the need for which the contractor has perceived. The goods or services may or may not be proprietary, but the idea must originate with the proposer. If the proposal is accepted, a contract is negotiated. There is no competition because the idea originated with the contractor—theoretically. An unsolicited proposal coming "out of the blue" with no advance discussion is extremely unlikely to be successful. Successful unsolicited proposals are usually the result of a personal discussion of ideas with individuals in the agency and some advance expression of interest by the agency.

At the same time, many contracting officers are extremely suspicious of unsolicited proposals, suspecting that they may not be unsolicited at all but are a private arrangement between the individual government executive and a favored contractor and are being used to circumvent the normal competitive procurement system. Good evidence must be offered that the proposal qualifies as truly unsolicited and presents the contractor's unique ideas, products, facilities, and/or services.

There is danger here, too. A good unsolicited idea may be "pirated" by an agency and result in a bid open to everyone, using the idea. This is not common, but it has been known to happen.

My own experience suggests that there is no really good substitute for reading the CBD every day—and reading it most carefully—if you want to maximize your opportunities for bidding. This is not to say that the CBD should be your only source; the other methods suggested here, including as much personal marketing visitation as you can manage, should be used too, but not to the exclusion of studying the CBD every day.

Commercial Publications

There are some commercial publishers of information intended to aid the bidder in learning of opportunities (see the Appendix), but these are rarely complete substitutes for the CBD and (I believe) should be supplements to the CBD.

Making the Calls

Over the years, I have been able to win many contracts without personal marketing—without making marketing calls on the agencies— simply by learning of opportunities via the CBD, sending for the solicitation package, and responding with good enough proposals to win contracts. This is not, however, an argument for doing it this way. It's "doing it the hard way."

Making personal calls on agencies is just as effective as making personal calls on any other kind of business prospect. You learn more and more about each agency's programs and needs. You learn which agencies are the best prospects for whatever you offer. You get to know the people and what their preferences are. And you make your name known, which helps a great deal also, of course, especially if you are in some business where proposals are required and at least some subjective judgment will be involved in the evaluation. But perhaps most important are these two factors: (1) you generally learn of impending procurements far in advance of the time you would have if you waited for the CBD to advise you, and (2) you learn things that will help you to write more effective proposals.

One most important factor is that you may be able to make some across-the-counter sales—small purchases (up to $10,000) that the agency can make via the informal process of issuing purchase orders. These are not insignificant sales. If you are a small contractor, each and every sale has significance for you of itself, and whether you are small or large, each sale is an opportunity to prove yourself, to get your foot in the door of the agency, and to win bigger and more important jobs later on.

$65,000 from One Call

When I walked into the Labor Department's OSHA, some years ago, I spent several hours tracking down my first customer there, but I soon had a purchase order for $2,400 as a result. That led to another for $2,500 and to still more work, totaling about $23,000. As a result of pleasing this customer, I was recommended to others, winning still more small contracts, which led to larger ones. In all, as a result of that first day's personal marketing, I subsequently won over $65,000 worth of government business.

Even individuals and very small companies win substantial government contracts. The awards announcements of recent issues of the CBD reveal these rewards, for example:

- Labor Department, to James Russo: $164,000 for audit services
- NASA, to Stanley Pollaseck: $48,000 to write a handbook compiling non-metallic materials
- Veterans Administration, to Gust Lagerquist: $29,800 for elevator repair
- GSA, to Ben Rose, Inc.: $50,000 for draperies and upholstery fabrics
- GSA, to Don Swann Sales Corp.: $63,000 for paper napkins

A Few Guidelines on Where to Sell

By now you will have realized that the government market is so huge and diverse—and dynamic, too, as new programs and new agencies come into being—that it is most difficult to make any absolute statements about it. Some general guidelines can be provided, however, to save much of your learning time.

1. If your main field is HRD services—training/training development, behavioral research, surveys and studies involving the human element, aid to the disadvantaged, etc.—HEW, with all its agencies and bureaus should probably be your prime target, although you will find many targets of opportunity throughout the agencies.

2. If technical/scientific research in physical sciences is your field, look primarily to military R & D (research and development) facilities (listed later in this chapter), but keep an interested eye on DOE, NASA, DOT, and EPA as good secondary targets.

3. If you sell common commodities, pursue the Federal Supply Service of GSA and the Defense Supply Service of DOD by all means, but at the same time, don't neglect the Postal Service. And if your commodities include tools, machine parts, etc., some of them may be items purchased regularly by the military service.

4. If you are an A & E (architect–engineer), by all means get a Standard Form 254 on file with the Public Buildings Service of GSA, the Postal Service, and the Corps of Engineers. And keep a few spare ones around for hastening to the many, many other agencies who list A & E requirements in the CBD every day of the year.

5. If your field is computer software development and services, watch the entire government market carefully, for targets pop up everywhere for this service, with many major annual contracts coming out of NASA installations and DOD installations.

6. If you are in management consulting and handle a wide variety of custom services, see Item 1 in this listing, but be most alert for targets of opportunity almost anywhere in government.

7. If you sell strictly consumer goods, some of them may be of interest to the Federal Supply Service, but the military exchanges will probably be a better target, and these may be approached both centrally and individually. Addresses will be found in the Appendix.

R & D Targets

There are numerous military and civilian R & D laboratories: Army, Navy, Air Force, USDA, Commerce, EPA, HEW, HUD, Interior, NASA, DOT, Postal Service, and others. Listings of these will be found in the Appendix.

Special Targets

With Congress in session almost all the year and the great influences for change exerted by the administrations of modern times, many new programs and bureaucratic reorganizations take place. In President Johnson's administration, the Office of Economic Opportunity, with its Job Corps, Head Start, Community Action, and VISTA programs, created quite an enormous market for services and products related to the programs. Those companies and individuals who spent enough time at OEO headquarters in Washington were almost assured of contracts, and many, many new companies were launched on OEO contracts. It is a literal truth that I stumbled over a completely unexpected contract for $50,000 by sauntering past the office of a Ph.D. who called me in, on the spur of the moment, to challenge me with the prospect of doing a six-month study in 30 days. In a fairly short time, this casual conversation led to a six-week contract for nearly $50,000.

A number of years ago, I was able to assist the predecessor agency of EPA, the Air Pollution Control Office (then part of PHS), in publishing its first set of standards, under contract. EPA has issued many millions of dollars in contracts since, and I have been rewarded with a small one now and then.

The new Postal Service Institute (as it was originally known) became an excellent market target and remained so for some years, and the Postal Service generally has spent a great deal of money for buildings and equipment, as well as for services.

A new major program, a new agency, a reorganization of agencies, and other such developments usually spell opportunities for business sooner or later. In most cases, it is later, however, for it generally takes a few months—sometimes longer—before a new agency begins to get itself well enough organized and its programs well enough defined to determine exactly what it is going to need in contract support.

The Department of Energy is the newest such development. As in the case of DOT, DOE is a compilation of older agencies, reassembled as a new entity under a cabinet officer. It will undoubtedly continue its programs, which are already in existence, for a time but will almost assuredly drop some, restructure others, and introduce new ones in time.

The alert marketer will pay a great deal of attention to new agencies and new programs, spending as much time as possible learning where it is, who it is, and what it is. With DOE's $10.4 billion initial budget, it will certainly become a worthwhile target for business opportunity.

5

Get Help from the Government to Sell to the Government

The government will help you to sell to the government. Just push the right buttons.

 ### *Small Business Administration and Its Programs*

Many people have heard about the Small Business Administration (SBA) and its loan/loan-guarantee programs for small businesses. But that isn't even scratching the surface of government aids to businesses, small and large. Government aid to business is a major concern of the administration.

SBA pursues several programs to aid small business:

1. Training and education, through publications and direct counseling by experienced business executives.
2. Loans and loan guarantees—the latter, primarily—to aid small businesses in getting launched successfully.
3. Set-asides for government contracts. The SBA sets "size standards" for various kinds of businesses and causes other government agencies to set aside certain procurements, disqualifying all except those firms meeting the SBA size standards for small business.
4. Procurement assistance, which includes the 8(a) program. This program is designed especially to aid minority firms in winning government contracts set aside especially for minority firms. In

actuality, the contracts are awarded by the other government agency to SBA, who then awards the contract, as a *subcontract*, to the minority firm.

5. A certification program in which the SBA demonstrates to other government agencies' contracting officers that the given firm is technically qualified.

6. An information service to other government agencies to aid them in identifying/locating small business firms that can handle their requirements satisfactorily.

Department of Commerce

Two agencies within the Department of Commerce offer special aids to businesses, large and small. One of these is EDA (Economic Development Administration), and the other is OMBE (Office of Minority Business Enterprise). EDA makes grants and loans or loan guarantees to communities and to private businesses, as well as to organizations, to stimulate the economy—specifically, to provide or save jobs. (This program was covered in Chapter 3.) OMBE offers aid to non-profit organizations, primarily, whose missions are aid to minority-owned businesses. Both grants and contracts are offered to organizations to provide minority firms with various technical assistance and training aid functions, somewhat after the manner of SBA but not necessarily confined to small businesss: size is not a criterion in this case, although the nature of the program is such that it is primarily small businesses that are affected.

Department of Defense

DOD has an active small business program, making earnest efforts to aid small business in winning contracts and subcontracts for defense work of all kinds. In many cases where defense contracts are large, a small-business representative is stationed in the contractor's facility and actively pursues the interests of small businesses in winning subcontracts. That is, he works with the contractor's purchasing officials to aid them in identifying subcontracts that can be handled by small businesses and in finding small business firms to bid for these subcontracts. A small business firm seeking subcontracts is well advised to seek the small-business representative out in these locations and to solicit assistance.

Other General Provisions

In general, all government procurement officials are empowered to make certain special provisions in special cases, where federal law has stipulated that certain bidders are entitled to special consideration, for example, when the bidder's facility is situated in a "labor surplus" area—an area of excessively high unemployment. Given such a situation, the contracting officer may give preference to such a firm. Physically handicapped persons are also entitled to such special preferences, and may invoke such preference in bidding government contracts.

Laws of recent years have recognized the difficulties that women proprietors of businesses have in becoming established, and certain special preferences may be accorded female business proprietors.

All government agencies are required, by law, to provide general aid and guidance to small-business people seeking business. In most major agencies or agency headquarters offices, an employee of the agency, and/or an employee of the agency especially designated as the small-business representative, may be sought out to guide and direct you to the right people to see in the agency. NASA headquarters in Washington, D. C., for example, has two such people: one a general guide/information service, the other specifically responsible for small-business interests in the agency.

GSA Business Service Centers

The General Services Administration operates business service centers in each of its regional offices. In the center are counselors whose specific responsibility is to aid business people in finding their way about in government agencies, offering information and guidance, which includes a number of official government publications explaining procedures for pursuing government business. These are good starting points for businesses. (They explain how the entire system is supposed to work, although it does not always work that way!)

Types of Assistance for Minorities and Small Businesses

A visit to one of the GSA business service centers is worthwhile for anyone unfamiliar with the federal procurement systems. The visitor will get an armload of publications describing the systems, the procurement functions and facilities, and the location of the nearby federal establishments. Counselors are available for personal discussions and counseling services.

Local SBA offices provide a similar service—publications and counseling. However, in the case of SBA, the visitor will also get a great deal of information and counseling on the various SBA programs and how to take advantage of them.

Department of Commerce OMBE offices also provide a variety of publications and counseling services for those qualifying as minorities under the law. In the case of OMBE, there are federal (Department of Commerce) OMBE offices, local-government (state, city, etc.) OMBE offices, and non profit organizations supported with OMBE funds (grants and contracts) for the purpose of aiding minority enterprises in getting started and succeeding in business.

In addition, both SBA and OMBE enter into contracts with for-profit firms to provide training and technical assistance to minority firms. In each service area—and a service area is a single city, in one case, and a much larger area, in another case, according to the estimate of the population to be served—the contractor agrees to provide personal consulting—training services to minority firms, as ordered by SBA or OMBE. The services are according to function: accounting, technical planning, marketing, etc. The contractor must demonstrate a staff including experienced professionals for each functional service category. When a minority firm finds itself in need of assistance to improve its accounting system, write a proposal, prepare an annual report, improve its inventory plan, find better sources of supply, or solve other business problems, it may appeal to its sponsor (SBA or OMBE) and request assistance. The sponsoring agency, if it agrees that the request is justified, then orders the contractor to provide the needed service.

SBA also operates a technology assistance program, under which the agency will aid small firms in getting professional technical assistance to qualify for federal contracts requiring technological sophistication.

Another SBA program is the issuance of certificates of competency. It works in this manner. Should a contracting officer deem a small business firm to be unqualified technically for a project the firm has bid on, the firm may appeal to SBA. SBA will cause the award of the contract to be delayed while SBA checks on the firm's technical qualifications. If SBA is satisfied that the firm is qualified technically to perform the project, SBA will issue a certificate of competency to the firm, and the contracting officer in question will be enjoined from disqualifying the firm from the contract competition. But if the firm were disqualified on the grounds of being unstable financially (i.e., if the firm does not appear to be able to handle the financial burden of funding the project), SBA may again hold up the award while investigating the possibility of finding funds under a loan guarantee to assist the firm in achieving financial stability.

Some Other Programs That Aid Minority Enterprises

NASA and the U.S. Navy have announced, during congressional subcommittee hearings on new revisions to the Small Business Act, that they are pursuing a policy requiring major contractors to present specific plans and programs for significant efforts to subcontract to minority enterprises to the maximum extent possible. When the prime contract is sizable (over $500,000), the bidder must include at least a general plan for subcontracting to minority enterprises. Before final contract award, the contractor must submit a more detailed plan, and in some cases, this plan may be a final determining factor in who is favored with the contract award.

There is increasing emphasis on promoting the cause of small business generally and minority-owned business especially, and more and more congressional attention is being focused on this. The 1977 public works programs, under which $6 billion in grants were issued to approximately 8,000 communities and under local governments for public works projects, provided that at least 10% ($600 million) was to be spent in subcontracts with minority enterprises. That program has been contested in the courts and found unconstitutional by the California Supreme Court and may ultimately go to the U. S. Supreme Court for final adjudication. Meanwhile, a U. S. Appeals Court has found the 10% minority set aside constitutional.

Foreign-Import Damage

A little-known EDA program provides financial assistance to businesses that have been injured by low-priced imported goods. (The shoe manufacturing industry is a special case in point.) The focal point is the effect of the import damage on jobs, as in all cases of EDA assistance. Therefore it must first be established that the foreign import threatens the jobs of United States workers. That certification is done by the Department of Labor, and the application for it is often initiated by whatever labor unions the workers belong to. Once Labor has performed its investigation and issued its certification that the workers of any given employer are in danger of losing or have lost their jobs as a result of imports, the employer may apply to EDA for financial assistance, which is usually a loan guarantee (the loan to be used in some manner to combat and overcome the damage, such as retooling for more efficient production or major marketing campaigns to stimulate sales).

SBA has recently appointed another assistant administrator, a woman whose job it is to create and implement an SBA program to aid women in business enterprises, just as SBA aids others in the until-now male-dominated business world. This administrator is Patricia Cloherty, formerly with a venture capital firm. She joined SBA in 1977 to increase the number of business firms headed and/or owned by women and to offer several programs of assistance to women in or preparing to enter business.

The initial plans call for $400 million in fiscal 1978 business loans to women, and SBA is currently conducting 90 one-day seminars for women who want to enter into business but haven't made definite decisions yet. Fifteen two-day seminars are planned for women who have definitely decided to go ahead with business ventures or are already engaged in a business enterprise.

Among the SBA programs involved in these activities are one for financial assistance (loans and loan guarantees), another for aid in winning government contracts, and still another of internal orientation and training of SBA personnel in the overall program. Details of these programs are not yet available, but the processes will probably follow established lines. Certainly, if the women involved in a business venture belong to a minority covered by the 8(a) program, 8(a) procedures may be followed for government contracts.

Meanwhile, congressional subcommittees are working on revisions to the Small Business Act, which would aid small businesses generally in winning federal contracts. Specifically, S-2259, the Small Business Procurement Expansion and Simplification Act, would give SBA more power and authority in setting federal procurement policies than it now enjoys. As now written, the act would also make all procurements under $10,000 automatic small-business set-asides, and procurement procedures would be greatly simplified.

Under present law, any purchase under $10,000 is a "small purchase," and procurement may (and should) be by government purchase order, rather than by formal contract. This procedure is simple, compared with formal contracting, but it is still somewhat laborious and can easily take two or three weeks to effectuate after the decision has been made to make the purchase.

Meanwhile, while an estimated 160,000 new bidders have sought government contracts in the year past—many unsuccessfully—the General Services Administration and the Department of Commerce are engaged in a joint program to find more bidders and provide more bid opportunities to small business!

Each quarter, GSA and Commerce issue jointly a list of items for which the government would like to have more bids—to increase the competition, on the one hand, and to provide more small-business opportunity, on the other hand. Each of the three lists issued so far (at the date of this writing) has included about 50 to 60 items, many of the items common commodities: commercial-grade office furniture, hand tools, carbon paper, kitchen ware, dining room utensils and crockery, paper goods of various kinds, and other such consumer items.

The anomaly arises from the fact that the government has available, as its media, only official government publications in which to announce these items. The CBD is virtually the only source through which the government agencies may reach potential suppliers with information concerning needs. For some reason, the nation's financial press, including the financial sections of the daily newspapers, choose to ignore news of government markets for their businessmen readers. Or, at the least, they choose not to pursue this field actively and cover it only in the most general of terms and in fragmentary fashion.

Government centralized procurement—Federal Supply Service, Defense Supply Service, and the Postal Service supply depot—stockpile billions of dollars worth of inventory, comprising something on the order of 1.5 billion different items. Merely maintaining the stocks of commonplace items represents in itself a huge market.

6

The Mechanisms of Government Procurement

The alphabet soup continues: government contracts may be FP, CPFF, T & M, BOA, and many other types that are hybrids of basic contracting ideas.

The Two Basic Contractual Approaches

You have already learned that the government generally enters into either fixed-price or cost-reimbursement contractual arrangements and that there are numerous hybrids and variants of each of these. As in all things governmental in the United States, the standard arrangements are soon known by their initial letters, or an acronym.

Fixed-price contracting is, of course, the simplest arrangement, under which the contractor agrees to supply some specified goods, services, or combination of both at an agreed-upon fixed price to be paid after delivery, usually, although "progress payments" are often made. A fixed-price contract may be of any size, from a government purchase order for a few dollars to a formal contract for millions. A fixed-price contract may result from any type of solicitation, too: IFB, RFP, or RFQ. The factor that generally influences what general type of contract will be offered is the degree of specificity that can be agreed upon or with which the government can solicit the procurement.

For example, if the government wishes to buy 1 million commercial-grade No. 2 lead pencils with end erasers mounted in metal ferrules, enameled with yellow paint, and inscribed, "Property of U. S. Government," these become the *specifications* and are generally sufficiently detailed so that there would be no significant difference between the pencils offered by one contractor and those offered by another. In practice, the solicitation would probably also specify the length of the pencil and perhaps the wood of which it was to be made and might even indicate something like "Dixon or equivalent."

In such a case, the only advantage one contractor might offer the government, compared with another contractor, is price; hence, an IFB would normally be used to solicit the bids. However, since the government knows exactly what it wants and exactly what quantity it wants to buy and can specify a delivery schedule, there is no reason for the contract to be other than for some fixed price.

On the other hand, if the government wanted a special pencil designed for some special purpose, an RFP might be issued to solicit bids—if the government could not specify exactly how the pencil was to be designed, assembled, and delivered.

Suppose, for example, the government wanted a pencil that was indelible for ordinary erasers but was equipped with a very special eraser that could erase its markings. The government agency would invite bidders to write proposals describing how they would make such a pencil, what it would look like, how long it would take to develop, when delivery could be expected, and what it would cost.

⟶ Unless the technology already existed for such a pencil, an R & D (research and development) effort would be required, and it would be nearly impossible to predict exactly how much the development of such a pencil would cost. The contract would then be some form of cost reimbursement: the government would guarantee to pay all costs plus some fixed fee or profit. That's the whole basis for cost-reimbursement contracts: the difficulty or impossibility of predicting costs accurately.

There are many circumstances that might make it difficult or impossible to predict costs. A stretched-out delivery schedule of several years makes it difficult to price because of the difficulty of predicting inflationary effects. If the government cannot predict exactly what quantities will be required, it might be difficult to predict costs, because the contractor can't predict what quantity discounts he might be able to get. In such cases, the government usually asks the contractor to estimate the probable costs and base a fixed fee on those probable costs. Here's how such a program might actually work:

The government requests the development of a new type of radio receivers. The contractor estimates that it will take one year (or the government has specified one year as the development time) and $25,000 worth of direct labor, plus $15,000 worth of other costs, for a total of

$40,000. He requests a fee of 8%, or $3,200. If the government accepts his proposal as the best one offered, a contract will be written in which the contractor will bill the government his actual costs plus $3,200 profit or fee. A ceiling cost might be set at $50,000 or some figure close to it. The exact figure is not important, because the contractor will be reimbursed only the actual costs plus the $3,200, which is fixed. The final contract may run the nominal $43,200, or it may run over or under that, depending on various circumstances. Whatever it runs, unless some unforeseen circumstance arises that causes a contract amendment the contractor will get his costs back plus the $3,200 fee.

This is a typical cost-plus contract, often referred to as CPFF, cost plus fixed fee.

Variants and Hybrids

The contracts just explained are the typical fixed-price and cost-reimbursement contracts. But there are many variants of these. One of these is CPFF/AF, which is the cost-plus fixed-fee/award fee. In this arrangement, a small fixed fee is established, and the contractor is awarded an additional fee, periodically, based on the government's evaluation of his performance. If the contractor has saved the government money by bringing the product in well under the original estimated cost or if he has delivered other benefits, he will get a generous award fee. If he has failed to do more than the conventional job, he will get an average award fee. If he has done a poor job, he will get a small—or possibly no—award fee. This is generally referred to as incentive contracting, and there are several possible variants to this basic arrangement, but all are based on the idea that the contractor's fee will be based on the quality of performance and contract management, with especial attention to cost-reduction success.

T & M contracts are time and material agreements. In these, the contractor is paid agreed-upon rates for labor and materials, as actually used, plus some agreed-upon profit percentage. These types of contracts are generally used when the government really has no firm idea of how much service they will require but wants a contractual agreement that services and materials will be provided at agreed-upon rates, when and as needed.

BOA (basic ordering agreements) are similar to T & M contracts and are sometimes referred to as task order contracts. Here again, the contract provides what is often referred to as a laundry list of services and materials, at fixed rates, with the agreement that the government will order and receive services and/or materials at these rates within the maximums and minimums stipulated in the contract.

To illustrate how such arrangements work, suppose you are a publications department in a government agency and you know that you will have certain peak loads of work, when you will need writing, editing, proofreading, typing, typemarking, paste-up, and illustrating help. But you don't know exactly when and how much help you will need. The solicitation you issue would ask the bidders to list hourly rates for each category of labor, or it might request hourly rates for writers and editors and page rates for typing, or any other such basis for unitizing prices. The quotation form for the solicitation might look something like this:

Category	Estimated Quantity	Rate per Unit	Total
Writing	600 hours		
Editing	300 hours		
Proofreading	750 pages		
Illustrating	180 hours		
Typemarking	750 pages		
Paste-up	300 pages		
Production coordination	75 hours		

Now note that some services are in terms of hours, while others are in terms of pages. The solicitation provides an estimate of hours required or pages required for each category, and you, the bidder, are asked to estimate your rates, but you will guarantee those rates for the term of the contract, which is probably going to be for one year.

You might respond with a quote something like this:

Category	Estimated Quantity	Rate per Unit	Total
Writing	600 hours	8.50/hr	$5,100.00
Editing	300 hours	6.00/hr	1,800.00
Proofreading	750 pages	2.00/pg	1,500.00
Illustrating	180 hours	6.00/hr	1,080.00
Typemarking	750 pages	5.50/page	4,125.00
Paste-up	300 pages	4.00/page	1,200.00
Production coordination	75 hours	5.99/hour	375.00
		Total	$15,180.00

Supposedly, other things being equal, the bidder with the lowest total would usually be the winner. Not so! Later, in Part II of this book, you'll learn why the lowest total is not necessarily the lowest bid!

Standard Form 33 (Figure 4) is ordinarily used as the first page of a solicitation or bid package. This form may be used for either an RFP (Request for Proposals) or an IFB (Information for Bid), which requires only price information from the bidder. One or the other will be checked in Block 2 of Standard Form 33.

SOLICITATION, OFFER AND AWARD		3. CERTIFIED FOR NATIONAL DEFENSE UNDER DPS REG. 1 AND/OR DMS REG. 1 RATING		4 PAGE 1	OF 4
1 CONTRACT (Proc. Inst. Ident.) NO.	2 SOLICITATION NO. 03-79-13 [X] ADVERTISED (IFB) [ ] NEGOTIATED (RFP)	5 DATE ISSUED 11/6/78	6 REQUISITION/PURCHASE REQUEST NO.		

7 ISSUED BY CODE	8 ADDRESS OFFER TO (If other than block 7)
USDA Forest Service Black Hills National Forest Custer, South Dakota	Contracting Officer Black Hills National Forest P.O. Box 792 Custer, SD 57730

In advertised procurement 'offer' and 'offeror' shall be construed to mean bid and bidder

SOLICITATION

9. Sealed offers in original and ____0____ copies for furnishing the supplies or services in the Schedule will be received at the place specified in block 8, or if handcarried, in the depository located in ___See Block 7___ until ___2:00 P.M.___ local time* ___12/6/78___

*at place of bid opening   (Hour)   (Date)

If this is an advertised solicitation, offers will be publicly opened at that time.

CAUTION – LATE OFFERS: See pars. 7 and 8 of Solicitation Instructions and Conditions.

All offers are subject to the following:

1. The Solicitation Instructions and Conditions, SF 33 A ___7/77 edition.___ edition which is attached or incorporated herein by reference.

2. The General Provisions, SF 32, ___4/75___ edition, which is attached o̶r̶ i̶n̶c̶o̶r̶p̶o̶r̶a̶t̶e̶d̶ h̶e̶r̶e̶i̶n̶ b̶y̶ r̶e̶f̶e̶r̶e̶n̶c̶e̶

3. The Schedule included herein and/or attached hereto.

4. Such other provisions, representations, certifications, and specifications as are attached o̶r̶ i̶n̶c̶o̶r̶p̶o̶r̶a̶t̶e̶d̶ h̶e̶r̶e̶i̶n̶ b̶y̶ r̶e̶f̶e̶r̶e̶n̶c̶e̶ (Attachments are listed in schedule.)

FOR INFORMATION CALL (Name & telephone no.) (No collect calls) ▶ ___Leslie Vallie: 605/673-2251___

SCHEDULE

10 ITEM NO.	11 SUPPLIES/SERVICES	12 QUANTITY	13 UNIT	14 UNIT PRICE	15 AMOUNT
	SEWAGE TREATMENT PLANT COMPONENTS See page 4 for list of attachments and schedule of bid items.			DO NOT WRITE IN THIS SPACE.	

See continuation of schedule on page 4

OFFER (pages 2 and 3 must also be fully completed by offeror)

In compliance with the above, the undersigned agrees, if this offer is accepted within _____ calendar days (60 calendar days unless a different period is inserted by the offeror) from the date for receipt of offers specified above, to furnish any or all items upon which prices are offered at the price set opposite each item, delivered at the designated point(s), within the time specified in the schedule.

16. DISCOUNT FOR PROMPT PAYMENT (See par. 9 SF 33 A)

% 10 CALENDAR DAYS.   % 20 CALENDAR DAYS.   % 30 CALENDAR DAYS.   CALENDAR DAYS

17. OFFEROR CODE FACILITY CODE	18 NAME AND TITLE OF PERSON AUTHORIZED TO SIGN OFFER (Type or print)
NAME AND ADDRESS (Street, city, county, State and ZIP code) AREA CODE AND TELEPHONE NO. ▶ [ ] Check if remittance address is different from above – enter such address in Schedule	19 SIGNATURE 20 OFFER DATE

AWARD (To be completed by Government)

21 ACCEPTED AS TO ITEMS NUMBERED	22 AMOUNT	23 ACCOUNTING AND APPROPRIATION DATA

24 SUBMIT INVOICES (4 copies unless otherwise specified) TO ADDRESS SHOWN IN BLOCK __26__	25 NEGOTIATED PURSUANT TO	10 U.S.C. 2304(a) ( ) 41 U.S.C. 252(c) ( )

26. ADMINISTERED BY (If other than block 7) CODE	27 PAYMENT WILL BE MADE BY CODE
USDA Forest Service Boxelder Civilian Conservation Center P.O. Box 47 Nemo, SD 57759	

28 NAME OF CONTRACTING OFFICER (Type or print)	29. UNITED STATES OF AMERICA BY ____(Signature of contracting officer)____	30 AWARD DATE

Award will be made on this form, or on Standard Form 26, or by other official written notice

33-131

Standard Form 33 Page 1 (REV. 3-77) Prescribed by GSA, FPR (41 CFR) 1-16.101

Figure 4. Standard Form 33.

    In addition to this form, a requester generally receives a package of information, which will include specifications of what is to be supplied, terms and conditions, relevant procurement regulations, and other forms that the bidder must make out—usually check-offs—that are required to conform to various regulations concerning proprietorship of the bidder's firm, compliance with equal employment opportunity laws, etc.

    In many cases, the bid package will contain a statement of work, describing the requirements, and a separate pricing form (Standard Form 60 for civilian agencies and Standard Form 633 for military agencies).

In some cases, where the bid requires only a single price for a fixed lot and cost analysis is not required, the bid package may call for the bidder to indicate his price directly on Standard Form 33. The bidder signs in Block 18. He has, in effect, signed a contract in advance. If the government accepts the bid, the government official need merely sign Block 29, with the other data required in the bottom section, "Award," and a contract has been completed. That's the meaning of the words at the top: "Solicitation, Offer, and Award." In fact, Standard Form 33 implements all three functions.

Before all of this confuses you, please note that there are three basic types of *solicitation*—IFB, RFP, and RFQ—but many types of contracts. Each type of solicitation may result in any of a variety of contract types: fixed-price, cost-plus, basic ordering agreement, time and material, cost reimbursement, basic purchasing agreement, etc. In this book, we are most concerned with the RFP because our basic purpose is to teach the writing of superior proposals, but it is useful to know about and understand the entire procurement system under which the federal government operates.

Although the RFQ is not used nearly as often as the IFB and RFP solicitations, there are many occasions on which an RFQ (Figure 5) is issued, and you should have at least a general understanding of this. Strictly speaking, an RFQ is not a bid solicitation at all—or isn't supposed to be used as one. The term stands for "Request for Quotations," and it is not a contractual instrument, as Standard Form 33 is. The prices quoted by a respondent do not commit him to the price as do the other forms, for example.

In issuing a bid solicitation, the government executive is required to furnish an "in-house estimate" of probable costs. Obviously, he must stay within his budget, and he cannot ordinarily get approval to issue the solicitation without furnishing an in-house estimate. The RFQ is one means for getting such figures together. The form simply asks respondents to furnish estimates of the job or goods described by the RFQ. However, it is fairly common practice to select one of the respondents and negotiate a contract as a result of RFQ responses.

Practice varies. Some agencies will use RFQs to get prices only when the job is expected to be under $10,000, and then they issue a purchase order to the respondent selected. (We say *respondent* because, strictly speaking, those who submit RFQs are responding and not bidding.) In

OMB Approval No. 029-0188

STANDARD FORM 18, MARCH 1971 GENERAL SERVICES ADMINISTRATION FED. PROC. REG. (41 CFR) 1-16.201	**REQUEST FOR QUOTATIONS** *(THIS IS NOT AN ORDER)*	PAGE OF **1**

1. REQUEST NO.	2. DATE ISSUED	3. REQUISITION/PURCHASE REQUEST NO.	4. CERTIFIED FOR NATIONAL DEFENSE UNDER DPS REG. 1 AND/OR DMS REG. 1 RATING:

5. ISSUED BY

6. DELIVER BY *(Date)*

7. DELIVERY

FOR INFORMATION CALL *(Name, area code and tel. no.) (No collect calls)*

☐ FOR DESTINATION   ☐ OTHER *(See Schedule)*

8. TO NAME AND ADDRESS *(Street, city, state, and ZIP code)*

9. DESTINATION *(Consignee and address including ZIP code)*

10. Please furnish quotations to the issuing office on or before close of business (date) _____ . Supplies are of domestic origin unless otherwise indicated by quoter. This is a request for information, and quotations furnished are not offers. If you are unable to quote, please so indicate on this form and return it. This request does not commit the government to pay any costs incurred in the preparation or the submission of this quotation, or to procure or contract for supplies or services.

SCHEDULE

11. ITEM NO.	12. SUPPLIES/SERVICES	13. QUANTITY	14. UNIT	15. UNIT PRICE	16. AMOUNT

17. PRICES QUOTED INCLUDE APPLICABLE FEDERAL, STATE, AND LOCAL TAXES

DISCOUNT FOR PROMPT PAYMENT _____ %10 CALENDAR DAYS _____ % 20 CALENDAR DAYS; _____ % 30 CALENDAR DAYS; _____ % _____ CALENDAR DAYS.

NOTE: Reverse must also be completed by the quoter.

18. NAME AND ADDRESS OF QUOTER *(Street, city, county, State, including ZIP Code)*	19. SIGNATURE OF PERSON AUTHORIZED TO SIGN QUOTATION	20. DATE OF QUOTATION
	21. SIGNER'S NAME AND TITLE *(Type or print)*	22. TELEPHONE NO. *(Include area code)*

18-112

Figure 5. Request for quotations.

other cases, a formal contract might be negotiated. Therefore, while the form itself stipulates that the request is for estimates or quotations only, you may receive an RFQ with a statement of work and a request to submit a proposal. That is, the issuing agency may not have an in-house estimate and may be utilizing this means of avoiding the normal requirement to furnish one.

The fact is that it is a Catch-22 situation: federal procurement regulations are so voluminous that an agency can find regulations to cover virtually anything they wish to do, once we depart from a few basics, such as small-purchase provisions, required competition, and justifications for avoiding these.

7

How to Prepare and Submit Your Bid

How not to do it, particularly when it's an IFB. The basic road map for proposal writing, with dos and don'ts.

Some Rules about IFB Bids

One day I received a telephone call from the contracting officer at the naval Oceanographic Office. It was during the Vietnam war, and the U.S. Navy was letting a few small contracts for technical translation of documents in French, Chinese, and other languages. For example, the only good pilot's guide for the Mekong was in Mandarin Chinese, and I had earlier had the difficult task of finding a translator for it. (I found one in NASA.)

The contracting officer had tears in his voice. "You're the low bidder," he advised me, "but you forgot to sign your bid!"

My secretary had mailed out the bid, after typing it up, without bringing it to me to sign (Block 19 of Standard Form 33), and I hadn't given it another thought.

"Can I come right over and sign it now?" I asked.

"No way," he said. "I wish you could, but the law is the law. I just thought I'd let you know for future reference."

This was an IFB, and IFB-type procurements are subject to stringent laws. They are opened publicly—anyone may attend—and the bids are read aloud at the exact hour and date stipulated. The low bid almost invariably takes the award, unless there are irregularities—such as not signing your bid!

Any fraud or misrepresentation is also cause for disqualifying a bid, as is an apparent inability to deliver the goods or service as promised. The latter, however, is extremely difficult to prove legally and is rarely pressed, although the contracting officer may suggest that the bidder withdraw his bid.

Technically, the government may hold you firmly to your bid, in an IFB bid, even if you have made a serious error in your figures. In practice, they do not, because it is not in the government's interest to risk your defaulting on the contract. At the same time, IFBs are usually accompanied by a sheet cautioning you to check your figures carefully before signing your bid.

IFBs generally bring out a great deal of competition, and it is sharp competition. Unless you are one of a select few able to supply the goods or service called for and the competition is thus severely limited, you are going to have to bid low to win in most cases. Therefore, people who bid this type of solicitation are not always looking for profit margins of any size but are seeking other benefits:

1. A "base" for their businesses, that is, an annual contract that guarantees them a certain amount of business or income to meet basic overhead and operating expenses, yet leaves them capacity for more profitable work. This, of course, allows them to be somewhat "independent" and selective in pricing their commercial (nongovernment) work.
2. Something to tide them over a slow period so that they can meet the payroll, that is, so that they can keep their staffs together, rather than laying people off.
3. An expansion of their purchasing power, which results in lowered costs.

In some cases, a bidder may have a more efficient plant so that he can underbid others and still take a normal profit. Or he may have made an exceptionally good buy on raw materials. But whatever his reasons, he knows that he must be extremely competitive in pricing. If you bid in this manner, it is a good plan to personally attend a few bid openings, at least in the beginning, so that you can sit and record the bids. You will soon learn what prices you must bid to win, and the education will be worthwhile.

What Is an RFP?

You've learned now, if you didn't already know, that an RFP is a Request for Proposals and that you are expected to write a formal document in bidding for the contract. But there is far more implied in the question, "What is an RFP?" Again and again I have heard proposal writers poring over the statement of work and muttering to themselves, "What the hell do they *want?*" Some marketing people have said to me, "I won't write a proposal unless the customer tells me what he wants to see in it. I make him write my proposal." This latter statement is made frequently, in many different forms, by those who believe, apparently, that the government officials are playing games with them, withholding information from the statement of work and making the proposal writer guess at what's wanted. It's a most common myth that contract winners are those "in the know" somehow.

All of this is sheer nonsense, with an occasional exception. Certainly, the federal procurement system is less than perfect, but there is far less hanky-panky or bending of the basic rules and principles than such people believe. They are the exceptional cases, not the usual cases.

To answer that frustrated proposal writer muttering to himself (or herself) they don't *know* what they want! That is, they are asking the proposers to suggest—*propose*—a program to meet their requirements and/or solve their problem. In most cases, the statement of work has told you everything they know about their need, and they are saying, in effect, "We have a problem (a need for a certain result), and we don't know the best way to handle it. You experts out there in the great world of trade and commerce (or engineering, or computer sciences, etc.), tell us what we ought to have or ought to do, what you can do for us. Tell us exactly; give us a *program. Sell* it to us—show us that it's the best possible way to go. We'll buy whichever program (proposal) appears best to us, price considered, but not necessarily the lowest price, if we like the program well enough."

There are several possible reasons for issuing an RFP:

1. Specialized skills and/or equipment are required and are not available in the agency.
2. There just aren't enough people available in the agency, and it is impractical to hire more, for any of several reasons.
3. It is considered less expensive to have an outside contractor do the job.
4. The job must be done quickly, and an outside contractor can get the job done more quickly than the agency (again, for any of several reasons).

Therefore, the requirement may not necessarily be a problem to be solved but may be strictly a set of routine services, such as everyday computer programming or writing technical manuals, or a production run on a piece of equipment.

An obvious question arises, then: If that is the case—that the services or products are strictly "routine" and well defined, and the government knows *exactly* what it wants, why an RFP at all? Why not an IFB?

Again, there is more than one reason—at least two, in fact. One is that the agency issuing the RFP may not want to hem the bidders in too closely with tight specifications. Leaving something for the bidders to suggest in their proposals often results in many new and worthwhile ideas for improving the service. In fact, this is one reason that some statements of work are not in painstaking detail: the agency is inviting the bidders to propose their own ideas and does not want to hamper proposers by hemming them in too closely with specifications.

Another reason for using the RFP is that the agency does not want to be compelled to accept the low bid, as they are in the case of an IFB. Low bidders are not always the best-qualified performers of the work to be done, and their low bid sometimes reflects ignorance rather than efficiency. An RFP or "negotiated procurement" enables the agency to utilize their own judgment and not be at the mercy of low prices.

An RFP, then, is sometimes an appeal for help, but it is always an invitation to present and sell your own ideas on how to best satisfy the customer's need.

To be sure this is clear, let's illustrate with several typical examples of the different cases.

Suppose that the military have decided that their latest fighter aircraft has been obsoleted by some new Soviet weapon and needs to be replaced by one that is faster and more heavily armored or armed, presents a smaller radar image, etc. They believe that the technology exists to improve the plane, which is some years old now. So they develop an RFP and work statement and go out with it to the companies that do such work. This would be a rather large requirement, with many technical problems to solve, of course, and would almost certainly be a cost-plus contract. A considerable effort and expense would go into writing the proposal responses, too, of course, It's not unusual to spend upwards of $1 million for such proposals. The aircraft companies bidding would write multivolume proposals, going into considerable technical detail.

The above is an an R & D (Research and Development) contract. But there are many small research and development contracts too. An agency might want a survey to be made. Perhaps the Department of Energy wants to find out how many householders keep their thermostats below the comfort level and how many are motivated to do so by energy consciousness versus cost consciousness. The proposer would probably have to make a preliminary study to design the survey so as to be sure of getting a representative sample, properly stratified and properly analyzed to draw reliable conclusions.

Writing a proposal for such a requirement may be quite difficult, especially if the agency has merely stipulated a desired result, without indicating whether they have any ideas of their own about survey design. It may be that they have no one on the staff who knows any of the technicalities of making surveys and working with probability statistics. Or it may be that they do have such an authority and are deliberately saying little so as to be able to judge the proposer's own competence in that technical field! In any case, it will be necessary to demonstrate not only an understanding of the problem or requirement but the proper technical capability to design and carry out the survey.

Another RFP may call for the relatively simple technical service of mailing out thousands of forms, with bursting and collating, labeling, record keeping, etc. This may seem to be a relatively uncomplicated job of work, but it is still necessary to demonstrate your competence at the work.

In another case, an agency may wish you to provide computer personnel to work for a year on their own site, operating their own computer. Here, there is probably no problem per se, but there is a requirement for people of certain technical and professional skills. In this proposal you will have to demonstrate the ability to provide people—reliably—having the proper skills and experience.

An RFP may be likened to your own situation when you take your new car into the dealer and complain about a funny squeal whenever you turn the corner. Similarly, the service writer will ask you questions to pin down whatever you can tell him about the symptoms—and RFP work statements sometimes describe only symptoms, rather than problems—and may possibly ask you to leave it for an estimate. The estimate he provides later is his proposal: he will tell you what he believes to be the trouble and what cure he proposes, as well as what it will cost. You will decide whether you are satisfied or want to get a "proposal" from someone else. One thing is rather sure: if his "proposal" calls for spending a fairly large sum of money for the repairs, you are going to want to be convinced that (1) he knows what he is doing and has diagnosed your car's problems accurately, (2) he is dependable and can handle the job well, and (3) his price is reasonable for the job.

Essentially, you have to do the same thing when you propose to the government.

What Is a Proposal?

In answering the question "What is an RFP?" we have at least begun to answer the question "What is a proposal?" That is, we have answered it in rather general terms of function: what the proposal must *do,* rather than what it *is.* What it is must be answered in two ways. First, we'll answer it by functional characterization and, second, by a definitive and detailed description of its component parts and why they exist.

We can characterize a proposal, as we already have, by regarding it as our suggested program to meet the customer's needs, for it is that. But you may remember that we also said that the customer is going to "buy" whatever he deems to be the best program or the best solution to his problem.

Any good salesman will tell you that people do not buy; you have to *sell them.* And we recognized that previously when we put the words "sell me" in the customer's mouth by interpreting an RFP as saying, "Sell me your program." In short, we should think of ourselves as salesmen when we write proposals, for the proposal is—must be—a sales presentation.

In most cases, the winning proposal becomes part of the resulting contract. Therefore, some proposal writers tend to regard the proposal as a contractual document and are greatly influenced by contractual/legal/ fiscal considerations when they write a proposal. Here's what's wrong with that: the proposal may *become* a contractual document—*will,* if it's the winning proposal—but at the time you write it and during the time the customer considers and evaluates it, it is a *sales presentation.* If it is not, you have wasted your time in writing it! Later, when we get into *proposal-manship,* as compared with proposal writing, you'll see the truth of that more clearly perhaps. But remember that your success or failure in winning the contract depends largely, almost entirely (entirely, in many cases), on your proposal. You may not get any other chances to do any selling of your program, your company, and your capabilities.

How Important Are Proposals?

Talk to a marketer whose job is to make the calls, learn about requirements, and pick up bid sets, and he'll tell you that proposals are pure formalities, that contracts are awarded as a result of his hard work in the field. Talk to a proposal writer whose proposals rarely win, and he'll tell you that most bids are "wired" and that proposals coming in cold don't count for much, no matter how good they are. Talk to government officials who evaluate proposals and select winners for contract award, and you'll hear something else, as we have:

- The chief contracting officer of one agency told us that about one out of three proposals submitted to his agency, in most competitions, survives the first reading by the evaluators. He also told us that it is not at all unusual for as many as nine out of ten proposals submitted to be rejected immediately after the first reading.
- A divison chief in another agency confided that he often rejects a proposal upon reading the first page, refusing to "waste time" even turning to page 2.
- And an official in another agency stressed that he has canceled procurements entirely in some cases, when he judged none of the proposals received worthy of being selected for contract award.

All the government officials with whom we have discussed this—and we have talked to hundreds—agree that they will not—cannot—award a contract in response to a poor proposal. And all agree that a truly superior proposal can win a contract without any other marketing activity.

The question naturally arises: What is a good proposal? Or, conversely, what makes a proposal a poor proposal?

Understanding the Problem

The solicitation package or bid set includes a statement of work (sometimes referred to as the specification). This explains what the government wants. It may describe a set of services to be performed, an end product to be developed, or a problem to be solved. This is the requirement. Whether the requirement involves a specific problem to be solved or not, it is commonplace to evaluate whether the writers of a proposal understand the problem that is, of course, whether they understand the requirement.

By far the most common failure, leading to swift rejection of proposals, is failure to understand the requirement, and that factor is often specifically named as one of the criteria for evaluation of the proposal. This writer has seen the notation made by evaluators in the margin of proposal pages: "They don't seem to understand the problem."

Many proposal writers—I am one—use a special section of each proposal to demonstrate good understanding of the requirement. In my own case, I generally have a brief section headed something like "Appraisal of the Requirement," followed by another section that is a detailed discussion of the requirement.

One singularly unsuccessful proposal writer in my own experience always started his proposals with his purported understanding of the requirement—and demonstrated his lack of understanding immediately! If he was answering a request by the Postal Service to devise an accounting system or anything else the Postal Service felt a need for, his "understanding" always started out with a "gloom of night and heat of day" speech about the overall mission of the Postal Service, rather than about the specific need for which the RFP was issued. And for other agencies, he would seek out the official government publications that stated the agency's overall mission and responsibilities in equally dramatic and pompous language and quote directly. This invariably led to a muttered "Madison Avenue" and swift rejection by evaluators. Few of them are so unsophisticated as to buy snow jobs like this, and most are deeply offended by such apple-polishing efforts.

Most proposal writers whose proposals convince the evaluators that they do not understand the problem are guilty either of attempted snow jobs (albeit more sophisticated efforts than those of our "gloom of night" friend) or plain shoddiness. Both faults reflect an assumption that the proposal—what the proposal says, that is—does not mean very much and that the requesting agency will accept a bland assurance that the proposer will do the job admirably. Such proposals always appear to be saying, "I can't take the time now to analyze just what it is that you want, but I can handle it, whatever it is. Just pay me the sum I name in my cost proposal, and all will be well."

No government proposal evaluator in his right mind would risk accepting such a proposal, much less recommending contract award to the contracting officer responsible for the legal actions required to actually execute the contract. This is the kind of proposal that does not survive the first reading and often does not even get a complete reading.

Some Other Common Proposal Faults

It is fairly common knowledge that the quality of the staff proposed for the program being bid is almost always a critically important consideration. Some proposers base their entire proposal on the résumés they include as the proposed staff. And many do not even do a good job of that. Here are some common faults with résumés submitted:

Boilerplate résumés. Some organizations have standard résumés for their entire professional and subprofessional staffs and use these, without variation, for each proposal. The problem with this is that most people who have been in the working world for any length of time have had many different kinds of jobs and experiences. Their résumés can be written in many ways—"slanted," that is, to the particular requirement. A standard résumé rarely makes the individual appear as well qualified for the given program as he can be made to appear by writing his résumé differently, stressing the experience that is most relevant to that program.

This writer, for example, is an experienced professional writer, training-materials developer, training-systems designer, and a few other things, with many publication credits. He is also a lecturer, expert in electronics, experienced in safety and health requirements. etc. Putting all of that (and a few other qualifications) into one résumé, with suitable credentials to back up the claims, is entirely impractical, for several reasons. For one, the resulting résumé would become a much-too-voluminous biography. For another, it would have the adverse effect of being unconvincing. And for still another, there would be no control over the net impression gained by the reader. He might, for example, judge the individual to be an electronics engineer who happened to have some writing experience, when the desired effect might be something entirely different.

It's well worth the time and effort to structure each résumé specifically for the proposal. Some proposers use only those résumés they believe to be most impressive generally, without regard to their relevance to the program being bid. That is, they trot out the resumes of all their Ph.D.'s, former high-ranking military officers, former high corporate executives, inventors, etc. This is another kind of snow job that doesn't work at all well.

Suppose, however, that the proposer does, in fact, carefully prepare an outstanding set of résumés and incorporate them. Fine. The proposal will get high marks for the qualifications and experience of proposed staff. But that's only one area of evaluation. No matter how important good project staff may be, it will not carry the day alone. It's still only one of several areas in which the proposal will be evaluated.

Another common fault—and again, an attempted snow job—is the effort to be glib, while using a torrent of "buzz words," jargon, technological terms, and plain gobbledygook. This not to say that technical language and jargon should not be used at all. It is inescapable that the language must communicate with the evaluators. An engineering proposal must use engineering terms; a training-development proposal will probably have to use the terms of behavioral psychology; etc. But these terms and this language must be used to communicate, not to obfuscate. Proposal evaluators will not be impressed, much less swayed, by 64-dollar words and obscure scholarly references. Tortuous language and terms that send the evaluator to the unabridged Webster's will try his patience and may cut his reading of a proposal short.

At least one government executive applies the term *professional* to a factor he looks for in reading and evaluating proposals. By this he means the writing style, the grammar and punctuation, the organization, and the use of language. His attitude is that he is seeking work by professional people and that they should be able, at the least, to convey their thoughts clearly and to use the language with reasonable care and accuracy. Otherwise, he finds, the proposal appears "unprofessional" to him and suggests that the staff will perform unprofessionally also.

This is not to suggest that proposal writers need be "authors" in their writing skills, but they should be able to organize their thoughts in some orderly fashion and present their ideas clearly. The tendency of some proposal writers to use buzz words and weighty, ponderous langauge is bad enough when done properly. When such words and terms are used incorrectly, they are ludicrous. "Impressing" readers with erudition and vocabulary in a proposal is a dangerous, and usually losing, game.

Some evaluators have also told us that such usages always make them paraphrase the Shakespearean observation: Methinks he doth protest too much!

Another common failing is the failure to propose a sound plan for program management and quality control. The government official responsible for the program is going to be concerned that the program will be adequately managed. He knows that technical skills alone are not enough. If he has managed contracted projects in the past, he has probably had the experience of projects staffed with good technical skills that foundered because of poor management. Unless he has specifically stated that proposed management will be evaluated, he is likely to find that many of the proposals submitted say little about project management.

Proposal requirements ordinarily require a sort of "company résumé"—a statement of the bidding organization's experience and other qualifications, as distinct from the individual staff members' qualifications. Here again, too many proposers use boilerplate statements, with all the hazards already stated with regard to individual résumés. If your forte appears to be radar design it will not be interpreted as strength in computer programming.

The Most Basic Proposal Fault

A most basic fault in many proposals—unrelated to what have already been pointed out as common faults—is general vagueness. This may be the result of shoddiness—simple reluctance to make the considerable effort required to write a good proposal—or it may, and often is, deliberate. Many proposal writers do not appear to understand what the government agency is saying when it issues a Request for Proposals. Just as every proposal has a general message that may be read between the lines, so does every RFP.

We covered this point earlier when we stated that the RFP is an appeal for help or, at least, an invitation to suggest a set of remedies and sell them. However, many proposal writers are afraid to be precise and definitive, reasoning that the client may not like what he reads or may not agree with the program. That's what they refer to when they mutter to themselves, "I wonder what they want." They seem to think that the writer of the statement of work had some definite plan or program in mind and that the proposal is a contest to see who can guess what the government requesters were thinking.

Reasoning thus, some proposal writers deliberately are vague and general, hoping that the customer will accept their bland, if vague, assurances that the company proposing is the best and its staff is the best and that all that stands between the customer and salvation is a contract and money! It doesn't "play in Peoria." Just as you would not pay some mechanic $300 to fix your car, without a clear understanding of what he was going to do—exactly—and good evidence that he could do so capably, the government is not going to award you many thousands of dollars on your bland assurances.

Is there some risk in being specific? Certainly. But there is no risk in being vague. No risk because it is certain rejection. You might as well save your time and money and "no-bid" the RFP.

This is a subject that will come up again later, when we are dealing with proposalmanship.

What Should a Proposal Contain?

Some RFPs include a detailed description of what the customer wants in the proposal, and some even dictate *how* they want it—a specific format mandate. Most, however, content themselves with telling you *what*, not *how*.

What all RFPs demand, whether specified absolutely or only implied, is this:

1. Clear evidence that you understand the problem or requirement.
2. Evidence that you understand the technical, professional, or craft fields necessary to do the job properly, as well as to understand it.
3. Your approach to the job and evidence that it is the right approach or at least a good one.
4. A specific program laid out in enough detail to be evaluated properly.
5. Evidence that you can manage the program adequately, with proper quality control.
6. A plan for staffing the job with well-qualified people, and an estimate of the tasks, subtasks, functions, materials, manhours, schedules, etc. (This is really a subset of item 4 above: a detailed program.)
7. Information about your organization's experience, achievements, facilities, technical and personnel resources, and, in some cases, financial resources. (Financial resources, like costs, belong in a separate cost proposal, however.)
8. Résumés of the key staff, especially those to be assigned directly to the proposed program, demonstrating their individual education, skills, experience, achievements, and other suitability for the roles assigned them.

The Logic of the Proposal

There is a certain logic to the organization, format, and flow of a well-organized proposal, which should dictate the format. (We refer here to the technical proposal. Costs are presented separately, in a cost proposal, so as to not influence the judgment of those who make technical evaluations.)

The logic of the organization and flow that I use and recommend is this: The first item should be a restatement of the problem or requirement, as the proposal writer understands it. A general discussion of that problem or requirement should follow, in terms of the state of the art or current technology/resources/knowledge dealing with that field of endeavor. This is an analysis and examination of the alternatives, with technical arguments leading to a conclusion, which the proposal writer is recommending to the customer and proposing as his approach, resulting from the logical analysis. That conclusion and approach are next implemented in a proposed program that results logically from the discussion. And the final section should contain the company's qualifications and résumés, which are the qualifications of the staff generally, but especially of those personnel proposed for staffing the program.

In general, unless the customer has dictated a specific format or there are special considerations dictating a change from standard format, I use the following general format, with minor variations:

I. *Introduction (Section or Chapter I)*
    A. Who the proposer is and his general qualifications, stated briefly. (Anywhere from one-half page to several pages, depending on the size of the proposal overall.) Subtitle: "About the Offeror" or a similar phrase.
    B. Understanding (appraisal) of the problem (requirement). A brief restatement of the requirement, in the proposer's own words (*do not copy the customer's words*) to demonstrate understanding, although understanding will also be demonstrated throughout the proposal. Several possible methods, including restating the most critical elements of the requirement or the essence of the requirement. Should lead logically to the next section/chapter. Size depends on the size of the overall proposal.

II. *Discussion or Technical Discussion*
    Take off and continue from understanding of the requirement, pursuing analysis and examination, leading to the approach and the specific program you are going to propose. Demonstrate in this that you are completely professional in your field, understand it thoroughly, and can identify and discuss all pros and cons of every possible approach and that you are exercising good judgment in the approach you select. Sell your approach here.

III. *Proposed Program*
    Organization of this chapter/section is optional. I recommend starting with a description of how the project will be organized and staffed, with a brief description of the credentials of the key staff and a notation that résumés appear later. A "man-loading" chart is very useful here, for several reasons. This identifies principal tasks/subtasks/functions, indicates who on the staff (by functional titles) will be responsible for and perform each, how many man hours or man days are anticipated for each, and what the total man hours or man days are for each key person. May include subordinate staff, if you prefer. This section may include some brief discussion of tasks and functions, too. Should include a detailed discussion of how the program will be managed and what procedures and management controls, especially quality control, are proposed. Should also include specific identification of all "deliverables" (end items to be produced for the customer), interim deliverables, and schedules. Résumés of proposed staff may be included either in this section or the next; I prefer to include them here.

IV. *Qualifications and Experience*
    In this section, describe your company, your past projects that are relevant (especially major achievements), your staff generally, how your company is organized, and what its overall size, strength, and physical facilities are. If project-staff résumés were in the previous section, include a few key resumes here of other professional staff who might serve as backup to the program or who might be indirectly involved, perhaps as management support, purchasing support, etc.

V. *Highlights and Summary*
    Many prefer to put this up front as an abstract of the proposal or as an "executive summary" for the customer's top managers to review. Up front

or in back as a recapitulation of key points, somewhere there should be a brief summary, focusing on the highlights—whatever you deem to be the most attractive features of your proposal and the principal reasons for awarding you the contract. (Some companies have made this a section titled something like, "Reasons for Awarding Contract to 3-M Corporation.")

Appendices

You may or may not have reason to add appendices. Here is the general rule covering the case: If there is detailed information or reference information that some readers may want to see but others will not wish to spend time on, put it in an appendix and reference it in the text. Examples are bibliographic notes you may have cited, copies or abstracts of professional papers, drawings, letters of reference from past customers (I'd rather put them in Section IV), detailed discussions of points you have made in the text, samples of products produced for others, etc.

Later, when we talk about *proposalmanship* you'll find that we recommend certain other inclusions. However, the above is typical of most proposals and represents the information normally expected by the reader of a proposal. It also has a logical format and flow of information and ideas.

Other Inclusions and Elements

Most proposals have at least some charts and/or drawings. If the subject is a highly technical one, there will probably be a number of drawings. But even a proposal of relatively simple proportions will have some sort of milestone chart and project-organization charts, and it will probably also include an organization chart of the company submitting the proposal. As noted above, there may be samples of past programs, such as copies of manuals and reports or, if the product is a "hardware" item, photos and drawings of the item.

If you execute the above well and communicate your information clearly enough you will have a professional and respectable proposal. However, whether you have the *winning* proposal or not will depend largely on how well your competitors have prepared *their* proposals.

This brings us to an essential element of the art we are talking about here, for *proposalmanship* is an art, not a science nor a set of mechanics. Proposal writing, by our definition, means depending, for your success, on what your competitors do or do not do—something out of your control, of course. *Proposalmanship,* on the other hand, depends for its success only on what *you* do. It does not gamble on the possibility that no competitor will do more than a workmanlike job.

In the next chapter we'll have a look at how readers typically evaluate proposals, and you'll then begin, we hope, to see the roots of *proposalmanship*.

8

How the Government Evaluates Proposals

The law requires "objective evaluation." For the most part, the system is eminently fair, with abuses relatively few.

What Is an "Objective Evaluation"?

Since a proposal competition is not strictly a price competition but is a technical competition, the evaluation of proposals and the comparison of one against the other are at least partly a matter of human judgment. Federal agencies are therefore required to develop and use "objective evaluation" schemes.

These usually take the form of setting up a list of criteria, assigning a point value to each, and awarding each proposal a number of points in each category. For example, a statement of work might say something like the following:

Evaluation Criteria

Understanding of the requirement, as evidenced by the proposal content	20 points
Validity and practicality of approach	15 points
Organization experience and qualifications	30 points
Staff qualifications and experience	25 points
Price	10 points
Total	100 points

The listed criteria may be either more detailed and more specific or less detailed and less specific, as presented in the RFP. Internally, the evaluation staff will have a lengthy list of factors upon which to arrive at point scores for each of the above or other criteria that they may establish, such as management, quality control schedule, or other factors. In each case, the customer must decide, of course, what is most important to him, and he conveys some of this, but rarely all of it, to the proposers.

It is not uncommon to be rather vague about the evaluation criteria, giving only a rather general idea and even not telling the proposers how many points are assigned for each factor. On the other hand, some of the RFPs are highly detailed in this regard.

The evaluation criteria plus careful review and evaluation of the RFP, give the thoughtful proposal writer a good indication of where he must lay his major stress in writing the proposal. Here again, effectiveness in doing this is *proposalmanship,* and makes a great difference in final results.

The factor of price is handled in a wide variety of ways. In some cases, it receives a simple point value, as in the example. In others, the statement is made that price will be a factor, but no points are awarded for low price. In still others, a rather elaborate scheme of trading off price against technical points is utilized, so that each proposal is evaluated for "cost per technical point," and the one rated best in this regard is the winner.

Even this scheme has many variations. One popular one is to take the proposal that has received the highest technical evaluation and use it as the reference for all by calculating how many dollars per technical point that proposal represents. The technical point score of others that are deemed technically acceptable is then developed to a cost per point to see which is the lowest according to that measure. A low bidder achieving a poor technical score may thus lose out, while a relatively high bidder with a high technical score may be the winner.

Most of these methods allow the evaluators some latitude of judgment, so that they do not have to accept a bidder whom they believe cannot do a satisfactory job. At the same time, it is difficult for them to play favorites, except by giving a slight edge in their judgments when a contest is a close one.

The fact is that it is a risky game for any evaluator to depart from the rules thus set because the losing bidders all have rights to a "debriefing," where they can cross-examine the debriefer, and all have the right of appeal, called a *protest,* when they feel that they have been unfairly judged. Then the evaluators have to back up their judgment, while the award is held up, usually for months, and the project is delayed.

In one contest between a large, well-known manufacturer and a relatively unknown small company, the large company won 238 technical points against 235 for the small company. However, the small company was considerably less expensive than the large company, and the 3 points were not enough to offset the price differential, so the small company received the award. A protest was lodged by one of the unsuccessful bidders and was promptly thrown out because the evaluators were able to demonstrate complete fairness in the award.

In a rather well-known case cited earlier (Chapter 2) NASA awarded a contract for approximately $65 million to GE for a satellite program, promptly challenged by Fairchild, who charged irregularities. The protest held up, in this case, and the GE award was vacated, the contract going to Fairchild.

In another case, an incumbent contractor lost its current contract, which went to another firm. The incumbent protested, and the agency responded that the successful bidder had scored 85 technical points against the incumbent's 80 technical points and was $10,000 lower in costs.

Protests against awards are lodged with the General Accounting Office, headed by the Comptroller General of the United States. This office (GAO) is not part of the executive branch but reports to Congress and serves as a watchdog over other agencies, monitoring current contracts and programs and reporting findings in formal reports to Congress and the public at large.

In the last case reported here, where the successful bidder scored higher in technical points than the incumbent, there is an interesting point that is highly relevant to the evaluation of proposals. This point came to light, as far as I am concerned, because I happened to have conversation with one of those who had evaluated the proposals.

The reason that the incumbent did not score as well as it should have is that it became careless because it was the incumbent, had been for some time, and had become secure and overly confident. The written proposal was rather diffident in the section calling for a description of the organization's qualifications and experience. The philosophy was that the agency knew the company well, through a long contractual association, and did not have to be bored with information it already had.

This was a fatal error for this reason: a proposal can be evaluated only *on what the proposal contains.* No matter what the evaluators happen to know about the bidder and no matter how prominent and well-known the bidder happens to be, no evaluator may read anything into a proposal. Consequently, the incumbent lost valuable points in that area.

In this respect, at least, all bidders, large and small, are equals. All get credit for what they say (as long as what they say is true, of course), and none gets credit for what it implies or hopes the reader will read in. Carelessness in providing all required information costs points, and lost points cost contracts.

I was the victim of my own carelessness in one such case. The contracting officer had advised me that he wished me to have the contract because he thought my organization was especially well suited to the need and would do an exemplary job. He cautioned me that I had to submit a top-notch proposal because the competition was going to be keen. I lost, to both his and my shock. Here is how it happened. I sent one of my staff over to gather up some information because of an obscure point in the statement of work. My employee talked to the wrong people and got the wrong information, and we wrote the wrong proposal. It was a well-written proposal, but the wrong one, and there is no credit for good writing per se. But the contract was one of several coming out in series, and we bid and won the next two. (Writing the right proposals, this time.)

This example demonstrates again the basic fairness of the system and refutes the myths about "fixing" and favoritism.

Best and Final Offers

Fortunately—or unfortunately, in some cases—the findings of the evaluators are not always the last word. While the government almost always reserves the right to make an award, following proposal evaluation, without further negotiation, they quite often pursue at least one more step before making a final decision. In fact, they almost invariably do so if the contract is a sizable one, has been closely contested, and has had a great many bidders and/or there are several neck-and-neck finalists. And they often do so even with smaller contracts, time permitting and given more than one bidder in the ball park, technically and costwise.

Usually, this further evaluation takes the form of what is commonly referred to as a *best and final.* Each of those considered well qualified technically and close enough in price so that it seems reasonable to assume that negotiations may produce a significantly lower price are invited in to "orals" first, as a rule. (There are exceptions.)

There are generally three to five such finalists, although there may be more in some cases. Each firm is invited to come in and discuss their proposal. The discussion usually takes the form of questions by government executives, designed to clarify the bidder's intent and proposal. He is given the opportunity to make a presentation and is usually invited to submit any technical modifications he wishes to present to modify his proposal. Then, almost as an afterthought, he is advised that he is free to look over his costs, too, and modify those figures, should he care to!

As a result, one is generally selected for serious negotiation, during which the price may be negotiated down further.

Bidders who anticipate this stage and deliberately start with a higher price than they expect to settle for are running a risk, however, since such orals and best and finals are not guaranteed. Bidders are generally exhorted to make every effort to submit their most favorable terms in their initial offer, for there may be no other opportunities!

Being called in for a best and final usually means that you are in the top few and are being seriously considered for contract award. However, there is usually at least one or two of your competitors in the same position, and there is usually only one award to be made. As a practical matter, most bidders coming in for a best and final do shave their prices a bit. How the best and final procedure is employed varies, from agency to agency, according to internal policies, which are far from uniform. In some agencies, the policy is to offer everyone who has qualified technically the opportunity to make a best and final, while in others, only the top three or four are selected for best and final. In at least one case I know of, best and final was handled by mail, which I believe to be an unusual procedure. But it was a small contract, and it was somewhat surprising to see a best and final at all for such a small contract.

There are rare occasions, too. In one, our technical proposal was so highly regarded that we received a call to this effect: "We love your technical proposal, but your price is outasight! Is there any chance we could negotiate a bit?"

We thought that we could, and we did manage to reach an agreement and sign a contract. But that was an unusual case, where they liked our technical proposal so much that they were willing to try, even though it appeared that we were far too high in price for any reasonable hope of getting down within range. This was a rare occurrence, not likely to happen very often.

Evaluation, then, while reasonably "objective," is not entirely so, nor can it ever be so, for human judgments are always involved in deciding whether your résumés rate 5 points or 8 points, etc. And it is even more difficult to be completely objective about rating such matters as your technical approach to a problem or your management plan. There is this to be said, however. The evidence is ample that a superior proposal by an unknown company is much more likely to win a contract than a competing mediocre proposal by a well-known company. Proposals are written by humans, and big companies have no monopoly on human talent and human energy.

The abuses in the system lie mainly in the contracts awarded without competition as "selected-source" or "sole-source" procurements. While the basis for all procurement regulations is competition, provision is made for those supposedly exceptional cases in which it is in the interests of the government to select a given source and negotiate without competition. In those cases, the agency must justify the procedure, and such justification should be exceedingly difficult. Once it was—and it still is in many agencies. But some agencies are lax and permit unwarranted selected-source procurement on rather flimsy justifications. This has come to the attention of certain people in Congress, and some action is likely to correct this as a result of the outrage in Congress already expressed.

Part II

PROPOSALMANSHIP: THE GRADUATE STUDY

9

Introduction to Proposalmanship

Some of the proposals we get are so bad that only one out of 10 even gets read all the way through.
—SMALL BUSINESS ADMINISTRATION OFFICIAL

Proposalmanship Isn't Necessarily Proposal Writing

The job was obviously "wired" for the incumbent contractor. The solicitation package described an amount of "cataloging" work—parts listing —to be done on site at a NASA installation and said very little beyond that. It wasn't even a Request for Proposals. It was an Information for Bid and required merely pricing an hourly billing rate for employees to do the work at the government's own facility.

Despite study of the slender work statement, I could find nowhere a specification of how many people were now doing the job or how many people were to be proposed. When I tried to visit the facility, which I wanted to do principally for the purpose of counting heads, I was put off with excuses until time began to run out. I could have made a formal protest, of course, and they would have had to arrange a site visit for me. But it would still have been easy for them to keep me in the dark about the information I most wanted. I decided against it. Instead I began the most intensive study of a work statement that I had ever made. Again and again I pored over the few pages, line by line, until I had almost memorized it. I came, finally, to two firm conclusions:

1. The volume of work required amounted to about one and one-half man years of effort.
2. Four people—two journeyman catalogers, an apprentice, and a clerk–secretary—were actually being employed.

Consequently I bid for *three* people: one journeyman, one apprentice, and one clerk–secretary. The contracting officer studied me owlishly and mumbled something along the lines of "You're right, of course; three people can do the job," as he showed me where to sign the contract I had won. Despite the fact that no proposal was involved, I had practiced what I call *proposalmanship* to win that contract.

Proposalmanship is not the art of writing proposals (that's proposal writing). It's the art of winning contracts. More specifically, it's the art of writing proposals (usually) that win contracts. The focus is on *winning,* not on writing. Not that writing is unimportant. Good writing is most important. Good writing is needed to communicate and to sell. But you have to have something to sell, of course. And that comes out of analysis and creative thinking: strategy.

How Many Strategies?

One knowledgeable gentleman, writing on the subject of writing winning proposals, concentrates on what he calls the "main message" or theme. He uses the competition for the TFX aircraft, which later became the F-111 after it was accepted by the Defense Department and became operational, as an example. The then Secretary of Defense, Robert McNamara, had made it clear that he wanted a new aircraft that could be used by both the U.S. Air Force and the U.S. Navy, which appeared to be a sensible idea. There were two leading bidders, General Dynamics and Boeing. One adopted the main message *Commonality.* The other pressed home the theme an *Aerodynamic Solution to an Aerodynamic Problem.* One proposed a swing wing; the other, a delta wing. The swing-wing design presented many problems, and to most experts, the delta-wing design was superior. Virtually all of McNamara's staff recommended the delta-wing design over the swing-wing design. The Secretary of Defense "voted" them all down and selected the swing-wing design, which, sure enough, turned out to be a dud in many ways.

Which message or slogan do you think the swing-wing advocates— the successful bidders for a huge contract—used? An *Aerodynamic Solution to an Aerodynamic Problem* makes a lot of sense. It's an entirely logical approach, and it was undoubtedly the right approach, since the proposed solution was a delta-wing design. The proposal clearly pointed out all the problems of a swing-wing design and all the advantages and the much lower risk of the delta wing. The problem with this strategy was that it was entirely logical, and logic doesn't sell well. Emotional appeals sell far more effectively than do logical appeals.

The magic word was *Commonality*. That was the word, the idea, that Mr. McNamara wanted to hear. That was his whole purpose in awarding the contract. And this is not to say that the delta-wing design did not offer the same commonality that the swing-wing design did. The difference is more subtle than that. The difference was that one proposal—the successful one—concentrated on the end purpose for the procurement and followed through with a constantly hammered-home theme that promised achievement of the end goal, the end goal that was so close to the defense secretary's heart that it had become an emotional desire.

Would the delta-wing design have won out if it concentrated on the end goal, rather than on the means to it? Who can tell? We know only that the winning theme caused Mr. McNamara to reject all the technical analysis and counsel offered him by a knowledgeable staff and to buy the promise. It was not one of his better decisions, as it turned out.

Using *Commonality* as a theme was strategy, successful strategy.

There are many possible strategies for winning. In the first case, at the beginning of this chapter, there was a case of basing strategy on cost: three people cost less than four people, and since it was an IFB, low bid was sure to win. The problem was how to become the low bidder, and the strategy was immediately apparent when my study revealed that the job was overstaffed. (I could safely assume that the incumbent contractor would try for a straight renewal, keeping his staff intact!)

The case of the F-111 is a bit different. Price was relatively unimportant here, as long as price was in the ball park. Here the successful strategy was *presentation* strategy.

In all cases, the burning question is this: What does it take to win? Cost? Approach? Credentials? Staff? End result?

This is not to suggest gimmickry. A promise, a theme, a main message, a presentation strategy—whatever you wish to call it—cannot win by itself. It must be backed up by a solid proposal, by successful persuasion that the program is well conceived and will succeed. That's the selling job the proposal must do.

In the case of the F-111, the successful proposer undoubtedly first addressed that question: What does it take to win? What does the customer want as an end result of the program? What is nearest his heart? Once that is decided upon, everything should be built around it. The logical next questions are these: What's the best way to dramatize and press home the main message? And what's the best plan for actually achieving that desired end result?

Evolution of a Strategy

Here's a case out of my own personal experience to demonstrate how a winning strategy may evolve in that manner. Several years ago, the Postal Service completed the first of its new bulk mail centers in Secaucus, New Jersey. The center was a literal maze of conveyors, machines, chutes, electronic sensors, control consoles, and other paraphernalia, all under the control of a central computer. The technical center of the Postal Service Training and Development Institute had trained technicians, electrical and mechanical, at their center in Norman, Oklahoma. Now they wanted a contractor to prepare on-the-job training, to be administered to the graduates, as the center began operations. Competition for the contract was keen, and I spent a great deal of time analyzing the work statement and struggling to find a winning proposal strategy. I proceeded from these basics:

1. The trainees had been through general technical training in mechanical and electrical technologies that was not specific to the equipment installed in the center. The on-the-job training must make them competent to maintain that specific equipment.
2. Characteristically, technical training is designed according to a designer's opinion of what a technician ought to know. Usually, the training designer is an engineer or a highly skilled professional who feels that the course should cover just about everything on the subject.
3. Most of the equipment in the center was new in design and even in concept, never proved in actual service.

I decided that we would avoid the typical overtraining of most technical training programs and pound home the theme of technical training completely specific to the need and only to that need. The benefits of the approach, I decided to point out, were at least three: economy, more effective learning because we would not distract the learner from what he needed to know by teaching him things that he didn't need to know, and reducing the personnel losses because the trainee would be knowledgeable about Postal Service equipment only, hence not able to use Postal Service training to get himself a better job elsewhere.

I built the sales arguments along these lines: we weren't interested in the "learner's needs" (again flying in the face of the traditional practice of training-needs analysts). We were interested only in the customer's needs, which were to maintain the equipment and the center. Any effort that did not address the customer's needs was a waste and unjustifiable. The criterion for deciding what materials belonged in the course and what did not was, then, simply this: What does the *equipment* (not the learner) need?

To find out what this was, I proposed, we would "ask the equipment." And we would do this by conducting what I then invented and termed a *failure probability analysis.* That would tell us what failures were most likely and could be predicted as most frequent. And that would also give us criteria for *weighting* the training or deciding how much effort to devote to each topic.

I then sketched in the outline of my failure probability analysis along the lines of such measures as the "known reliability" of given types of components, "component populations," "duty cycles," and other such commonsense measures, and I indicated how they would be assembled into an overall analysis. I then went even further, to point out that "oversimplification" was an effective way to teach maintenance technicians, by reducing all problems to "go/no-go" status; that is, a component was either good or bad (to be left alone or replaced), with the shades of gray between. And I expanded this theme too.

The latter nearly cost us the contract, because it offended the literal-minded engineers, who quarreled with the concept as not being strictly in accordance with scientific fact. However, in personal presentation, I managed to convince them that it was an eminently practical approach and entirely in keeping with their purposes, and we did win the contract.

The concept made good sense, but that wouldn't have sold the customer if we had not been able to come up with a convincing plan for making the concept work.

Here's another kind of case: As you should know by now, proposalmanship is strategy; it doesn't necessarily relate to proposals per se, but refers to any and every kind of bid, even to those so-called formally advertised bids where price is the only important factor. In one such case, I decided to bid for an annual contract that called for a "laundry list" of editorial services: writing, editing, illustrating, typing, proofreading, etc. I knew, of course, that I had to come in with the low bid to be a winner. Yet, the prices were very competitive, since the contract had been let year after year, and the current prices were public information.

I therefore set about analyzing each item in minutest detail, to see if I could find a foothold to come in with the low bid, yet be able to turn a profit and avoid high risk. Most of the services were to be quoted by the hour. But typing, characteristically, was to be quoted by the page. Now most people doing this kind of work know of two kinds of pages: double-spaced and single-spaced. And they assume an "image area" of approximately seven inches by nine inches. This means that a manuscript page, which is normally double-spaced, using a standard elite type (or 12-pitch IBM) is about 84 characters wide and 26 lines deep. And judging from current prices being charged, that was the assumption on which the current contract had been bid; that is, the prices seemed about right for that size of page.

However, the writer of this solicitation and statement of work had been most careful and thorough and had gone so far as to define what he meant by "a page." He had defined it as 54 characters wide and 18 lines deep! This comes to less than one-half of what most of us think of as a standard double-spaced page. When I priced it accordingly, I was the low bidder and winner, much to the consternation of competitors who hadn't bothered to read the work statement very closely.

Give the Customer What He Wants

Salespeople often talk about "creating wants." Whether you "create" a want or merely find one is probably moot but not really important. What is important is that you sense a customer's wants accurately and respond to them or make a customer conscious of wants he has not specifically recognized, which is pretty much the same thing. To do this, you must have at least a general understanding of your customer's "psychology."

Try putting yourself in the place of a government executive who is soliciting proposals for some job he wants done. And let us suppose that it is a substantial contract—let's say, $250,000. That's quite a bit of money, and it's no small responsibility to spend it wisely and effectively.

Now let us suppose that you get a number of proposals in response to your solicitation. Typically about two-thirds of them run the gamut from "impossible" to fairly good—but not good enough. You read and screen —you're probably leading an evaluation team of three people—and you're left with several acceptable proposals. You have two that are probably the best of the lot. They're about even with each other in technical quality. One is from a large and well-known corporation; the other is from a small, unknown company. "Mr. Big's" proposal is somewhat higher in price than "Mr. Small's" proposal, but it is still within what you have earlier established as the "competitive range."

Which one will you select?

If you're a reasonably cautious and conservative person, you'll probably select Mr. Big's proposal for this reason: should he falter and do a poor job, you can shrug and point out that you selected a well-known company with a good reputation. What more could you do? But if you select Mr. Small and he lays an egg, you will (you fear) be open to severe criticism for risking an important contract on a small, unknown entity, when the only difference between the two was a "few dollars."

There are exceptions. Some contracting officers are pretty tough about their role in the final selection process, and all contracting officers are sorely tempted to go with the lowest bidder. A tough enough CO may force the executive into taking the lower bidder if the technical difference is slight. Legally, any contracting officer can demand a written justification for selecting other than the low bidder under circumstances of nearly equal technical evaluation, and evaluators are not always eager to undertake such an arduous task.

It's useful to know the internal policies in an agency, and especially the relative characters of the evaluators and the contracting officer, when deciding on a strategy, especially a strategy that involves how much you will "sharpen your pencil" in pricing the job.

Proposalmanship therefore involves gathering intelligence about the agency, its policies, the people involved, and anything else you can get. There are many cases where it's virtual policy that the lowest *qualified* bidder will win. That is, winning technical points above the minimum necessary to be considered qualified doesn't help very much if you're not the low bidder. There are cases where cost is one of the criteria and is part of an entirely objective mathematical rating scheme. And there are cases where cost is entirely unimportant, as long as it is not more than the agency's budget for the job. And there are even cases where too low a cost is fatal, because the evaluators take that as a sign that you don't understand the requirement at all. (Or they may fear having too much money left in their budgets and favor the supplier who helps spend it all.)

There are also cases where evaluation is somewhat loosely structured, and some single point in your proposal intrigues the customer so much that he brushes all competitors aside.

In short, there is an almost infinite number of possible strategies and/or permutations of basic strategies. Strategies, however, do rely on an understanding of the internal situation in the agency, customer motivation, internal policies, and other factors.

Reading the RFP and Drawing Inferences from It

RFPs vary widely in their characteristics. Some are extremely detailed in all respects, some remarkably vague and uninformative; some appear to speak frankly, others appear guarded; some are highly specific in describing the evaluation criteria and how they are to be weighted and manipulated to arrive at a final score, others are simply too general; some go so far as to prescribe in detail how the proposal is to be organized and formatted; others leave it entirely to the proposer, merely listing the required information.

Many people try to read things into these characteristics. To some, a vague RFP (statement of work, that is) indicates that the contract is "wired"—some favored bidder has all the inside information and everyone else is being shut out by the withholding of information. On the other hand, some people read that same meaning into a highly specific, detailed RFP: the RFP, they believe, has been structured so that only some favored bidder can qualify with high marks.

There is an element of truth in both these sets of inferences. Occasionally, such characteristics do indicate an effort to wire the contract. But more often, they indicate nothing other than that in the one case, the customer does not know just how to attack his problem and leaves it entirely to the proposer to suggest approaches. In the other case, the customer knows exactly what he wants or thinks he should have and is saying so.

Ideally, the RFP and work statements—the latter, in particular—should be written this way, as they are by the truly knowledgeable government customers: the statement of work and other parts of the RFP should contain enough detail to guide the proposer so that he has ample opportunity to be "responsive," yet it should not be so detailed and restrictive as to prevent or inhibit proposers from offering innovative ideas and fresh approaches.

The Types of Strategies

Overall, we're interested in developing a win strategy or, as some people call it, a capture strategy. That could be price, technical program, presentation, or other—whatever we have decided is going to be the most critical area of the decision-making process leading to contract award. And, of course, it could be a combination of these. However, in most cases, there is some overriding consideration, such as price or technical innovation, as we have already seen. That decision leads us to another set of strategies: how to manage to come in with the lowest price, the best program, the most qualified staff, the most outstanding proposal, etc.

Obviously, it is to your advantage if you can have the best program *and* the lowest price *and* the most qualified staff *and* the most outstanding proposal presentation, and you should certainly try to excel in all areas. But realistically, you are not likely to be outstanding in all areas, if for no other reason than that proposal schedules usually do not allow you time enough to concentrate that kind of effort on all areas. You must therefore try to psych out the most important area and concentrate on it.

In my own past experience, I can think of cases where the success I had in winning a contract was due to one or more of these factors—to selecting the best strategy, that is. I believe that it is impossible to generalize and say that one or another is usually the decisive factor. As you review the many case histories you will find in these pages, you should be able to see that more and more clearly.

However, there are certain basics about which we can generalize. The blurb at the beginning of this chapter quotes an official who is lamenting about the poor quality of so many proposals he has reviewed. More specifically, when he calls them "bad," he is referring to one very common fault found among proposals in typical submissions: failure of the proposer to demonstrate that he understands the problem. There is probably nothing that brings swifter rejection of a proposal than that fault. If you manage to convince the reader/evaluator that you do not understand what he is looking for, he sees no reason to read further and goes on to the next one.

The head of a division at the new Department of Energy told me very clearly that he often reads a proposal no further than page 1. If he finds the copy on page 1 discouraging enough, he goes on to the next proposal.

Another government executive has told me that he often cancels a procurement entirely if he is dissatisfied with all the proposals he gets. He insists that he will not award a contract to "the best of a bad lot," as many others do, but will try again, in a few months, and see if he can get better responses.

Demonstrating understanding is done throughout your proposal by the various things you say and the ways you respond to the request. However, the matter of demonstrating understanding is so important that many experienced proposal writers insert a special section early in the proposal, called something like "Understanding of the Requirement." Here, they present a brief statement to demonstrate that understanding and try to tempt the reader into wanting to read the rest.

In a sense, we can get a message from that division chief who won't turn to page 2 if he finds page 1 bad enough. It's this: The main task of any proposal writer is to persuade the reader to *want* to turn to page 2—that is, *every* page should motivate the reader to want to see what is on the next page, every page should capture the reader's interest and *sustain* that interest throughout.

The art that I call proposalmanship includes some techniques for doing just that, and we'll be examining those next.

10

Step 1 in Proposalmanship: Analysis and Understanding

When all else fails, try reading the instructions.

The Importance of Doing Your Homework

My office was in the Maryland suburb of Washington, D. C., Rockville. The job I was bidding was at Fort Belvoir, Virginia, a few miles south of Washington. I had written the proposal in a frantic weekend effort, came in lagging the RCA Service Company by a few technical points (235 to 238), but was enough lower in price to be adjudged the winner—tentatively; "tentatively" because an inspection team was on their way from Fort Belvoir to look over our facility and satisfy themselves that we were capable of doing the work.

The team arrived and took the usual tour of the premises. We then gathered in my office to talk.

"I hope you found everything satisfactory?" I said, inquiringly, knowing they had, of course.

The head of the team fixed me with a cold eye. "It's over forty-five miles from the Fort," he said.

"How did you come?" I asked. I'd expected the comment and was, fortunately, prepared for it.

"Beltway. Fifty-six miles."

I nodded. "That's about right, I think."

He looked a bit exasperated. "The RFP says forty-five miles is the limit."

It was a challenge, of course. He expected an argument.

"It says 'radius,' " I answered. "Forty-five mile radius. Straight-line. You can't measure that by road. You need a map and a ruler. I used Rand McNally figures. Radius."

Consternation is the best word to describe their looks. The RFP had indeed said "radius," and they hadn't given a thought to what the word meant.

The law is the law. Like it or not, they had to sign the contract.

I had been well aware that the driving distance was more than 45 miles, and I had been at great pains to get official Rand McNally figures for straight-line distance. If they had caught me unaware, the outcome might well have been different—and probably would have been.

As in the case in the previous chapter (concerning the definition and cost for a page of typing), the answer lay in doing the homework—reading the RFP and the statement of work thoroughly. Undoubtedly, a large percentage of proposal failures are due to failure to read, digest, and analyze the RFP and the statement of work.

RFP Analysis and Reading between the Lines

It is not enough to read the RFP. That is, it is not enough to read the lines of the RFP. You must also read *between* the lines. Sometimes you find more there than on the lines. Given the facts (1) that the RFP may be badly written because the executives who write them are not always particularly gifted writers or even clear thinkers and (2) that the customer may not even know exactly what his problem is but is describing only symptoms, the art of reading between the lines assumes some importance.

There is a third reason for RFPs' often being less specific than you hope they will be: in many cases, the customer is reluctant to tell the world the whole truth about his problems and why they exist.

For example, suppose he has a badly written computer program that he wishes to have cleaned up and put in order. He is likely to employ many euphemisms to describe his problem. Will he admit that his staff is inefficient and has permitted the data base to accumulate an intolerable number of errors? That he himself has not been more on the ball about it?

Perhaps his agency's policies have produced problems, or he is in a nasty battle with a rival for something or other in his office.

In any event, there are any number of reasons for concealing some of the facts, despite a desire to elicit the best possible proposal. He might want to know, for example, the condition of the data base before estimating the cost of reprogramming a system. These things, therefore, often require some deductive analysis: assembling odd and assorted bits of information from which to draw reasonable conclusions.

It was reading between the lines that enabled me to judge accurately that four people were employed at NASA as catalogers—many readings and rereadings, assembling the bits, and drawing logical inferences led to an accurate conclusion. Without that search, I could never have conceived the winning strategy.

I didn't have to read between the lines to learn the government's definition of a page of typing, but neither did the information leap off the page at me. It was fairly well buried in all the paper of the RFP and had to be ferreted out.

The relative importance of any single item or evaluation criterion may be other than it appears to be. The RFP may assign 30% for staff qualifications, yet the quality of staff résumés may actually be of far greater impact. Perhaps the customer feels that it would appear unreasonable to assign more than 30% to résumés, yet he may know that he will be far more influenced by the résumés than that 30% figure suggests.

The RFP may invite innovative ideas, yet the chief evaluator might be a conservative who is heavily inclined toward established, conventional approaches.

There are several methods for gathering intelligence to arrive at accurate answers to these problems. But the first method is RFP analysis itself. A surprisingly large number of answers are there in the RFP all the while. But frequently it takes effort and shrewdness to entice them from the paper.

A Graphics Method for Analysis and Design

Brainstorming is an idea invented by a New York advertising man to get a mental synergy going among a group of people. It requires a leader, who poses a question or a problem and guides the session, and someone to record the ideas. The group is encouraged to spew forth all ideas that come to mind, no matter how wild or impractical they may appear. The members are also enjoined from making any judgments of ideas emitted, so as not to inhibit others from throwing ideas out. And anyone may take an idea just emitted and resubmit it with new twists or variations.

Later, when the people have run down and all the wild ideas have been noted, they are evaluated, the ones showing no promise of usefulness thrown out, and the remainder considered seriously.

Proposalmanship entails a variant of the brainstorming idea to help analyze the RFP. (It also produces a useful by-product, which we'll discuss later.)

Many RFPs—statements of work, that is—are somewhat involved in what they ask for, calling out work by a succession of phases and tasks and even subtasks. Simply digesting what the customer has requested—trying to visualize the program he has in mind generally—can be difficult under those circumstances.

An excellent way out is to develop a flowchart depicting the program as suggested by the statement of work. Such a chart presents the program in a form in which the various functions and phases of the work can be viewed together and compared with each other without the need for mental gymnastics.

Let's take, first, a relatively simple case: responding to the requirements for a Job Corps training center. Each curriculum to be taught in the vocational courses offered in these centers was to have various "step-off" points—points at which the trainee could enter into apprenticeship or even journeymanship in one of the many job opportunities for which he was to be trained.

Basically, the concept was simple enough. The trainee was to be given the opportunity to proceed through a number of preparatory courses in each given career field, with the option of proceeding all the way to the most advanced courses offered in that field, yet with the option of "getting off the train" at any point where he might be ready for work, at some proficiency or skill level lower than those at the end of the trip.

The proposer had to demonstrate not only understanding of the concept but the ability to identify each vocational career field, develop and structure the courses in an ascending order, identify all terminal specialty courses, and, at the same time, identify all the appropriate step-off points.

It would take a great many words to handle all this in text, if it could be done adequately at all that way.

Once the basic idea was laid out on paper, as a flowchart, the pieces began to fall into place. The finished chart (Figure 6) is shown for one of the fields, automotive/automotive body repair curriculum.

This chart, and most others developed for the same purpose, did not spring from the mind onto paper at one leap. Such charts must be developed, starting with a very generalized, rough sketch, setting forth the customer's basic ideas. It then goes through a series of refinements until the designers are satisfied that they have developed a plan.

The chart should be developed, at least in semi-final form, *before* writing begins. There are at least two reasons for this:

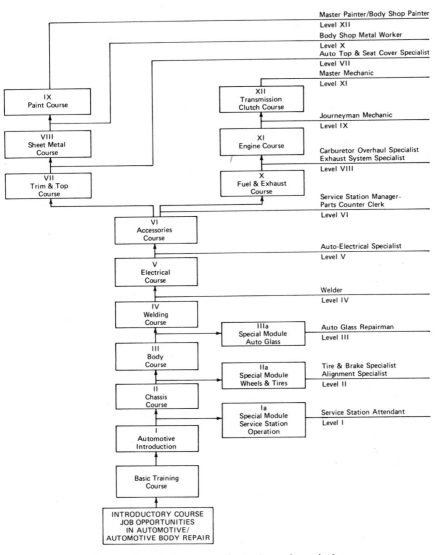

Figure 6. Automotive/automotive body repair curriculum.

1. The chart puts the problem and the tentative program into perspective. Until you develop the chart, the possibility is excellent that you won't know what you are talking about but will merely be winging it on paper—doodling, in effect.
2. If the chart is well done, you have relatively little writing to do, except to present your technical arguments for the plan depicted. The chart is—should be—self-explanatory. If it is not, it is a poor chart and should be done over.

Here's a good rule: Every graphic presentation—chart, photo, drawing of any kind—should "displace its own weight of language." That is, the chart should reduce materially the amount of text that would otherwise be required.

Here's a corollary: If any graphic illustration requires extensive explanation in words, it is probably a useless and is almost certainly a poorly conceived illustration.

That latter is, in fact, a test that any wise editor applies to graphic presentations.

Take the famous photo of the World War II raising of the flag on Iwo Jima by the U. S. Marines. How much text does that require?

Developing such charts, to return to our main subject, is not always as simple as the example we have just seen. In many cases, I have found it necessary to develop a chart so that I myself could understand fully what the statement of work was saying! It is not at all unusual for words to be entirely inadequate to explain a complex concept.

Here is where that special kind of brainstorming proves its worth. Through it, I have been able to lead, write, develop, manage, coordinate, and otherwise produce winning proposals in technical/professional areas where I myself had little or no expertise! Until that time, I was in the habit of developing my own preliminary flowcharts and then turning them over to others to refine and improve. That is, I gave the staff my own basic concept of what the customer was asking for and how I proposed to respond by charting it roughly. Then, in a series of meetings, the staff of proposal writers would work together to add ideas, critique what we had done to date, etc.

But the day finally arrived when I was asked to organize, manage, lead, and coordinate a team in a field about which I knew very little.

My first effort to chart the customer's requirement was pretty bad. It was childishly simple and said very little. It contained only the most basic blocks of the requirement—blocks that required no insight into the technical field.

The answer turned out to be this: I assembled the leading technical experts of the company, who were assigned to give at least part of their time to the proposal effort. I seated them in a conference room and stood before them, chalk in hand and a large blackboard in front of me, on which I had sketched my own, greatly simplifed chart. I then led them, reading from the statement of work, through the development of a more detailed chart. Present also was an individual assigned to copy the chart on paper as we developed it together.

This process can take a few hours, or it might take several days and repeated sessions, periodically, in a large and complex program, such as the designing of a new, high-speed aircraft. However, a synergism results as the experts advance ideas, argue them, trigger each other into new thoughts, and critique and rebut each other. Ultimately, they come to agreement, point by point, as the chart develops, and the overall picture begins to emerge.

In this manner, we gain the combined thinking of all the expert talents and knowledge and argue the concepts out before spending time and effort in writing that will largely be scrapped. Because the picture of the requirement and the program proposed is almost literally that—a picture —the team arrives at a true agreement and a common understanding of the program proposed. Communication among the team is vastly improved, and objectives are much more clearly understood. Strategies begin to emerge as a result.

Here is a case in point, to illustrate how that can happen: For some years, the military services have been experimenting with various methods for improving the presentation of maintenance information, especially for the complex systems in use today. Many schemes have been tried out, such things as "SIMMS," "PIMO," and "JPA" have emerged from these efforts. Recently, one of the services decided that it was time to do something more with the JPA (Job Performance Aids) technology. They issued an RFP. The statement of work was lengthy and involved. It called for studies of the JPA technology to date—the state of the art— experimental developments based on findings, and several other aspects of a program, the main objective of which was, apparently, to get JPA technology out of the laboratory and into production. That was not their language but is a translation of their language.

As the customer saw the requirement, there were three major tasks or phases of work, which they identified as JPA Technology Definition, Criterion Data Collection (for each of several test cases), and Job Performance Aid Package Development (again, for each test case). The statement of work saw these as totally separate and independent tasks/ phases and suggested that the government might award three separate contracts, one for each task/phase.

Following the system outlined above, I assembled my client company's experts before a blackboard and set to work.

Long before we had finished developing a fairly complicated flow-chart (see Figure 7), it had become readily apparent that these three tasks or phases were not as independent of each other as the customer appar-

TASK 1: JPA TECHNOLOGY DEFINITION

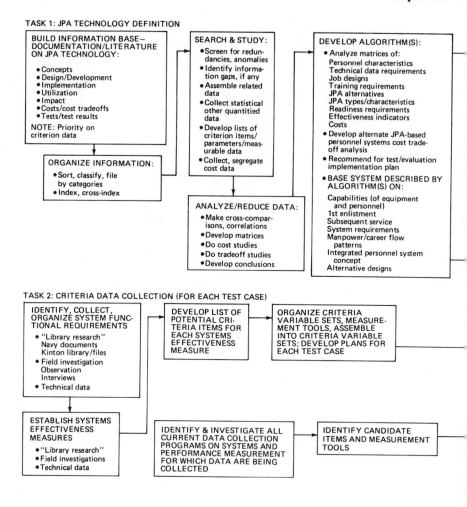

Figure 7. Example of a flow chart.

ently thought they were. In fact, analysis of the chart showed clearly that if three contracts were awarded, much of the work would be redundant; that is, knowledge gained in Task 1 was essential to the performance of Tasks 2 and 3.

Obviously, presenting that chart to the customer in the proposal was going to demonstrate a deep understanding of the problem and a much more efficient way of doing the job than would be the case were three contracts awarded.

Nor was that the only benefit derived from flowcharting before writing. As a result of having the chart developed and available—during its

TASK 3: JOB PERFORMANCE AID PACKAGE DEVELOPMENT (FOR EACH TEST CASE)

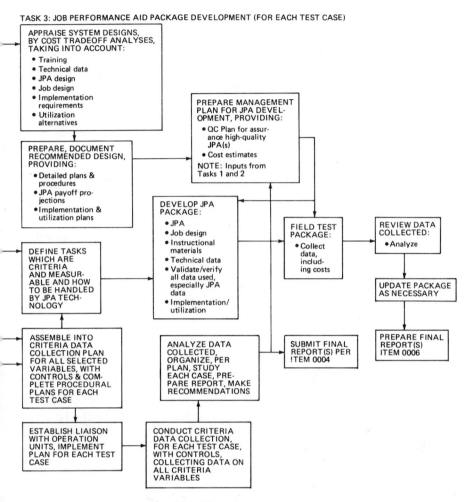

Figure 7. *(Continued)*

development, that is—we gained a far better understanding of the problem than the customer had! The statement of work had no charts but relied entirely on language to present the complex set of functions shown. The text was full of redundancies and anomalies. (It appeared to have been written by a committee, and probably was.) Without the chart, the proposer might well have prepared a proposal equally confused and contradictory.

This goes straight back to the question of what the customer is looking for when he issues an RFP. It is dangerous to take for granted that the customer knows exactly what he wants—except that he does know what final result he wants. But as to how to achieve that result, the customer is asking you, as the expert, to tell him, to propose a program that will achieve the desired result.

The system of working as a team to get the requirement down in the form of a flowchart of some sort, therefore, has these distinct advantages and benefits:

1. It is, of itself, an analytical tool, helping to define/identify what the customer has in mind, even if the idea that the customer has is a rather vague one.
2. It's a communication tool among the proposal team members, enabling them to arrive at commonly understood and agreed-upon definitions and technical approaches.
3. It's a springboard for new ideas, insights, strategy developments, and cost-saving techniques.
4. It simplifies the writing enormously, a special advantage for those of the team who are not particularly gifted writers, and it is also a far more effective means of communicating your ideas to the customer than words alone.
5. It's clear evidence of your understanding of the problem and adds to your general credibility because it's easier to follow than text and proves that you have, indeed, made a penetrating analysis.

There are some other spin-off advantages. One of these is that the development of the chart facilitates making writing assignments, because specific and distinct areas of the program have now been identified. These can be used advantageously as the basis for writing assignments.

These, in turn, may lead to a second generation of charts or drawings, at more detailed levels. That is, one of the large blocks or a group of related blocks may be developed into another chart, more detailed, demonstrating how the functions or tasks will be carried out.

The same set of benefits derives at this more detailed level: less text required, better analysis of the area of effort, and better understanding, better communication with the customer.

The first flowchart should therefore be developed at the "top level," showing the main, overall functions, tasks, phases, etc. of the program. If the program is large enough and complex enough to require it, second-level charts may then be developed for some or all of the areas of effort identified in the first chart.

There is little doubt that graphics do help materially to sell your concept and proposed program to the customer.

Storyboarding Techniques

A spin-off and further expansion of this idea has been used success-fully by many proposal teams. It uses the basic idea just described and borrows the storyboard idea from the field of audiovisual presentation.

A *storyboard* is a device for planning and presenting an audiovisual program. The visual is sketched in (at an early stage, it may be described in words), and the audio text—the script that accompanies it—is typed alongside. Figure 8 illustrates a portion of such a storyboard, taken from an audiovisual program on value engineering.

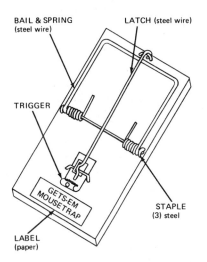

When a mouse decides to sample the cheese that has been carefully deposited on the trigger, his first nibble springs the latch and releases the bail, which then comes down on the unsuspect-ing creature, under the force of the energy stored in the spring, thus exterminating the mouse. All of this Rube Goldbergian sequence of events has one purpose. We cannot take the time now to build up this *fast* diagram, piece by piece, but we will present the diagram to you, *without scope lines.* Where would you put them? That is, what would you designate as the basic and higher-order functions?

MOUSETRAP

Component	Function
Base	Holds parts
Bail & Spring	Store energy
Trigger	Releases latch
Latch	Holds bail
Staples	Locate parts
Label	Identifies maker
Mousetrap	Kills mice

Figure 8. A typical storyboard.

This idea can be used effectively in proposal planning, in this manner: Select a block or a related set of blocks from your chart and use it as the "visual" for one section of your storyboard. Then develop the concepts that you will use in the proposal. An example is shown in Figure 8.

Once developed, it may be worth another flowchart (Figure 9) showing how the subtasks/functions relate to each other, or it may be handled with language (text) alone. Each individual case must be studied to determine which is the best alternative, which communicates best with the customer, and which makes the most credible and convincing presentation.

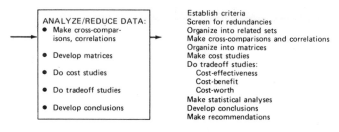

Figure 9. Spinning-off another flow chart.

Whatever the final decision, the exercise has at least enabled you to identify and decide upon some logical set of actions—subtasks or functions—to carry out the objectives identified in the box. Later, when you are ready to "man-load" the project, you will find that this work serves another useful purpose and gives you the foundation for realistic costing of the project.

Storyboarding has still another meaning for some proposal writers, especially for those proposing some complex piece of hardware, such as a new fighter aircraft.

Characteristically, hardware RFPs usually have long and detailed lists of specifications: what the customer wants the finished piece of hardware to weigh, how big it should be, what it should be able to do, etc. The proposer is expected to respond to each and every one of these specifications in the proposal and to demonstrate an understanding both of each individual specification and of the overall significance of the entire set of specifications.

In nonhardware RFPs, such as the one just discussed, the specifications are often rather general and buried in the text rather than being distinctly listed. Quite often, specifications must be inferred in those cases, and they really don't deserve the word *specifications,* because they are not truly specific. However, such contracts are usually not of the magnitude of large hardware procurements, and it is possible to identify (or infer) the specifications, use them to formulate a flowchart, and develop a preliminary design, all in a single session, as described.

With large hardware procurements, the proposal-planning job becomes more complicated. Steps preceding the development of a flowchart and a preliminary design are necessary. One system has proved highly successful in producing winning proposals:

The first step is to prepare a complete list of all proposal requirements—the specifications for the program or the equipment itself and any other requirements that the RFP and statement of work have stipulated—a master checklist for the entire proposal, in fact. Each of those items on that master checklist becomes a storyboard in itself. The storyboards are reviewed by the specialists, usually in teams and employing a form of brainstorming to analyze the specifications and interpret their meanings, their significance, the alternative ways of meeting them, the problems they pose, their effects on overall design and/or performance of the equipment, and all other such matters. The specifications are also addressed and studied for their meanings and effects on proposal strategies by raising such questions as, Why is this specification included? What does the customer hope to accomplish by it? What should we say about it in our proposal?

The answers arrived at are recorded on the appropriate storyboard, along with any sketches or other relevant information. Suitable headlines and blurbs are recorded also, if the proposal is to use the format favored by those using the storyboard technique. (These formats will be shown in Chapter 13.) When a response to each specification has been agreed upon, the set of storyboards may be assembled and used as the basis for the proposal and for any charts to be developed.

In the simpler case used to introduce this subject, we did the entire thing simultaneously, in a single session, because it was a relatively small project. In one session, we identified and analyzed each specification and charted our response to each, assembling an entire program in a single flowchart. The principles, however, are the same:

1. Identify the requirement in terms of specifications, to the maximum extent of specificity that the work statement provides.
2. Analyze, translate, and interpret each specification/requirement. (When stated requirements are not highly specific, as they often are not, we hesitate to use the word *specification* for fear of causing confusion.
3. Develop proposed response to each requirement.
4. Chart responses, and relate all to a flow in a flowchart.

A proposal team is not ready to begin serious writing before they have arrived at this point and have identified/developed a basic attack strategy.

Whether these things are done on the decentralized basis described for a major procurement or on the simplified, one-session basis is primarily a matter of the size and complexity of the procurement and the proposal.

The important factor and the *raison d'être* of all of this is simply to ensure that the proposer does in fact have a complete understanding of the customer's need—perhaps even a better understanding than the customer has.

Merits of the Vague versus the Detailed RFP

In the proposal business, you soon learn that you may expect an RFP and a statement of work to fall into at least one of three categories: terribly vague, terribly detailed, or somewhere between those extremes.

As we have already explained, an RFP may be detailed or vague deliberately. But it is more often detailed or vague as a result of the RFP writer's own insight or lack of it into his own problems. The characteristics of an RFP, in this respect, are factors to consider in arriving at bid or no-bid decisions. That is, is it better to bid the vague or the detailed RFP? Which offers the better chance for success?

In my own view, the vague RFP offers the better chance for a contract. I am almost always more attracted by a vague, presumably poorly written RFP, as compared with the highly detailed and specific RFP.

One of the reasons I advocate that approach and am motivated by it is that it is a decidedly minority opinion: most people are repelled by a vague RFP and far prefer to bid the highly detailed, specific one.

The logic of my opinion is that because it is a minority opinion, the more vague and obscure the RFP, the fewer the number of proposals submitted in response to it: competition is almost always far less severe when the RFP is vague than when it is clear, largely because responding to a vague RFP is much harder than responding to one where the response is virtually dictated by the RFP. This discourages many bidders.

However, even more motivating than the fact that competition will almost certainly be reduced by a poor RFP is the far greater freedom of choice that a vague RFP affords proposers. You may philosophize, speculate, and propose over an extremely broad range of possibilities without running very much risk of nonresponsiveness.

In the vague RFP, unless the customer has been deliberately vague to give an edge to an insider, the customer is pleading for help. He is admitting that he has little idea of how to solve the problem or meet the need and desperately needs help. This is opportunity. It's hard work, but it's opportunity. I can state unequivocally that my success ratio has always been greater in responding to vague RFPs. And it's not a coincidence.

In proposal writing, as in most other things, difficulties are not problems—they're opportunities. The difficulties of vaguely written RFPs offer opportunities to be innovative, opportunities to be imaginative, opportunities to develop strategies.

Conversely, you may expect that those of your competitors who choose to respond to the vague RFP tend to be equally vague in their responses. At least some of them will proceed on the naive notion that the customer is deliberately withholding information to test them, and they think that they are being foxy by being vague in response. They tend to believe that they are playing it safe that way.

The opposite is true. The risk of going counter to a customer's notions and prejudices by being specific where he has been vague is a small risk, compared with the risk of turning the customer off completely by being so vague in your response that he really does not know just what you are proposing!

Many unsuccessful proposals are written just that way: full of smug assurances that the proposer is an expert organization, full of the finest staff people, dedicated to producing fine results for all clients, with an impeccable track record. Claims, rather than evidence. No evidence, no logic, no arguments—just claims . . . self appraisals.

Here again is a rule—with an occasional exception, perhaps, but nonetheless a general rule that is true: the more detailed your proposal, the more credible it is and the greater is its chance for success. Far better to provide excessive detail (more than is needed) than insufficient detail (less than is needed) to establish credibility.

The first flowchart presented in this chapter came out of a successful proposal for a Job Corps center, which contract produced over $25 million in billings. The proposal was in three volumes, totaling almost 1,000 pages. One of the volumes was an appendix, with long lists of reference data, the source for which cost us $3.00! The entire proposal cost us $12,000 to prepare. The customer estimated that we had spent at least $50,000. That reflected his amazement at the wealth of detail we had included, but it also impressed him mightily and gave us tremendous credibility. Details are accepted as evidence. And evidence makes you believable.

11

Other Intelligence-Gathering

Geting the right information is at least one-half the battle.

Ask and You Shall Receive . . .

I tried to be tactful. I was testing the new Freedom of Information Act, or "Sunshine Act," as the newspapers were calling it. The place was the contracts office at NASA/Langley, in the Norfolk/Hampton/Newport News area of Virginia, and I was there to gather information in connection with a possible bid for an annual support contract.

I asked the contracting officer, "Under this new law, I suppose I now have the right to ask what the current rates are on the present contract?"

He grinned at me. "I wouldn't have offered, but since you ask . . . ." He reached up on his shelf, handed me a document. "I'm going down and have a smoke," he said, and left.

He had handed me his file copy of the existing contract and left me alone to make any notes I wanted to. In my hands was the complete proposal submitted successfully the year before, the prices, the staffing—the "whole nine yards."

. . . But You Can Receive the Wrong Thing . . .

I was strolling through the halls of the Postal Service Training and Development Institute in Bethesda, Maryland. I waved to the contracting officer, an old acquaintance from many contracts past. He beckoned me in response. I went into his office behind him, and he closed the door.

"Look," he said, "You'll be getting an RFP from us in a day or so. It's perfect for you. I want you to have this contract. I think you'll do a great job for us on this one. Just be sure to give us a real good proposal."

I assured him that I would indeed turn in a proposal of my usual high quality and went on without much more thought.

The RFP, when I got it in the mail, was pretty vague and difficult to follow. I decided I needed more information. I therefore sent one of my assistants out to the institute to run down the information and get us some answers.

I subsequently submitted my proposal—and lost.

The contracting officer was stunned. "What happened?" he demanded. "You usually turn in a crackerjack proposal."

I admitted I didn't know, but I requested a debriefing. Then I went back to see the contracting officer.

"We were way off base," I told him. "The job they wanted done was entirely different from what O'—— told us, when we checked with him."

He groaned. "You talked to the wrong guy. He doesn't agree with the way K—— wants the job done, but K—— is the boss. You should have talked to K—— ."

Moral 1: Even when the contracting officer *wants* to give you the job, you have to give him a good enough proposal to warrant the award.

Moral 2: You can't write a good proposal without good information.

We were done in on this one because we were careless. We got information that was in contradiction to the RFP, and we accepted it instead of checking it out. We deserved to lose.

The Importance of Intelligence

Marketing intelligence is critically important. In the last chapter, we talked about proper RFP analysis, the first line on market intelligence. Far too many marketers do a great job of getting field information but fail to do a proper job of RFP analysis, which is somewhat absurd when you consider that it is in the RFP that the customer is trying especially to tell you what he wants!

On the other hand, RFP analysis is sometimes not enough. Aside from the fact that the customer may not be giving you enough of the right information because of any of several problems, no RFP can furnish some of the information obtainable by other means.

Here are a few things you want to know about most procurements:

1. Who are the proposal evaluators (i.e., the psychologists, the engineers, the managers, etc.)
2. Agency policies, such as relative importance of costs, how much the contracting officer presses for low bidders, etc.

3. Political, management, personnel, and other internal problems in the office or bureau soliciting proposals
4. The history of the agency in conducting "best and finals" versus awarding without further negotiating
5. Past and/or incumbent suppliers of similar or related services
6. The agency's past tendencies to stick with established suppliers versus openmindedness to new suppliers

All these are factors that help you develop strategies, judge the most acceptable technical approaches, and even establish the tone of your proposal.

For example, if you are bidding a training-development requirement and the evaluators are primarily psychologists and/or professional educators, you will want to trot out your best "behavioral" terms. But if the evaluators are engineers, you'll want to address the subject matter. And if they are managers, you'll want to slant your proposal in their direction by addressing the effects of good training on management.

In bidding to the Postal Service Training and Development Institute, for example, I used one set of terms with the technical/engineering staff at the Norman, Oklahoma Technical Training Institute and another set of terms at their management-training establishment in Bethesda, Maryland. To have done otherwise would have been fatal.

"The government" is people. It's "they," not "it." Each agency is a set of individuals, and agencies have their own characteristics. One agency tends to favor its "old-time," established suppliers and to regard with some distrust any bidder unknown to them. Another agency has a true open-door policy, and everyone receives equal consideration. Still another favors "new blood" and welcomes new contractors.

One agency prefers to deal with large, established firms, while another likes small, new firms.

Dealing with government agencies is not much different from dealing with commercial corporations, in fact. Thus the need to know your customer.

This is reflected also in how contractors regard the agencies and the government market generally. Some refuse flatly to bid "cold." They insist that they will bid only to an agency where they have had advance notice of the procurement, an opportunity to discuss the requirement with principals in the agency, and some indication that their proposal will indeed be welcome!

Some contractors grind out boilerplate proposals—in great quantity, at low unit cost, and with a low ratio of success. Their philosophy is that they make out about the same in the long run. They may be right. They appear to survive. But they undoubtedly miss many contracts that they might have had.

In any case, the more you know about the agency to whom you are bidding, the more likely you are to meet with success.

The Preproposal Conference

Many procurements, especially large ones, include a preproposal conference. All prospective proposers are invited to a hall where they are confronted with the contracting officer and the technical experts for whom the job is to be done, usually along with their staffs.

The broad purpose of such a conference is to enable the government to provide any needed clarification of the RFP and to enable the prospective proposers to get answers to questions that have occurred to them while reading the RFP.

The usual routine in such conferences is to have the contracting officer and the technical expert(s) each deliver brief orientations and then to throw the floor open for questions. In some cases, attendees have been invited to submit their questions in advance; in others, questions are accepted from the floor.

To the experienced government marketer, such conferences may be extremely helpful, although not in terms of answers and information provided by the government officials.

One thing you almost invariably find at such conferences is that a great many "dumb questions" are asked. They are dumb questions, usually, because they are either totally irrelevant or totally unnecessary: either the answer is obvious to any experienced government contractor, or the answer is already in the RFP.

The reason dumb questions occur is twofold. Many of those asking the questions are marketing people who have absolutely no technical knowledge concerning the requirements. This means that the company has unwisely sent the wrong personnel. (They sent someone who was readily available, rather than someone who could evaluate the information!) The other reason is that many of the companies attending such conferences are totally unqualified and inexperienced in the field of activity but are hopeful that they can bluff their way through to a contract.

The really experienced government marketer at such a conference rarely has anything to say. He comes to listen and observe, not to talk. He knows that for the most part, the answers to his questions are already in the RFP and that they can be ferreted out with patience and persistence. He knows, too, that many of those in attendance are relatively green or unfamiliar with the field of interest; therefore his questions will give them more information, relatively, than he will get. It's an uneven trade, which helps the competition. Hence, better to remain silent in most cases.

On the other hand, by listening, he is getting an idea of the quality of the probable competition, and he can usually judge which of his competitors represent serious competition. He can judge, too, how many competitors he is likely to have for the contract.

The preproposal conference can be valuable for the experienced government marketer who is wise enough to listen instead of talking.

I have attended many preproposal conferences. I have rarely, if ever, gotten useful technical information that I didn't already have. But I have gotten:

1. An insight into the size, nature, and quality of the competition
2. An insight into the characteristics of the contracting officer and the technical or "program" people
3. A sense of those factors of greatest importance to the agency in selecting a successful bidder
4. Background information on the requirement—history and reasons for the requirement; predecessor work and contracts, if any; and insight into the agency's greatest concerns

Other Sources of Intelligence

Poking around the agency and asking questions while a proposal effort is in progress is delicate business. Again, agencies vary. Some agencies and some individuals will welcome you and help as much as their consciences will permit, while others will tell you in the most direct terms that you have no business being there while a proposal contest is going on. Many will tell you that the only person you should be talking to, until the proposals have been submitted, is the contracting officer.

Therefore, this direct method must be used with some caution, lest you prejudice the agency against you.

The agency's library may be of help. There, you may be able to uncover reports describing the predecessor's work and history leading to the present requirement, and that can be helpful information.

If the requirement is a large one and the time scale permits, there is still another way that some companies have employed with great success. I have used it myself:

There is a large government facility that the government owns but that is operated by a contractor. It's a major installation, including computers, printing presses, and much other equipment. The operation and maintenance contract, at the time of my interest, was approximately $5 million a year, and the contract was let in three-year terms.

At the time of my interest, I knew only vaguely about the operation, although I knew its size and importance. At the preproposal conference, each of us was given a large carton full of manuals, books, drawings, specifications, and other data, which constituted part of the RFP. After studying this material, I was still in the dark about many things. I decided to resort to some help-wanted ads in the local newspaper, written especially to attract some of the individuals working at that facility.

Over the next two weeks, I interviewed a number of employees of the incumbent contractor. I learned the exact number of people there, was able to judge the total payroll with great accuracy, and gathered a great deal of other highly reliable information. Perhaps the most valuable intelligence I gathered was that the agency was dissatisfied with the incumbent contractor and was determined to make a change. I was also able to estimate the price at which the job should be bid—and with precise accuracy, as it later turned out. I believe that never, before or since, have I had such a complete and such an accurate set of intelligence data about a potential contract.

As it turned out, my company decided, at the last moment, not to bid because of other pressing requirements; that is, they couldn't spare the staff for a major proposal effort. It was a decision they regretted later when we learned that the contract had indeed changed hands at the exact figure I had estimated and that the winner was a new firm that we should have been able to beat easily. (In fact, we had other contracts with that same agency and were well regarded, having been renewed again and again.)

How the company who did win the job went about it is an interesting sidelight, too, demonstrating the uses of strategy.

In fact, it was a new company, but it was not a new company. It was an entity formed by two small companies for the express purpose of bidding this contract. And the reason the two companies formed a partnership, establishing a third company, was simple enough: neither of the two companies was large enough to win the job.

It is rare that a contracting officer will award a contract that is larger than the annual volume of the contractor; that is, a company doing $2 or $3 million a year has difficulty proving "financial capability" to handle a $5-million-a-year contract.

The two companies were in the same boat that way. Only by pooling their annual volumes could they demonstrate a satisfactory "financial capability." It proved a successful strategy, and that third company is in existence today, still being renewed every three years on that contract, which has grown considerably since then. The owners of those two companies judged correctly that it was better to have a good chance of winning half a loaf than a slim chance of winning the entire loaf.

One other amazing fact is that neither company had the technical-publications capability called for as a required qualification, but one went about recruiting technical-publications specialists and hastily created a technical-publications department, especially for that proposal. It proved satisfactory to the government evaluators.

An Intelligence Failure

If good marketing intelligence is a key to success, poor marketing intelligence may prove to be the key to failure. One such case is a classic demonstration of "snatching defeat from the jaws of victory."

At a major government installation some years ago, a great many job shoppers—contractor personnel working on the government site—were employed to support the technical-publications work of the facility. Several contractors were supplying personnel, but one in particular, whom we'll call the ABC Company, had the largest contract and the greatest number of employees engaged at work on the site.

It was determined, probably because of cries of outrage from federal employees' unions, that the arrangement was illegal: in violation of those regulations that define the conditions under which the government may employ contractor personnel on site. Accordingly, an RFP was issued to do the work off site, at some nearby contractor facility.

The ABC Company submitted its proposal, along with several competitors. The ABC Company clearly had an edge: a satisfactory record, experienced personnel immediately available and familiar with the government's requirements, and a good working relationship with the agency in question. To the end, the ABC Company was running out front. One disaster befell them: they had proposed a project manager who was unacceptable to the government's technical monitor, who was, of course, influential in the evaluation of the proposals. He couldn't tell them so directly, but he did try to get that message to them by indirect means. The ABC Company failed to get the message or, at least, underestimated the importance of the technical monitor's objection. The job went to another company, who had been second but not a strong second choice.

Years later, that second company lost the contract through an equally inexcusable failure to assess and use intelligence readily available: in a "best and final" session, following their proposal submission for their third three-year contract, the contracting officer tried tactfully for fully half an hour to advise them that while they were favored on the basis of past performance, their new prices were too high and would have to be reduced. Failing to get his meaning across, he finally grew impatient and bellowed, "Dammit, I'm trying to tell you that your prices are too damned high!"

Pressing now, the contractor learned that his prices were too high by approximately 10%. Therefore, in a back-in-the-office meeting, the contractor's project manager decided to cut his prices by 10%.

His marketing director objected. "Cut fifteen percent," he advised.

"Why? We know we're ten percent high. They told us so."

"But we're only one of six finalists, and everybody else has been given the same message. You can bank on it."

The project manager overruled his marketing director, cut his prices by 10%, and lost—by 5%.

12

Technical/Program Strategies

There's always a selling job to do, and selling is based on strategies.

The middle-aged gentleman approached the desk of Ted Bates, of the Ted Bates advertising agency in New York, and laid two shining-new silver dollars on Bates's desk.

He said, "I'm a brewer. I brew beer in Milwaukee. It's good beer. I have lots of competitors. They also brew good beer."

"He pointed to one of the silver dollars. "That's my beer." He pointed to the other silver dollar. "That's my competitors' beer."

"I want you to prove that this silver dollar—pointing to the one he had identified as "my beer"—"is better than that silver dollar." He pointed to the other silver dollar.

"Can you do it?"

Bates nodded. "That's our business, proving that one silver dollar is better than another. That's advertising. We can do it."

Bates accompanied the brewer to Milwaukee for a tour of the brewer's plant. During the tour, he watched in fascination as he passed a steam-filled room.

"What is that operation?"

The brewer shrugged. "That's where the bottles are cleaned and sterilized with live steam."

Bates's eyes lit up. He looked up and gestured. "Our bottles are sterilized with live steam. What a slogan. We can build your whole campaign around that idea."

The brewer looked skeptical. "I don't see how. Everybody in the business does the same thing. They all sterilize bottles with live steam."

Bates's eyes narrowed and he smiled slightly. "Yes, but nobody advertises it!"

He was right, of course. The public didn't know that sterilizing bottles with live steam was a common practice. And once this brewer advertised this way—which he did, in a successful advertising campaign—his competitors did not dare say, "Me too."

Bates calls that approach the "unique selling point." It embodies his whole philosophy of advertising and sales promotion. Find an attractive and unique point and build on it. And it does not necessarily have to be unique, except in the sense that no one has used it before in advertising.

A similar approach helps in proposals, for a proposal is a sales presentation too. (Some marketing people regard a proposal as a contractual document, and it usually does become one—*after* award. But while you are writing it and offering it, it is a sales presentation that you *hope* will become a contractual document!) Having a "unique selling point" in a proposal offers the same benefits:

1. It focuses both the customer's attention and your own efforts on a central theme.
2. It distinguishes your proposal, draws attention to it.
3. It's a selling argument in itself (if adequate arguments and proofs are offered).
4. It gives direction to your proposal, avoiding that unfortunate tendency of too many proposals to wander aimlessly, trying to be all things.

Obviously, if you are to have a "unique selling point," it must be carefully chosen. Winning a large contract is not exactly the same thing as selling beer!

If this is reminiscent of something said earlier about having a "main message," it is not a coincidence. It is, in fact, closely related: that main message may well be a unique selling point—unique in the sense that no other proposal offers exactly the same thing. It is closely related to, and expresses, your main technical or program strategy.

In one case cited earlier—that of the controversial F-111 airplane, which was in the headlines daily as the TFX while in development—the main message was *commonality*. This was not unique in the sense that it was a reflection of the customer's own goal, but it was, at least, a *main* selling point.

Every proposal ought to have a main selling point. If it can be made a unique selling point as well, so much the better. However, it should not be thought that risks should be taken with the sale merely to be different. Being different—even unique—is not of itself a persuasive tactic. The important thing is that your proposal have some main selling point—some main strategy: if without distorting or "gimmicking up" your proposal, you can introduce something fresh, different, innovative, unique, even controversial (as long as you can defend your position and present persuasive arguments) in the way you present your main selling point, you will have added a great deal to your proposal.

In the case of offering a fresh approach to developing maintenance training for the Postal Service's first bulk mail center, I managed to accomplish both. The concept of studying the equipment to assess its probable maintenance requirements was different from how such programs are usually planned. The methodology for doing so I had to invent: I borrowed from the engineering discipline of reliability analysis to invent my "failure-probability analysis." That gave our proposal a slant, an attention-getting theme, and credibility, because (1) I had a concrete plan for "asking the equipment" what it needed and (2) any knowledgeable reader knew that there was such a thing as reliability analysis and knew that therefore there was a precedent and basis for my plan; it was not a wild scheme or as radical an idea as it would have been had there been no such thing as reliability analysis.

Your plan must be credible. A large part of your writing effort must be devoted to making it credible, to *presenting the evidence*. (We'll be talking later about persuasive writing and technical argument.)

The Proposal as a Logical Argument

One way to understand the essence of proposalmanship is this: regard it as a syllogism—an exercise in logic. It presents one or more premises, then presents the corollaries, and then the conclusions, in a deductive or inductive series. *However—and note this—logic never sells anything by itself.* Yet, it is necessary to the entire sales process.

Later, when we discuss persuasive writing and effective sales presentation techniques, we'll discuss this point in greater detail. But, just in passing, note this: it is an article of faith in sales and advertising that people—and the government is people—respond to emotional sales appeals. Emotional appeals motivate. The logical evidence and arguments are necessary to establish credibility and to persuade the customer that his emotionally motivated decision is a logically sound one. Mr. McNamara desperately wanted to believe that an airplane could be built to satisfy both U.S. Navy and U.S. Air Force needs: he made himself believe in the concept of commonality, despite counsel to the contrary.

You must therefore, when choosing your strategies, selling points, etc., look for the emotional appeal that also makes good sense and can be backed up by sound arguments. Resorting to the emotional appeal is not cynicism nor charlatanism—unless you make it so. You sincerely select whatever you believe is the best approach to solving the problem, but you *then* seek out the right appeals and messages with which to *sell* it. The best plan in the world won't help you or the customer if you fail to sell it.

Developing Program Strategies

If brainstorming is a good method for analyzing an RFP and developing a program flowchart, it is also a good way to develop program strategies. Properly managed, the method produces many ideas, and at least one or two of them turn out to be usable.

In one proposal, we managed to use the idea of brainstorming itself to help sell the proposal. The customer had a requirement to develop "educational" materials in the area of consumer product safety. The RFP spelled out the customer's goals clearly enough, which included getting materials together for use in public schools and among community organizations. It included general suggestions for posters, panel books, lecture guides, and demonstration kits, but it stipulated that these were merely preliminary ideas, and the proposer was expected to offer ideas and suggestions, both in the proposal and as a contractor, after award.

Thus the proposer was left with almost a universe of possibilities, tempting him to suggest highly improbable and wild ideas, which could easily prove a disastrous tactic. As we brainstormed the requirement, we came up with many, many ideas, some of which would have been prohibitively expensive, and some of which would have presented enormous difficulties to implement.

We sensed that the customer wanted to be closely involved in the selection and identification of products to be developed and program strategies to be pursued, although the RFP offered no new ideas. We finally hit upon this general strategy for the proposal: we offered a series of ideas, stipulating that we did not expect to implement all but would confer with the customer to screen these and any ideas the customer cared to offer and that we would together make the final selections. We then described the brainstorming technique and proposed to conduct a brainstorming session, with the participation of both our and the customer's staff, to develop new ideas together.

That developed into our main selling point and proved highly effective: the customer *loved* the idea! We had no difficulty negotiating a contract shortly after.

In another case, bidding for a training-development contract, it was necessary to provide detailed explanations of how the curriculum would be developed before the writing of actual materials would begin. This is somewhat typical of such projects, especially where the evaluators are part of a formal training organization in the government and consist of professional trainers and educators, devoted and dedicated to the "behavioral" theories of educational development.

The classic and accepted approach is to perform a "task analysis" in which the desired end result—knowledge and/or job skills—is identified as individual "behaviors," and behavioral objectives are identified and documented. The curriculum plan is then built directly around these objectives. According to widely accepted educational theory, this is the can't-miss system.

One of the problems in all training development, which this system should solve (but rarely does), is identifying what material belongs in the program and what is unnecessary. In theory, one can demonstrate that doing the task analysis and developing the complete set of behavioral objectives will accomplish this end of identifying all necessary material and all "nice to know, but not necessary" information. But, of course, every bidder writing a proposal would make the claim that his task analysis would accomplish this. And saying, "Me, too," would not be very helpful to our own goal of winning the contract.

In flowcharting the requirement, we hit on an idea. We developed this approach into our "CPM Method for Task Analysis and Program Design." Briefly, it was as shown in Figure 10.

CPM means "critical path method." It is related to PERT (program evaluation and review technique) and is used widely in the construction industries for planning. The idea is to record in each circle, as shown in this greatly simplified sample, a step in the process. In construction, that might mean such things as pour foundation, erect steel, paint structural members, lay bricks, glaze sashes, etc.

Once all steps are identified, they are arranged in a sequence that defines those steps that must be performed in sequence e.g., you must go through 1, 2, and 3 to reach 4 and those that are not dependent on a preceding step but may be performed concurrently or independently e.g., 2a may be concurrent with 1, 2, and 3 and/or may be an alternative way to get to 4. (Alternative to 3, that is.)

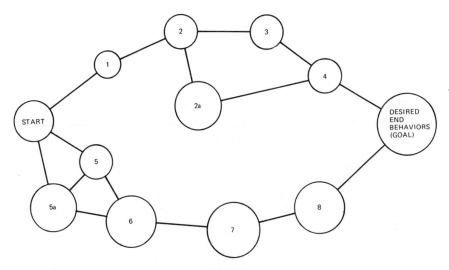

Figure 10. Adapting the CPM concept.

The "critical path" is that series of steps that *must* be performed to reach the end goal. Steps 1–4 may be performed concurrently with steps 5–8, but some of the steps are alternatives and not necessary.

To adapt this idea to training development, we simply arranged a similar plan, with training topics as the numbered items. We proposed then to identify the various sequences and critical paths, including all alternatives and all "nice to know, but not essential" information. This would be done after developing a complete set of *candidate* behavioral objectives, none of which would be finally accepted until they had been *validated* by this CPM methodology.

It was a successful idea, as it deserved to be, because it was a meritorious idea. It had to be sold, however, by describing it and pointing out that it was an adaptation of an already proved idea. The name we assigned it helped, too, giving us a main selling point that was unique also and offering the customer something new.

Take note that these two ideas were not totally new and dramatic breakthroughs but were improvements on existing methods and borrowed from already respectable ideas.

In some cases, a new name for an old idea helps. The term *task analysis,* referred to earlier, has become pretty hackneyed and today actually refers to something more than mere task analysis itself. One gentleman in the training-development business has built himself something of a reputation as the creator of the more imaginative and more descriptive term *front-end analysis*, although he uses it to describe what others propose to do as "task analysis"!

How to Brainstorm for Ideas

Brainstorming is not completely casual and unstructured. If it were, it would be quickly out of control and unproductive. It is essential that it be controlled to the extent that it sticks to its purpose and is not allowed to degenerate into philosophical or other kinds of arguments or into general discussions.

The first rule is that each session address one specific question—or, at least, one question at a time. Here are some suggested general questions. (Specific questions should be asked, too, with reference to the project.)

1. Do we have any natural advantages in this contest? (Identify.)
2. How can we overcome our disadvantages or liabilities? (Or can we?)
3. What is the true goal of this RFP in its simplest terms? (What does the customer really want? What the RFP says? Or what it implies?)
4. How can we improve the usual method/equipment used for this kind of job?
5. What's a better name/term for ———?
6. What is (are) the major problem(s) in this project?
7. What are most proposers likely to offer?
8. Are there any effective cost-cutters we can think of?
9. Has anything like this been done before? (If so, what, where, how?)

How to Develop a Flowchart

Developing a flowchart is akin to making a systems analysis. That term, *systems analysis*, has been bruited about as a "buzz word" for years by many who haven't the foggiest idea what it really means or how to go about doing it.

There are only two places one can begin, logically, in developing a flowchart: at the beginning or at the end. My personal preference is for starting at the end, for reasons that I hope will soon be apparent, and I hope that you will be persuaded to this belief also.

Computer people are fond of drawing flowcharts vertically on a page, starting (usually) at the top of the page and descending. I find this objectionable, for the reason that most of us are trained, educated, and conditioned from childhood to read from left to right. Why add to the reader's difficulties by compelling the learning of a new reflex? In any case, my own charts almost always wind up reading horizontally, from left to right, and along the longest dimension of the page. When I refer to the "beginning" and the "end" of the chart, I refer to the left- and right-hand ends, respectively.

When I begin a chart, I usually know what my objective is. If it's for a proposal, the objective is whatever the customer (RFP) has identified or defined as the desired end product or end result: a manual, a piece of equipment, a report, the completion of some service, etc. I therefore start by describing this briefly in a box at the right-hand edge.

If the customer has specified certain initial aids to me (e.g., source information he will provide, first steps he stipulates as necessary), I will identify those at the left-hand edge of the sheet in one or more boxes. My job is to get from the left-hand boxes to the right-hand boxes by the most effective route possible, indicating each step/leg of the journey and possibly including other interim products/functions that the customer has stipulated.

There are cases where the customer has called out most of the major steps—functions, tasks, etc.—and these can simply be recorded, as described, in a preliminary chart, which you will later work over and refine. On the other hand, he may not have told you very much beyond where you are to start and how/where you are to finish. The rest is up to you!

In such cases, I find it best to work backward, from the right-hand edge to the left-hand edge.

Figure 11 illustrates the beginning of such a flowchart, which we are going to develop here. We're going to keep this one pretty simple, but the principles apply, no matter how simple, no matter how complex. The difference is a matter of size and of complexity, not of kind.

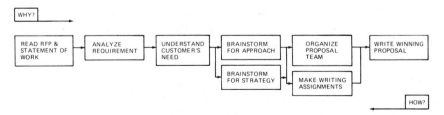

Figure 11. First steps in flowcharting.

The flowchart we are going to develop is one of the processes this book is about: developing a winning proposal. We know, therefore, that the right-hand block is "Winning Proposal." The left-hand block is "Read RFP and Work Statement." We must now get from "RFP and Work Statement" to "Winning Proposal"!

One clue to developing an analytical flowchart is that each block has an answer to "How?" and "Why?"in this manner: if you read the block and ask "Why?" the next block to the right should answer that question. Conversely, if you ask "How?" the block to the left should answer that.

Even on the level at which we are beginning this flowchart, the right-hand block, "Winning Proposal," answers the "Why?" you might ask of the left block, "Read RFP and Work Statement."

Ask yourself those two questions, as you develop the chart. They help you decide what should go in the next block.

Why read the RFP and work statement? Assuming we have already decided to bid and are reading in preparation to propose, we are reading the RFP/SOW (Statement of Work, which some of us like to abbreviate SOW), our first purpose is to analyze the requirement. If we make "Analyze Requirement" our next block, it's "How?" is answered by the block to the left. Why? To understand the customer's need, which is our next block to the right. Why? To brainstorm for an approach and a strategy. These are concurrent: we want to do both in our brainstorming session(s), so we make them concurrent in the chart.

The next step is to organize the proposal team and make writing assignments, and these, too, are concurrent activities, logically, if not chronologically.

Let's read the chart now, right to left: "Write Winning Proposal." How? By organizing a proposal team and making writing assignments. How? By brainstorming for approach and strategy (to identify writing and technical skills needed for writing the proposal, that is, and to issue proposal instructions and assignments.) How? By understanding the customer's need. How? By analyzing the requirement. How? By reading the RFP/SOW.

Let's try it the other way: "Read RFP and Statement of work." Why? To analyze the requirement. Why? To understand the customer's need. Why? To brainstorm for approach and strategy. Why? To organize a proposal team and make writing assignments. Why? To write a winning proposal.

If there are weaknesses in this logical how–why chain—and there are at some points, or we should not have had to add the explanations we did —our chart needs some more work. It is not detailed enough until the how–why explains the chart completely, without the reader's being forced to fill in logical gaps or information that may be implicit but is not explicit.

The chart is far from complete enough or detailed enough, but it illustrates the main message, and we would amplify it later, filling in the many steps necessary to develop a really superior proposal, the only kind that wins contracts consistently.

For example, following "Brainstorm for Approach" and "Brainstorm for Strategy," we should add boxes that detail the results of that brainstorming, such as "Identify critical points in RFP/SOW" and "Identify Technical and Writing Skills Needed." And there is a large gap between the right-most block and the ones left of it. There are also review cycles, illustrations to be made, editing to be done, revisions and rewriting to be done, etc. And there are many other factors, which we'll discuss too.

Ideally, the chart should show *what* we propose to do, *how* we propose to do it, and *why* we propose to do it.

Types of Flowcharts

Flowcharts and other illustrations can—and should—be used for other purposes than RFP analysis and general program presentation. First of all, if the program is fairly complex, it is often advisable to use a simplified, "high-level" flowchart first and then several lower-level flowcharts to detail important portions of the program. In fact, if you wish to stress some portion of the program above others, this is an excellent way to do so.

In one proposal, which was successful in winning a contract for nearly $20 million, the RFP called out a fairly lengthy number of specific items that required response. The job was a logistics job in support of a major program being conducted overseas by the Corps of Engineers (U.S. Army). It required the contractor to receive, at a location in the United States, quantities of furniture, building materials, equipment, and other supplies; conduct receiving inspections; warehouse the items; assemble and pack the items for shipment; transport them overseas; and receive them for warehousing and transportation at the other end of the supply line. Much record keeping and reporting was involved, of course, requiring data processing, among other things.

We identified three major activities—actual materials handling and flow, data processing, and reporting—and we began the development of three sets of flowcharts to present these. (Initially, we developed these as a graphic explanation of the RFP, for our own understanding of the program.) We wound up with a number of charts for each activity, which we assembled into sets.

Tentatively, we assembled each set into a single flowchart, indicating which section of each set covered which phase or aspect of the overall function. We now had three rather long flowcharts. At that point, we conceived another idea: Since the three major activities of materials flow, data processing, and reporting were all concurrent or parallel activities, could we present this idea in a single chart, showing the three activities graphically, and indicating the interrelationships among the activities at the appropriate points—for example, what step/phase/action of materials handling resulted in a computer entry and/or a report generated—and also showing all the major cause–effect relationships? We managed to do this successfully, producing a six-foot-long chart that presented the entire program in fairly detailed fashion.

It turned out, ultimately, to be highly effective. But we didn't stop with that. We had decided that several specific areas were critical. One of these was the safety area. Aside from being required by presidential order to observe safety precautions compatible with the Occupational Safety and Health Act, the U. S. Army is safety-conscious on its own. The RFP called for a complete safety program, including a project safety manual, safety publications, and safety training.

We therefore analyzed the safety requirements by developing a detailed flowchart, and we then used that as a basis for our safety presentation, which was also most helpful in winning a high technical score. (The proposal came in Number 1 technically!)

The flowchart you develop as an analytical aid, which also helps the proposal team communicate among themselves and reach a common understanding, is often the basis for the flowcharts you will later present to the customer in your proposal, but it is not necessarily the same. Flowcharts developed for analytical purposes tend to be rough, of course, and often overly detailed. They should be refined before being adopted for proposal use, and the terms used should be "selling words" as much as possible; that is, they should be selected so as to stress benefits to the customer. (For example, regarding you as my customer, "Write Winning Proposal" is better than "Write Best Proposal," since it stresses the one benefit you want to achieve—to win.)

Flowcharts should be developed, in many cases, to describe the management process, the quality control methods, the delivery schedules, your company's normal procedural chain and/or chain of command, and whatever other points you find to be critical.

For example, many contracts are of the type described by the government as a "task-order" type or a "basic ordering agreement" type. That is, you demonstrate some set of capabilities and provide a "laundry-list" set of prices: dollars per labor hour for each class of labor, cost per hour of computer time, cost per page of copy, cost per square foot of engineering drawing, etc. Once a contract has been negotiated, the government issues a "task-order" each time it has a need, and you, the contractor, must estimate the job (using the laundry-list prices). The government then issues a work order (negotiating with you about the task, if they do not accept your estimate), and you do the job.

Now, in such requirements, the government is usually quite interested in exactly how you process and estimate such task-order requests. The RFP, in these cases, usually requests that you explain your process in some detail. This is a situation in which flowcharts explaining your processes will serve you well. You'll want to show the care with which you develop estimates and verify them before you submit them and to show the system you use, which ensures a swift response to such requests.

If your proposal embodies a significant amount of proposed subcontracting, the government will want to know at least two things about it:

1. How you solicit subcontracts to ensure both adequate quality and cost control (with competitive bidding usually required).
2. How you monitor and control subcontractor performance to ensure an adequate final result (since you are the responsible prime contractor).

Flowcharts are a material aid in getting these messages across.

If the contract will entail a great deal of buying of supplies or parts from vendor companies, the RFP will probably ask you to explain your purchasing system in some detail.

If you propose to or will have to use a large number of special consultants to get the project done, the government will want to know how you propose to identify the suitable consultants and recruit them.

And if you propose on a project that will require considerable hiring of regular, full-time employees, the government will want to know all about your general recruiting capabilities and your special plans, if any, for this particular recruitment.

You must always bear in mind that while a private corporation to whom you might submit a proposal will ordinarily take your capability for granted and not require this kind of information, the U. S. government never takes capabilities for granted but always wants evidence.

The "evidence" is usually what you say in your proposal, but for really critical areas that will receive extra-close scrutiny by the customer, flowcharts are a far more effective way of saying it than words.

Other Types of Charts and Illustrations

Flowcharts are not the only kind of chart you can use, of course. Flowcharts are probably the most effective way to present any kind of process: flow. They show *how* and *when* in relation to the events represented. They do not ordinarily show when in relation to calendar time or contract days. And if *when* certain things happen, with relation to calendar time or days after award of contract, is important to the customer, either a time scale must be added to the flowchart or a separate chart must be developed.

"Milestone" charts (Figure 12) are popular for this purpose. On such a chart, you indicate each major event or function—a meeting, a report, a delivery, completion of a phase, etc.—by some symbol, with a time scale that shows when the milestone should be reached.

The simplified milestone chart shown illustrates the principle. In this

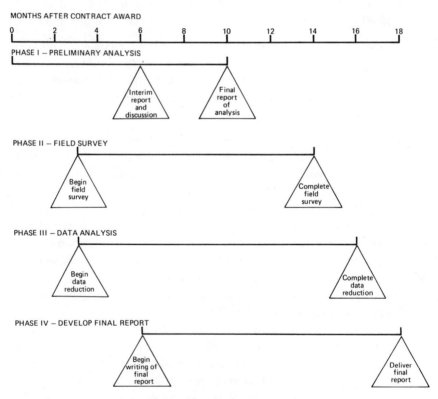

Figure 12. A simple milestone chart.

case, the time scale is "Months after Contract Award." In most cases, this is more appropriate than calendar time because it is usually almost impossible to predict exactly when a project will begin or a contract will be awarded after a proposal competition. Government estimates of such times tend to be overly optimistic, and frequently the start of the project is delayed.

Such a chart does show the relationships of different milestones, of course, much as a CPM or a flowchart shows how events relate to each other in time of their occurrence. For this reason, placing a time scale on a flowchart often accomplishes the same purpose as developing a milestone chart. However, frequently the milestone chart is used in a different section of the proposal and for a different purpose than the flowcharts are. Too, flowcharts are often fairly complex, and adding a time scale to them makes them rather difficult to use as milestone charts or schedules. And finally, flowcharts do not usually identify what you prescribe as milestones or key events in the project. For all of these reasons, you will find it best to use separate milestone charts in most cases.

Bear in mind, when you do so, that you are identifying all the critical or key points in the project. These may have been already described to you in the RFP, but you may wish to add several of your own in accordance with whatever you have said about the program in your discussions.

There are, of course, many other kinds of illustrations possible: engineering drawings, artist's concepts of a finished (proposed) project, floor plans of a proposed facility, line drawings of every other type, and even photographs, where these are appropriate.

In the case of the Corps of Engineers logistics support proposal, the contractor was required to stipulate and describe the proposed receiving and warehousing facility. In our case, we made arrangements to take an option on a dockside warehouse in a port with many advantages, and we managed to get a good aerial view of the entire dockside area. On this, we superimposed "call-outs"—lettering that identified the various buildings and facilities of interest, such as heavy cranes, tugs and barges, warehouses, outside storage, loading platforms, access roads, etc. We were able to use this large photograph (about 16 by 20 inches) to great effect. It described the proposed facility and its benefits to the corps far more eloquently than any number of words, and relatively little text was therefore required.

One Overall Technical/Program Strategy

Aside from all the many twists and variations possible in presenting an effective technical or program strategy, the mere fact of having voluminous and painstaking detail is in itself a major strategy. Detail creates a great deal of credibility; vague generalization creates skepticism.

It is fairly well known in professional advertising and marketing circles that the more information you present a prospect with, the more credible and persuasive your presentation is—provided, of course, that you can persuade your prospect to read all the detail. There is always the hazard of wearying your reader and saying too much.

Two ways of dealing with this hazard are (1) the use of graphics, such as we have been describing, to reduce the weight of words otherwise necessary, and (2) the use of appendices, which we shall get to a bit later.

If you can read much of what the customer is *really* saying between the lines of his RFP and work statement, *he* can—and will—read between the lines of your proposal, too. And every proposal says things between the lines—has a general impact, that is. For one thing, every proposal says either of these two things:

1. I'm not exactly sure what you want (I haven't taken the time to analyze your package, or I am not experienced in this field), but if you'll pay me enough money, I can "wing it" and do a good job for you.
2. I've been doing my homework, and I've worked hard at it, developing a thoroughly detailed plan. I know my business, and I am confident that I can get you exactly what you want, through the detailed plan presented here.

Item (1) is, of course, what the vague and completely generalized proposal appears to be saying, whereas (2) is what the painstakingly detailed proposal appears to be saying.

I happened to be visiting a customer in a U. S. Navy office in town one day when I overheard an admiral explode at a salesman who was working on him.

"I'm tired of salesmen coming in here to tell me what you want," he boomed out. "When will one of you get smart enough to come in and offer me what I need?"

That, in a nutshell, is what your proposal should do: offer the customer what he needs. Be a technical consultant. "Listen" to what he is saying (in his RFP and work statement) and take the time to really analyze the need and develop an effective program *in terms of his need and not of your desires*. Sincerity of this kind in your proposal will come out between the lines, just as self-serving disregard for his real needs will be discernible. In the end, it's the best strategy possible.

13

Other Strategic Areas

Pricing is a strategy, too.

We have talked of technical/program strategies, which are quite often the most decisive factor in proposal evaluation—but not always. There are many cases where the questions of management, staffing, quality control, and other aspects are of at least equal importance, even in highly technical programs.

It is against the law for civil service personnel to manage or supervise contractor personnel and vice versa: contractor personnel may not supervise civil service personnel. Even when the project is on site—when contractor personnel are physically located on the government's own premises, as in the case of computer operations or "facilities management" contracts—the government's project official may give only "technical direction" to the contractor's project supervisor.

It is therefore illegal for a government agency to hire contractors and their personnel as extensions of the agency's staff or as "contract employees" of the agency. Most government solicitations specify that the contract will stipulate that the contractor is not "an agent of the government."

This means that the government personnel must be careful in how the relationships between government personnel and contractor personnel are specified and are actually conducted. The distinctions of the above provisos of the law are quite important and can create severe problems if not handled carefully.

At the same time, the government's staff are often extremely influenced, in proposal evaluations, by the contractor staff offered in the proposal, even when the work is to be conducted at the contractor's facility. Whether the law makes a distinction or not, government officials responsible for the success of the project tend to appraise contractor personnel in much the same way they would appraise applicants for direct employment by the agency. These—the people the contractor proposes to staff the project—are the people upon whose skills the project's success will depend. Therefore, a great deal of weight is often placed on staff résumés included in the proposal, and quite often this is the most critical of all the evaluation points, even when the stated criteria do not suggest this.

Some organizations that write proposals regularly have boilerplate résumés. That is, they have file drawers full of staff résumés, which they have standardized to some preferred format, and these are the résumés used in all proposals.

This approach can be a serious error, tactically and strategically. Most individuals who have been in the working world for more than a few years have accumulated a variety of experience and skills. Therefore, each could write his or her résumé in many different ways. An engineer, for example, could stress any of different types of equipment he has designed or technical problems he has solved. Some engineers have done a great deal of technical writing, some have spent more time in the laboratory than at the drawing board, some have managed many products, some have been engaged in marketing and sales, etc.

A résumé for a given engineer might present him as a technical writer, a sales engineer, a safety specialist, an engineering manager, a mathematician, or any of many different engineering specialties. Of course, the same considerations usually apply to others: lawyers, architects, psychologists, physicists, sociologists, etc. How then can any single version of any individual's résumé be equally appropriate to all government project requirements?

It is somewhat futile to spend the time, effort, and money required to prepare any proposal and then risk its success by saving a fraction of that time, effort, and expense by using boilerplate résumés. Staff should be selected and their résumés prepared with the same planning and care that go into the proposal generally. And this is especially true of the senior proposed staff: the proposed project manager and his immediate subordinates.

We are in an age of specialization, and the consciousness of that present-day trend toward specialization influences the judgment of many. In TV production years ago, when TV was in its infancy, a TV manufacturer might assign one engineer to design the third intermediate-frequency stage and another to design the second such stage. Another might be assigned to the horizontal oscillator, another to the high-voltage circuits, etc. Each became a specialist—for that design effort, at least—in his assigned area.

It is hardly stretching things to say that specifying such details in one's résumé could cause an evaluator to consider the designer of the third IF stage to be somewhat less than qualified to design a second IF stage, much less a horizontal sweep circuit! This has frequently been the case with technical writers, and the candidate must qualify himself as a "radar writer" or a "computer writer," if he is to have any hope of being favorably considered.

Whether this is a foolish orientation or not, it is a fact that such seemingly trivial considerations can greatly influence the score accorded a given proposal. Given a collection of competitive proposals, the evaluator is going to make every effort to select the one that appears best for the project.

Personally, I have found the time invested in preparing résumés to match requirements as closely as possible to be time well invested. And I find this to be especially true if the staff is to work on site, in close communication with the government's staff.

"Management control" is another consideration that often gets close scrutiny and heavily influences final evaluation and rating. This is linked to the tendency to consider contractor staff as extensions of government staff. Many government officials are inclined to think of *management control* as referring to *their* control of project management. They sometimes put this into words in the RFP by stipulating that they want the contractor to establish a "responsive" project organization, meaning responsive to the government project manager's ideas and wishes. He is legally responsible for only "technical direction," which we might interpret as guidance in what final results the government wants to achieve. In practice, he wants to be sure that the contractor will follow his directives as though they were orders.

For this reason, most agencies will object to any management structure that does not indicate direct communication or liaison between the contractor's project manager and the government's project manager.

Figure 13 suggests a plan of organization in which the government's project manager does not have direct access to the contractor's project manager but has to go through some other layers of command before he reaches the individual who is actually running the project. The govern-

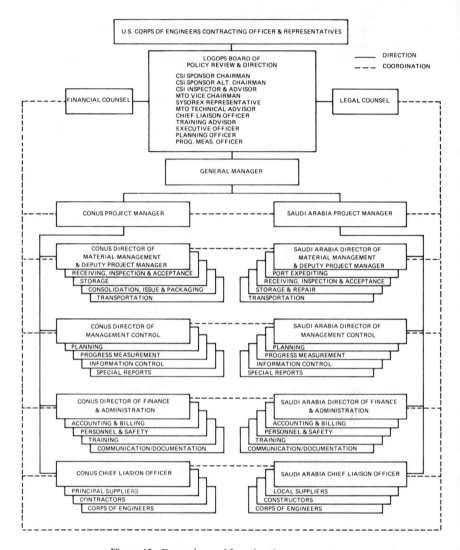

Figure 13. Executive and functional management.

ment's project manager, who is probably the leader of the proposal-evaluation team, is likely to object violently. Figure 14 is more along the lines of what he would like to see. It shows a direct link between the government's project manager and the contractor's project manager, and a direct line-of-command of the project.

As a rule, the government would prefer to see a "dedicated" project and a "dedicated" project manager and senior project staff. To gain maximum points in this area, it is almost always advisable to stipulate that a special project staff will be created, with the senior members having no

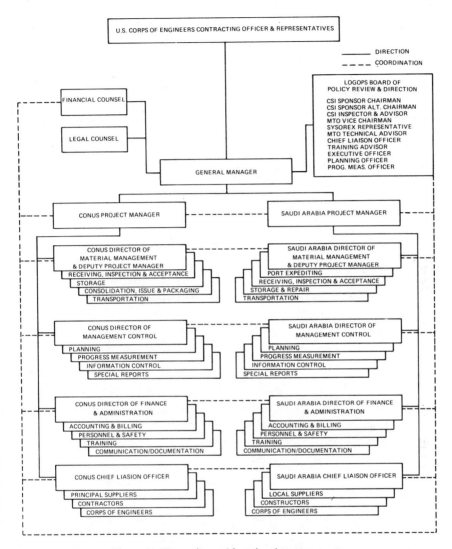

Figure 14. Executive and functional management.

other duties and assigned 100% to the project for the duration of the project. The customer does not want to feel that he—his project—will have to compete with other projects or duties for the time and efforts of the senior project staff. He wants a full-time project and a full-time project staff. And it is not enough to imply this in your proposal: it should be stipulated as specifically as possible.

The levels of the staff are another important consideration, especially in the case of the proposed project manager. Whether the project is one of your more important ones or not, it is always important to the customer, and he wants a contractor who considers the project important. Assigning a relatively junior employee as project manager suggests that the project is not considered very important. At the same time, the customer is not naive. He does not expect a large company to assign a vice-president of the company to a relatively small project, and he will not believe it if you so propose.

Of couse, this can create a dilemma. Suppose the job is for $500,000 and you are a large company, doing $100 million or more. The project is not of critical importance in your overall sales, yet it is not a small job either. You do want the job badly enough to spend the time and money to write a proposal. What do you do?

One thing you can do, in such a case, is to present your staff and your proposal as representative of and submitted by a *division* of your corporation and concentrate on that division status, of which your proposed project manager is a senior employee. This makes him credible, yet high-level, at least as far as the division's status is concerned!

Some companies indulge in a practice known as *hanging paper*. This quaint expression refers to a practice of stuffing a proposal full of first-class resumes with no intention—and perhaps no ability—to actually supply and employ those people on the project! This basic scheme has several variations:

1. A small company may actually have extremely few permanent staff members, but it comes up with résumés, acquired by various and sundry means, of individuals who do not even know that they are being "bid on the job." The company submitting such proposals intends to hire whoever is readily available if and when they win the contract.
2. A small company has advertised and got résumés from qualified people who have indicated that they would probably be available, if the contract is won, and who have given their permission to have their résumés submitted.
3. A company bids a number of top employees, having especially impressive résumés, on just about every job, with no intention of having the individuals serve beyond the first few days (if that long) following contract award. In fact, these people have been bid on many jobs, and it would be all but impossible to use them on more than one, even if they did not already have full schedules writing more proposals!

The first scheme is thoroughly disreputable, of course, and is actually a gross misrepresentation, since the proposer, who has at least implied that these résumés are of his own staff members, has no intention of providing them in any case.

The second is not as bad because the individuals have agreed to have their résumés submitted and to be available for the project in the event of victory.

The third scheme is perhaps even more vicious than the first one in many ways, because it is completely cynical. Unfortunately it is practiced fairly widely.

Little by little, government officials are catching on to some of these schemes and taking preventive steps. One such step is to stipulate that the successful offeror cannot substitute others for the proposed key personnel without submitting the résumés of proposed substitutes and getting the approval of the contracting officer. Obviously, when you bid, you cannot guarantee that some key member of your proposed project staff will not resign, retire, become ill, or otherwise become unavailable for the project, when and if the project becomes a reality. The government recognizes this. But if you can produce *none* of the proposed key staff after the contract is awarded, that is going to be regarded by the contracting officer with a great deal of suspicion and a fair amount of hostility! He is going to become convinced that you either faked your proposal from the start, or that you used the résumés of high-level, well-qualified professionals to win the contract but plan to use lower-level, possibly unqualified people to actually do the job. Hence the growing tendency to make the stipulation in the contract that prevents you from arbitrarily substituting staff of lesser caliber than those you originally proposed.

Cost Strategies

Technical and program strategies are not the only strategies possible. There are many cases where the success of your proposal is going to depend heavily on the costs you propose, and certain cost strategies are possible. It is possible, for example, to *appear* to be a lower bidder than you really are in many cases. There are also many ways to *avoid* costs, rather than "reduce" costs. In fact, just as it's easier to anticipate and avoid a problem, it's better to anticipate and plan avoidance of costs rather than to find yourself overspending and forced to embark on a frantic cost-cutting campaign.

Even for purely psychological reasons, it is better to think in terms of cost-avoidance than of cost reduction, because cost-avoidance implies anticipating costs and planning to avoid them, whereas cost reduction or cost cutting implies a salvage effort, after you have already wasted money in unnecessary costs.

One rule to follow, if you are going to avoid unnecessary costs, is this: don't reinvent the wheel. That is, don't make what you can buy cheaper.

The cost of producing art work for illustrations is a good example of people reinventing the wheel. In many cases, organizations charged with developing training or other printed information automatically assume that they will have to create all illustrations, and they immediately calculate the costs of illustrating and photography as part of their cost estimates.

In one case, by using illustrations available in government publications which are in the public domain—owned by the public and not copyrighted (true of most government publications)—we cut our illustrating cost from $6,000 to $2,000 and had money left from that budget.

In several other cases, we simply sent out a letter to a number of manufacturers of types of equipment we were training people in, requesting their photos, drawings, and other literature and permission to use these, giving the source a credit line or an acknowledgement. (In any case, we would have wanted to identify the equipment illustrated!) We had no trouble piling our desks high with usable material, saving us many thousands of dollars.

Bear in mind always that you must face make-or-buy decisions in estimating costs and that it is often cheaper to buy than to make, even when the cost of buying appears high. *Always* check out whether the item can be bought and, if so, what it will cost before you make that decision. Never assume that you can make it more cheaply than you can buy it.

These are not the only possibilities, however. Costing, particularly in the large organization, is not a simple matter. Many costs and many cost-avoidance possibilities are hidden in accounting labyrinths and in the accountants' technical jargon.

Before we tackle some of the other, more sophisticated cost-avoidance methods and cost strategies, let's have a look at just what "costs" are and how they get that way.

Costs and Costing

In most solicitations that call for proposals, cost is only one of many factors and is usually—but not always—not the decisive factor. In many cases, cost is relatively unimportant, as long as it is within the bounds of what the contracting specialists refer to as the competitive range. There are several basic situations as regards cost and its influence on the evaulation and the final decision:

1. The case just cited, where technical rating is all-important and cost almost unimportant, as long as it is within whatever the agency has budgeted for the job.
2. The case where cost is given an actual numerical weight and influences the final decision only to the extent of that weight.
3. The case where the agency has an evaluation scheme in which a cost per technical point is arrived at and all proposals are so rated, with the award going to the proposal with the lowest cost per technical point.
4. The case where cost will "be considered," the RFP says, and there is no indication as to how much influence cost will have.
5. The case where the award will go to the lowest qualified bidder, that is, the low bidder among those whose proposals are considered technically acceptable or within the "technical range."

An important element in your proposal strategy is, of course, judging which of these five situations you are in with your proposal. Usually, if you are dealing with case 2 or 3, you will know it because the RFP will have explained it. Otherwise, you are in one of the other three situations, and you will have to make a judgment as to which one.

When the RFP says something such as that the award will go to the proposal that "is in the best interests of the government, cost and other factors considered," the agency people are being cautious and conservative, leaving themselves as many escape hatches as possible.

There are some cases where the contracting officer is a firm and literal-minded official who will demand written "justification" for any award decision that is to other than the lowest qualified bidder. In such cases, the "program" people, who have made the technical evaluations and pointed to the proposal that they believe should be the winner (at which point they do not know the price tags on each proposal), often are reluctant to take the time (and the risk) of writing such a justification, and the award will then go to the lowest qualified bidder.

But there are cases where the contracting officer will shrug indifferently and go along with any decision of the technical evaluators, as long as they can get approval for the funds required. So it may come down to a simple matter of the personalities of the individuals involved: easygoing contracting officer versus strong-minded project officer or vice versa.

In some cases, a given agency may run to a pattern; that is, in some agencies, awards usually go to the lowest qualified bidders, whereas in others they rarely do.

These are some of the factors about which you have to gather marketing intelligence, as well as make gut-feeling judgments and decisions resulting from logical analyses.

There are also cases where it is fatal to come in at too low a price, thereby convincing the agency staff that you don't understand the problem and/or that you will surely be unable to do the job without getting into trouble. (There is also the problem that the agency staff want to spend a certain amount of money on the project so that they are not "stuck" with leftover funds, which is usually an embarrassment for a government agency.)

One other factor enters into costing: the probability—or improbability—of being invited to make a "best and final" offer, which gives you a last chance to change your price. If you can be sure or reasonably sure of being called in for best-and-final and final negotiations, the price you quote in your proposal is not quite so important—again, as long as it is in the competitive range. But you can't be sure of that as a rule.

Some agencies make a practice of holding best-and-finals on every procurement. Some do it only on the large procurements. And some do when time permits but forego it if there is pressure of some sort to get the award made quickly.

There is only one really sound procedure: don't guess at the price, but estimate it. And estimating the price means that you do your homework. You work out a program and plans of action in as much detail as possible, do your man loading, and base your price on that *firm plan* for doing the job.

That approach does several things for you:

1. You can quote with some degree of confidence.
2. You have *quantified* your proposal, giving yourself the protection you may later need if and when the customer demands more of you than you had intended to deliver for the dollars.
3. The agency may (and probably will) compare your technical proposal with your cost proposal (they are separate documents, of course) and see whether they "hang together." That will be valuable in several ways, giving you a sound basis for negotiations and defending your cost estimate.

What Are "Costs"?

Strangely enough, in far too many cases, those writing proposals do not understand costs at all but leave the costing to the company's accountants.

Clemenceau is quoted as saying something along the lines of "War is far too important a matter to be left to the generals." Paraphrasing, it is my belief that cost is far too important a matter to be left to the comptrollers. In fact, it has been my experience all too often that when the matter is left to the comptrollers, these worthy gentlemen will price you right out of the competition. And why not? Their job is to pay the bills, keep the books balanced, manage the cash flow, and show a profit, all of which takes money, of course. But it is not their job to win contracts: that's your worry.

If you are going to write winning proposals with any consistency, you are going to have to have at least some understanding of what makes up "costs" and what cost information the government ordinarily demands to support your estimate. Your accountants may make up the actual cost forms to be submitted, but they will be based on information *you* supply.

Accountants are like doctors, lawyers, engineers, and other professionals: they cloak their specialties in mysterious jargon that makes the entire craft seem far more complex and difficult than it really is. Some of them have even trained themselves to *think* in that jargon and are truly unable to translate their thinking into simple lay terms and concepts. Consequently we laymen tend to become frightened, even awed, by such cabalistic terms as *debit, offset, expense pool,* etc. and we may not even try to grasp this mysterious craft. The fact is that accounting is as much a commonsense concept as are most things and can be grasped, at least in its principles and basic concepts, by anyone—once the language is translated.

There are only two kinds of costs: direct and indirect. Every cost item, no matter how it's labeled, is a subset—an item of either direct or indirect costs.

Let us suppose that your company has six contracts in house, on which the staff is working. You probably have an individual number or code for each contract, and you are instructed to keep track of what job you are working on and to record that time as a charge against that job. If you work on more than one project, you keep track of how many hours you put on each and charge those hours against that job.

If one of those jobs requires a printed report and you send the report out to be printed, you record that project number on the printing order so the accountant can charge the printing against that particular project. Your labor and those printing charges are direct costs because they are incurred directly in connection with that particular job and are expended entirely on that job.

If you have asked one of the secretaries or typists to type your report, she may have asked you for a "charge number." That's because she too is instructed to keep track of her time and charge it against the right job. Her labor is a direct cost also.

If you make a trip in connection with a given project, your travel expense and per diem expenses are direct costs: they are associated directly with that job and only with that job.

Here's a flat rule: *any* costs that are incurred directly to do work of any kind on a given job and that can be *identified* quantitatively as connected with that job are direct costs.

There are good reasons, which we'll get to, for keeping as close track as possible of direct costs, and most companies do their utmost to identify all direct costs, even to keeping a telephone log so that toll charges can be charged against the jobs for which they were made. This system is particularly used in contract work, although it is practiced by many companies that are not in contract work.

If your company has a receptionist sitting at a desk, it is probably impossible to determine just how much of her time, if any, is directly chargeable to given jobs. One exception: many companies have receptionists help with typing and instruct receptionists to keep track of any "direct time" they put in. But even then, the time she spends answering the telephone and receiving visitors is in behalf of the company's operations overall and not for any single project.

Even if you keep a telephone log for toll calls, there is a basic telephone cost that cannot be logged against individual jobs. Rent and other building costs cannot be identified as connected with given projects (usually), nor can can the cost of furniture, typing paper, office supplies, and sundry other items.

Yet, these are all real costs. They have to be paid for, and the contracts have to do the paying, or the company will not survive long. They are *indirect* costs, which simply means that they are the general costs for doing business and cannot be definitely broken down and charged individually to each project.

Some costs may be either direct or indirect, according to how the company chooses to handle its books. If they do not have you keep a telephone log, all telephone costs will be indirect. If the receptionist is not ordered to keep track of which project she is typing for, all her time becomes indirect. And so on.

Fringe benefits—hospitalization for which the company pays, paid time off (vacations, leaves, holidays)—are indirect costs, as are payroll taxes and insurance. Exception: some cost-plus contracts will allow paid time off as a directly chargeable item, in which case it becomes a direct cost.

Both direct and indirect costs have subsets—subclassifications. Direct costs break down, usually, into direct labor—usually the largest item of direct cost—materials and supplies, if they are a significant item, and "other direct costs," which usually include travel, telephone, consultants, and any other special items, such as printing. Indirect costs have either two or three subclassifications: overhead and G & A (general and administrative) costs are the two major subclassifications, but some companies break overhead into "overhead" and "fringe benefits." For our purposes, to keep matters as simple as possible for these discussions, we'll include the fringe benefits in our overhead package.

The question that should arise now is this: If it is impossible to identify indirect costs in terms of charging the proper amounts to each project, how do we recover them? And, of course, we must recover them, as was pointed out a few paragraphs ago. The commonly accepted method for doing this is by establishing an acceptable *overhead rate*. This is perhaps what so many have difficulty in grasping. Yet, it is really simplicity itself.

First, a general definition: an *overhead rate* is that percentage of direct labor that represents overhead costs. For those to whom mathematics is a mystery and a frustration, that statement may be confounding. But look at it this way: Suppose that for every dollar I pay you as an employee, I have to spend 50¢ for rent, heat, light, and other overhead expenses. My overhead rate is 50%. That is, if I estimate that I will have to pay you $50 a day for 100 working days to get a certain job done, I will have paid out $5,000 in direct labor. Since I have to spend 50¢ in indirect or overhead costs for every dollar I pay you directly, I will encounter $2,500 in overhead costs—50% of direct labor. My total costs are therefore $7,500 (if I have no other direct costs, and we neglect G & A).

If a customer wants me to estimate a job, that's my formula: Direct labor + other direct costs, if any, + 50% of direct labor as overhead. (Plus G & A, in the actual case, *plus* profit or fee: *that's* my *price* to the customer.)

Now how do I know that it costs me 50¢ overhead for every $1 of direct labor, or a 50% overhead rate? Now *that's* where the accountants get their work in!

Overhead rates are, basically, *historical* overhead. The first year you're in business, you estimate your overhead, based on your known overhead costs (rent, heat, light, telephones, etc) and your best guesses as to other, as yet unknown, indirect costs. Since you know how much paid time off you're going to allow employees and what other fringe benefits you intend to provide, you can estimate that portion of overhead costs easily, based on your estimate of direct labor.

You must estimate how much direct labor you will use and divide your overhead estimate by your direct-labor estimate to arrive at a rate.

Suppose you estimate $60,000 worth of overhead costs for that first year and $90,000 for first-year direct labor:

$$60,000/90,000 = 0.667$$

To get a rate—a percentage—simply multiply $0.667 \times 100 = 66.7\%$.

Want to test it? Simply multiply the $90,000 estimated direct labor by the 66.7% and see if that produces the $60,000 overhead costs you estimated.

$$90,000 \times 66.7 = 60,030$$

During the year, your accountant(s) will be monitoring your business constantly, checking your overhead rate to see if it's adequate. You'll be told soon enough if it is too low!

Once you have completed your first fiscal (accounting) year, your accountant will be able to go back over your books and tell you *exactly what your true overhead rate was.* You will then have a "historical" overhead rate. And that, presumably, will be the rate you will be using for the next year.

But business is not static. Your volume is not going to be exactly the same each year. (Hopefully, it will go up every year.) Your overhead expenses are not the same either. They may even vary somewhat from month to month.

Some items are "fixed expenses." Rent is the same—for the lease period at least. Depreciation tends to be fixed, although it will rise if you buy more furniture, equipment, or vehicles. And many other expense items are more or less fixed and predictable.

Telephone costs vary somewhat. Secretarial help, temporaries, taxes, insurance, and many other items are likely to vary. These are "variable costs," obviously. They may change a bit, even if you do exactly the same amount of business you did last year. But if you do more (or less) business this year than you did last year, they are almost certain to change: more employees and more activity mean higher telephone costs, more office supplies, and more of many other things. You may even have to buy more furniture and rent more office space.

Historical overhead is, therefore, far from an absolutely reliable way of estimating costs. You may have an historical overhead of 66.7% (last year's overhead) but be operating, actually, at a far different overhead—perhaps higher, perhaps lower.

If your total business has increased appreciably, your overhead should have gone down—your rate, that is, not your total overhead dollars. The reason is that your overhead does not increase at the same rate as your direct costs do when you experience an increase in total sales. You still have only one receptionist, you probably have not rented more office space or bought more typewriters, etc. Your fixed expenses are still fixed—probably at the same point, or nearly the same point, as last year. Only variable overhead has increased.

Last year, you had $165,000 in sales. Your direct labor bill was $90,000, your overhead bill $60,000, your profit $15,000. (Remember that to keep matters simple, we are ignoring G & A and other direct costs for this example.

This year, sales increased to $245,000. Your direct-labor bill is now $140,000, your overhead bill is $80,000, your profit $25,000. Your overhead rate is:

$$80,000/140,000 = 0.571 = 57.1\%$$

If you are still estimating your jobs and charging your customers at the old overhead rate of 66.7%, you are making a good profit, and there is nothing wrong with that. But if you are bidding competitively against other companies, you are inflicting an unnecessary burden on yourself and probably losing some contracts you could have won. That's what's behind the frequent complaints you hear from marketing people about fighting a high overhead or an excessive "burden rate." And that's what's behind the constant efforts of good business people to reduce unnecessary expenses. Achieving a favorable (low) overhead rate enhances your competitive position.

Because of this uncertainty as to what your actual overhead rate is at any given time, the government usually accepts a "provisional" overhead rate. That's simply an estimated overhead rate, which will be verified by government auditors (accountants) at year's end or at the end of the contract. If the audit, which reveals the *actual* or "experienced" overhead rate, shows that the rate is different from that estimated, the bill is adjusted: you bill the government the difference (to the extent provided for in the contract) or you pay the difference back to the government.

Ordinarily, audits are performed only on contracts in excess of $100,000, although some agencies will reserve the right to audit contracts of $50,000. Cost-plus contracts are almost invariably audited.

Usually, a contract based on a provisional overhead rate includes a clause specifying the *maximum* overhead rate the government will pay you, should the audit reveal that your estimated overhead was lower than the actual overhead. If your actual overhead is greater than that contractual maximum, you will have to absorb the difference as a loss. That, of course, keeps you from using the provisional overhead as a device to appear far lower in your price than you really intend to be!

Where and when would you use a provisional (estimated) overhead rate? When is it in your interests to do so? Consider the following circumstances:

In your first year, you did $165,000 business and had an overhead rate of 66.7%. In your second year, you did $245,000 business and had an overhead rate of 57.1%. Now in your third year, you have good reason to expect to do $300,000 business and probably to drop your overhead rate a point or two further, although you are sticking with that 57.1% in the meanwhile. But you are preparing a proposal for a project that will require about $150,000 worth of *additional* direct labor, raising your direct labor "base" to about $290,000—more than double the direct-labor base you were previously expecting. What will that do to your overhead?

Almost certainly, while you will experience additional overhead *dollars,* your overhead rate will go down significantly. You estimate the actual dollars increase in overhead at $30,000, for a total of $110,000 overhead and $290,000 direct labor. This would mean an overhead rate:

$$110,000/290,000 = 0.379 = 37.9\%$$

What overhead rate should you bid, the 51.7% you are actually experiencing or the 37.9% you estimate, with the additional contract?

Obviously, you are going to be in a much stronger competive position at 37.9% overhead than at 57.1%. If you want the new contract badly enough, you should propose a lower overhead rate—perhaps not 37.9%, because that may be optimistic and represent a risk, but certainly not much over 40%.

If you are reasonably sure of that original $140,000 direct labor you expect and have some confidence in your own estimates, there is little risk involved because you will work at that lower overhead rate *only if you win the contract*. Otherwise you will still be getting that 57.1% overhead you have already been billing!

General rule (if you want new contracts badly enough): whenever a prospective new job is big enough to drive your overhead rate down, estimate the new overhead rate and bid at that rate, provisionally.

Of course, if you succeed in winning that new contract at your lower overhead rate, you will be in a much stronger position in terms of costs for every other bid you make. That's an additional bonus. It's the big advantage of large sales volume, if you keep a close watch on overhead dollars.

G & A

Let's have a look now at G & A (general and administrative costs). This is a relatively new concept, which arose primarily out of the heavy government contracting that began to take place after World War II, as our Department of Defense began huge procurement programs.

Defense Department contracting officials took a dim view of certain types of expenses that companies were charging to overhead—and consequently to the government. One particularly was the cost of marketing, a large item. For some reason or other, the government accountants and lawyers decided that marketing or sales costs were not "allowable" items of overhead expense. Yet, they were real costs for which companies were entitled to charge and be repaid, particularly in the many cost-plus contracts of that era. The government did not deny that these were legitimate expenses but only that they were not proper *overhead* expenses—the indirect costs of getting the actual job done.

The answer was a new indirect-cost category: G & A. Charged as G & A, the costs were acceptable. Some commercial companies have a G & A, but it's less common there than in companies doing business with the government generally, and only a handful of government contractors operate their books without a G & A category.

What goes into G & A, ordinarily, is advertising and other sales and marketing costs, corporate salaries, legal fees, and other corporate expenses. Unlike overhead, G & A is not a percentage of direct labor but is a percentage of *all* costs. (This will show up shortly, when we examine typical cost breakdowns.) In one sense, it's something like a "head tax" imposed on all the branches, divisions, departments, etc., of a large corporation to support the home office/corporate establishment. Typical G & A rates range from 2% or 3% to 15–20% but they tend to clump well below 10%.

Some corporations have a single G & A that is applied equally to all operating divisions or branches of the corporation. Others choose to allow each operating division or branch to establish its own G & A. The principle is the same, however, whichever way the G & A "pool" or "pools" is (are) established.

Let's take a look now at a typical cost breakdown for a cost proposal:

ESTIMATED COSTS

Direct Labor:

Project leader—400 hours / $25.00/hour		*$10,000*
Engineers—1,200 hours / $18.00/hour		*21,600*
Clerical—800 hours / $6.50/hour		*5,200*
	Total direct labor	36,800
	Overhead @ 57.1%	21,013
	Subtotal	$57,813

Other Direct Costs:

Travel—3 round trips to San Francisco		$2,100
Per diem—12 days @ $40.00/day		480
	Subtotal	60,393
	G & A @ 6.5%	3,926
	Subtotal	64,319
	Profit @ 12%	7,718
	Total Price	$72,037

Consider now what happens when you succeed in reducing your overhead and bidding at 40%:

Direct labor	$36,800
40% overhead	14,720
Subtotal	$51,520
Other direct costs	2,580
Subtotal	$54,100
G & A @ 6.5%	3,517
Subtotal	$57,617
Profit @ 12%	6,914
Total Price	$64,531

Because the overhead is compounded by the G & A and profit, since they too are percentages, a reduction of $6,293 in overhead dollars results in a total price reduction of $7,506.

That again serves to illustrate the importance of keeping overhead as low as possible—not to save the customer money *per se* nor to reduce your own sales volume, of course, but to make yourself as competitive as possible. Organizations with low overhead are hard to beat if their techni-

DEPARTMENT OF DEFENSE **CONTRACT PRICING PROPOSAL** *(RESEARCH AND DEVELOPMENT)*		*Form Approved* *Budget Bureau No. 22-R100*	
This form is for use when *(i)* submission of cost or pricing data *(see ASPR 3-807.3)* is required and *(ii)* substitution for the DD Form 633 is authorized by the contracting officer.		PAGE NO.	NO. OF PAGES
NAME OF OFFEROR	SUPPLIES AND/OR SERVICES TO BE FURNISHED		
HOME OFFICE ADDRESS			
DIVISION(S) AND LOCATION(S) WHERE WORK IS TO BE PERFORMED	TOTAL AMOUNT OF PROPOSAL $	GOVT SOLICITATION NO.	

DETAIL DESCRIPTION OF COST ELEMENTS

	EST COST ($)	TOTAL EST COST[1]	REFER-ENCE [2]
1. DIRECT MATERIAL *(Itemize on Exhibit A)*			
a. PURCHASED PARTS			
b. SUBCONTRACTED ITEMS			
c. OTHER - *(1)* RAW MATERIAL			
(2) YOUR STANDARD COMMERCIAL ITEMS			
(3) INTERDIVISIONAL TRANSFERS *(At other than cost)*			
TOTAL DIRECT MATERIAL			
2. MATERIAL OVERHEAD[3] *(Rate % X $ base =)*			

3. DIRECT LABOR *(Specify)*	ESTIMATED HOURS	RATE/HOUR	EST COST ($)		
TOTAL DIRECT LABOR					

4. LABOR OVERHEAD *(Specify Department or Cost Center)*[3]	O.H. RATE	X BASE =	EST COST ($)		
TOTAL LABOR OVERHEAD					

5. SPECIAL TESTING *(Including field work at Government installations)*	EST COST ($)		
TOTAL SPECIAL TESTING			
6. SPECIAL EQUIPMENT *(If direct charge) (Itemize on Exhibit A)*			
7. TRAVEL *(If direct charge) (Give details on attached Schedule)*	EST COST ($)		
a. TRANSPORTATION			
b. PER DIEM OR SUBSISTENCE			
TOTAL TRAVEL			
8. CONSULTANTS *(Identity - purpose - rate)*	EST COST ($)		
TOTAL CONSULTANTS			
9. OTHER DIRECT COSTS *(Itemize on Exhibit A)*			
10. TOTAL DIRECT COST AND OVERHEAD			
11. GENERAL AND ADMINISTRATIVE EXPENSE *(Rate % of cost element Nos.)*[3]			
12. ROYALTIES[4]			
13. TOTAL ESTIMATED COST			
14. FEE OR PROFIT			
15. TOTAL ESTIMATED COST AND FEE OR PROFIT			

This proposal is submitted for use in connection with and in response to *(Describe RFP, etc.)*

and reflects our best estimates as of this date, in accordance with the Instructions to Offerors and the Footnotes which follow.

TYPED NAME AND TITLE	SIGNATURE	
NAME OF FIRM		DATE OF SUBMISSION

DD 1 APR 68 **633**

S/N-0102-006-6501
C-32488

Figure 15. DD Form 633.

CONTRACT PRICING PROPOSAL *(RESEARCH AND DEVELOPMENT)*	Office of Management and Budget Approval No. 29-RO184	

This form is for use when *(i)* submission of cost or pricing data (see FPR 1-3.807-3) is required and *(ii)* substitution for the Optional Form 59 is authorized by the contracting officer.

PAGE NO.	NO. OF PAGES

NAME OF OFFEROR	SUPPLIES AND/OR SERVICES TO BE FURNISHED
HOME OFFICE ADDRESS	

DIVISION(S) AND LOCATION(S) WHERE WORK IS TO BE PERFORMED	TOTAL AMOUNT OF PROPOSAL $	GOV'T SOLICITATION NO.

DETAIL DESCRIPTION OF COST ELEMENTS

	EST COST ($)	TOTAL EST COST[1]	REFER-ENCE[2]
1. DIRECT MATERIAL *(Itemize on Exhibit A)*			
a. PURCHASED PARTS			
b. SUBCONTRACTED ITEMS			
c. OTHER—*(1)* RAW MATERIAL			
(2) YOUR STANDARD COMMERCIAL ITEMS			
(3) INTERDIVISIONAL TRANSFERS *(At other than cost)*			
TOTAL DIRECT MATERIAL			
2. MATERIAL OVERHEAD[3] *(Rate* %X$ *base=)*			

3. DIRECT LABOR *(Specify)*	ESTIMATED HOURS	RATE/HOUR	EST COST ($)		
TOTAL DIRECT LABOR					

4. LABOR OVERHEAD *(Specify Department or Cost Center)[3]*	O.H. RATE	X BASE =	EST COST ($)		
TOTAL LABOR OVERHEAD					

5. SPECIAL TESTING *(Including field work at Government installations)*	EST COST ($)		
TOTAL SPECIAL TESTING			

6. SPECIAL EQUIPMENT *(If direct charge) (Itemize on Exhibit A)*			
7. TRAVEL *(If direct charge) (Give details on attached Schedule)*	EST COST ($)		
a. TRANSPORTATION			
b. PER DIEM OR SUBSISTENCE			
TOTAL TRAVEL			

8. CONSULTANTS *(Identify—purpose—rate)*	EST COST ($)		
TOTAL CONSULTANTS			

9. OTHER DIRECT COSTS *(Itemize on Exhibit A)*			
10. TOTAL DIRECT COST AND OVERHEAD			
11. GENERAL AND ADMINISTRATIVE EXPENSE *(Rate* % *of cost element Nos.* *)*			
12. ROYALTIES[4]			
13. TOTAL ESTIMATED COST			
14. FEE OR PROFIT			
15. TOTAL ESTIMATED COST AND FEE OR PROFIT			

OPTIONAL FORM 60
October 1971
General Services Administration
FPR 1-16.806
5060-101

Figure 16. Standard Form 60.

cal competence and their proposal writing are as good as their overhead is low.

For most purposes, this method of cost breakdown illustrates how costs must be broken down for government agencies on government cost forms, except that special costs such as travel and consultants must be explained by notations in spaces provided. And if the contract to be is a large one, and especially if it is some form of cost-reimbursable contract, "expense pools" will probably be required to back up and demonstrate how you arrived at your overhead and G & A rates. These are ordinarily made up by your own accountants, of course, who have access to most of the figures required, but they will have to be based on your own information on such matters as how much direct labor will be increased by the proposed contract.

Government Cost Forms

If you are proposing to any military unit, you will probably have been supplied the DOD Contract Pricing Proposal [DD Form 633 (Figure 15)]. Civilian agencies generally use Standard Form 59 or Standard Form 60 (Figure 16), the latter most often.

These are not greatly different from each other, nor are they greatly different, in substance, from the examples we have just looked at. All have the same objective: to break down the various costs, direct and indirect, into their individual subcategories so that the government can study them and evaluate their validity. You could not, for example, propose to pay a typist $20 an hour or propose $150 a day for a hotel room.

In some cases—particularly for fixed-price, small contracts—cost breakdowns are not required at all but may be recorded on Standard Form 33 as a "for-the-job" price.

Expense Pools

Probably you will never have to make up expense pools (unless you are an accountant), but you should know what they are. In a word, they are the backup for your claimed or provisional indirect costs.

On large contracts, particularly cost-reimbursement types, the government will usually accept your stipulated overhead and G & A rates if they have been verified by a government audit during the preceding year. (Such audits are usually made by DCAA—the Defense Contracting Audit Agency—even on nonmilitary contracts.) In some cases, if you have never had a government audit, a preaward audit will be made to verify your claimed rates. However, it is not unusual, if you do not have an audit-verified rate or are proposing a provisional rate, for the agency to ask you to verify your rate by presenting the basis for such rates in your cost proposal.

To do this, you provide one or more "schedules," listing those indirect costs you anticipate in each of the two categories, overhead and G & A. These are the so-called expense pools. They show that $60,000 or $80,000, or whatever indirect expenses you claim.

The government reviews these schedules, as they do your DD Form 633 or Form 60, and judges whether all listed items appear to be reasonable and are allowable under the procurement regulations.

Figures 17, 18, 19, and 20 show typical expense pools. The various items listed are either expenses you are actually experiencing—fixed costs, for example—or expenses you expect to experience.

To keep costs down, the law authorizes certain actions, which you may want to suggest to the contracting officer. One of these is the provision of government-furnished equipment. The law says that if the government has equipment, machinery, tools, furniture, or other assets available

SCHEDULE
OVERHEAD EXPENSE POOL

Rent	$18,000
Heat and light	2,800
Insurance	3,650
Printing	900
Office supplies	1,100
Receptionist	8,000
Secretarial labor	22,800
Fringe benefits (paid time-off and hospitalization)	17,750
Depreciation, furniture and equipment	3,450
Withholding taxes	36,000
Unemployment insurance	2,100
Telephone and telegrams	4,800
Accounting	2,400
Legal costs	6,500
	$127,250

Total direct labor for
XYZ Division: $210,000
Overhead rate (127,250/
210,000) = 0.60 = 60%

Figure 17. Overhead expense pool to show derivation of overhead rate for operating division making bid.

SCHEDULE
G & A EXPENSE POOL

Officers' salaries	$78,000
Corporate offices, rent	5,600
Corporate offices, heat, light, telephone	1,200
Advertising	2,500
Marketing and sales	37,000
Depreciation, furniture and equipment	480
Accounting	11,000
Insurance	780
Secretarial	9,000
Legal costs	12,000
	$157,560

Total costs, all
divisions: $1,998,750
G & A rate (157,560/
1,998,750) = 0.07 = 7%

Figure 18. G & A expense pool to show derivation of G & A rate for corporation.

SCHEDULE
OVERHEAD EXPENSE POOL

Rent	$9,000
Heat and light	1,400
Insurance	1,825
Printing	450
Office supplies	550
Receptionist	4,000
Secretarial labor	11,400
Fringe benefits (paid time-off and hospitalization)	8,875
Depreciation, furniture and equipment	1,725
Withholding taxes	18,000
Unemployment insurance	1,150
Telephone and telegrams	2,400
Accounting	1,200
Legal costs	3,250
Total	$63,625

Figure 19. Overhead expense pool to show estimated actual dollars of overhead expenses anticipated.

SCHEDULE
FRINGE BENEFITS EXPENSE POOL

Paid time-off:

Sick/personal leave	6 days/year	
Vacation leave	10 days/year	
Holidays	9 days/year	
Total:	25 days/year	

Rate (25/235): 0.106 = 10.6%	10.6%
Hospitalization	3.0%
Total fringe benefits:	13.6%

Figure 20. Example of separate schedule to show fringe benefits portion of indirect costs when not included in general overhead rate.

and not in use, they may be loaned to the contractor to reduce contract costs.

In practice, the government has supplied entire buildings and full complements of furniture, computers, printing presses, machine shops, and much other material. And, in fact, in many cases the government has bought property for the sole purpose of lending it to a contractor, although this is not the intent of the law.

Another cost-saving possibility often employed is authorizing the contractor to buy from the General Services Administration. Many supplies and other items can be bought more cheaply from GSA than from an outside vendor, thereby reducing the contractor's costs and, of course, the cost to the government.

The advantage to the contractor is, immediately, that such arrangements place less strain on his cash flow and reduce his operating-capital needs. Aside from that, it is good "politically" to make helpful suggestions to contracting officers, who usually take cost-conscious contractors to their hearts!

Cash Flow

Cash flow is a major problem for many contractors and should be considered in calculating costs. If your company must borrow to finance your contracts, as many, if not most, companies must, you must consider interest costs on borrowed capital as an item of expense, for it is certainly that.

The cost of the money you borrow depends, of course, on how long you use it. Therefore, the more promptly you can get paid what the government owes you, the less money you will have to borrow. You should therefore calculate how much money you will need—that is, for how long you will have to lay out your own cash before you start to get some of it back from the government.

On a typical cost-reimbursement contract, you generally will bill the government every month. It will usually take the government from three to six weeks to pay you, depending primarily on how long it takes your customer to check your invoices and pass them on to the Treasury for disbursement.

That means that it will be from two to three months, after you begin work, before you start getting your money back. That is, you must finance up to three months' operations. You will therefore be using the bank's money for three months. Or, to look at it more realistically, you will be using three months' worth of bank money continuously, perhaps through the entire life of the contract. If it costs you $25,000 a month to operate the project, expect to pay interest on $75,000 throughout the contract, unless you can fund part of the cost out of available cash or defer payments on some costs until the government pays you. None of this is ordinarily your problem but is what your comptroller is responsible for. However, it is helpful to understand it, and it may be at least partly your problem if and when your comptroller asks you how the government will pay.

On the standard cost forms, provision is made for you to state whether you want government help in financing—for example, progress payments, government-furnished equipment, etc. However, even though you indicate here that, yes, you do want progress payments, you may find that the contract that has been drawn up for you to sign does not provide for progress payments (if the contract is fixed-price and not expected to run for long). Or you may find that a payment schedule has been set up that has pitfalls and can tie your money up for a long time.

Costing

Costing—estimating what the proposed program will cost to conduct —is always an important matter, of course. In some organizations, the technical/professional people who write the technical proposal describing the proposed project feel no responsibility for costing. They believe that to be the responsibility of the organization's accountants.

Even if that is so, costing would still be done on the basis of what the project designers—those people who wrote the technical proposal—proposed. It's inescapable that the costs, whatever they turn out to be, are the consequence of the technical proposal. It is in the technical proposal that the organization specifies the labor requirement, travel, consultants, schedules, and any other of the many activities that will cost money.

So, if you wrote the technical proposal and then turned the cost proposal over to your accountants, it is you to whom the accountants will address questions about who is to work on the project, for how many hours or days each, and what other things must be done or bought.

Ultimately, the proposal evaluators will compare your technical and cost proposals with each other, to see whether the costs you have estimated are reasonable for the effort you have proposed. You may expect that. If they are not compatible with each other, you may expect to be asked some embarrassing questions ''at the table'' (during presentations, best-and-final meetings, and/or negotiations), if, indeed, you get to the table.

In bidding for a Job Corps center, some years ago, we were required to perform a total logistics study, and some elements of our cost proposal became a bit ludicrous. For example, we stipulated a far greater number of typing stands than we did typewriters. At the table, we were a bit red-faced in admitting that this discrepancy was due to a foul-up and had no rational explanation. We also had a case of everybody putting salt in the stew, making it a very salty stew: for some reason, almost everyone thought of clocks, and we had listed some 200 wall clocks!

A Few Assorted Cost Considerations

The make-or-buy decisions discussed earlier have another aspect to be considered, an aspect that causes no end of difficulties in many situations. It is this: whatever you buy, as ''other direct cost,'' does not get overhead applied to it, whereas anything you ''make'' with your own in-house labor does have overhead costs associated with the labor you use. And when you get into situations where you must take that into account, you may well find false cost-savings; that is, ''on the books'' it can be made to appear that you have saved money, whereas you actually have not.

Let us suppose, to illustrate this, that you must write a lengthy manual as part of an engineering project. You estimate the cost of doing it yourself, with your own staff writing, editing, and typing, at $20,000. You go outside and get an estimate from a technical-publications firm, and you are given a firm price of $15,000. This is an apparent saving of $5,000. But is it? Let's analyze your in-house costs to see how you arrived at that $20,000:

Writing would be done by your engineering staff at a direct-labor cost of $8,000. Editing, illustrating, and typing would add $4,000 more in direct labor. Overheading that $12,000 of direct labor at your prevailing rate of 65% would add $7,800, for a total cost to you, befor G & A and profit, of $19,800. The saving of nearly $5,000 appears clear enough.

And so it is—provided that you have other work for that staff who would be working on the book, so that they are not idle and generating more overhead costs, and provided that you are on a fixed-price contract.

That's where the rub comes in. If going outside will idle some of your permanent people, you haven't really saved anything. On the other hand, if your regular staff have plenty of other work or you would have to hire someone from outside for the work, the saving is real enough.

The matter of fixed-price versus cost-plus contracting is quite another matter, and it creates special problems of its own. Here is a case in point:

A firm for whom I founded and managed a branch office had for some years had cost-plus contracts primarily, doing only a modicum of fixed-price work. But the contracts I won for my office were almost always fixed-price and bid as such at the company's approved overhead rate, which was relatively high for that type of company. In fact, it was so high that it imposed a substantial burden on me, trying to be competitive in price with firms having substantially lower overhead rates.

Accordingly, I constantly sought less costly ways of doing things. Even after I had won the contract and was deeply involved in getting the job done, I would study the alternatives and often modify my original plan when I found that I could bring in a consultant, buy services, or otherwise avoid the high overhead burden that was being charged to every hour of company labor I charged.

That created great difficulties for me in the company. Although my own projects were fixed-price and my cost avoidances were real savings and added profits, the comptroller became quite annoyed with me for not "supporting the overhead"!

In short, he expected me to generate unnecessary expenses to add overhead costs so that government auditors would find that the company's overhead was as high as was claimed for it.

In fact, the company's entire accounting system was geared to this concept. Whenever my monthly report showed fewer direct-labor dollars than I had predicted in my projections (which were, of course, based on proposals and contracts I had won), the computer reported a loss for my project: it had failed to "earn" its share of the overhead.

In short, if you are geared to cost-plus contracts, you may come to consider overhead to be part of your profits instead of part of your costs.

In this case, the problem was also that all branches of the company (and there were several branch offices) were on the same overhead base, whereas they should each have had their own overhead pool. If each branch had had its own overhead, the problem would not have arisen at all. Moreover, my office would have had a much more competitive overhead and would have been able to win more contracts and win them on more favorable terms. Much of what was charged to us as overhead was actually profit dollars, since our true overhead was much smaller than the rate being charged.

In another case, the services division of which I was a part was housed in the same building as a manufacturing division of that company (not the same company as in the preceding example). It is characteristic that manufacturing operations run a high overhead, usually two or three times that of service operations. Yet, because we were physically housed together, the comptroller insisted on compelling us to bid at the manufacturing overhead, an enormous burden to overcome.

When your company has separated itself into operating divisions or branches, it is often advantageous to calculate overhead for each individual operational unit rather than compelling one to "carry" another.

Given a realistic and accurate overhead, given a sensible accounting system, given enough work to keep all permanent members of the staff busy, and given an efficient operation overall, it is always wise to consider the situation from the make-or-buy viewpoint even for labor, in this sense: if you have a project or a task calling for special skills, it may be cheaper to hire a consultant on contract than to hire new staff members.

When you bring a consultant in to perform a certain special function, you do not "overhead" him because you do not experience overhead costs as a result of his labor: you don't give him paid time off, pay taxes for him, or pay for his idle time. You pay him a flat daily or hourly rate for the hours he actually works at the job and nothing more. It is not really different from buying a product rather than making it.

One former employer, alarmed at mounting printing bills, decided to buy an offset press without consulting anyone else. Once he had acquired the press, we became "pregnant," as one vice-president put it: we had to make further investments to protect the initial investment. We had to hire an operator, buy a plate maker, a paper guillotine, and a bindery. Then, when all that was done and we found ourselves unable to keep the press operator busy full time, we had to go seeking work for him. We soon found ourselves in the printing business, which was never our original intent at all! At that point, the employer finally admitted the mistake and divested himself of all this, at a substantial loss.

Games Competitors Play

One aspect of government contracting that is highly unpredictable is that of "changes." In custom work, particularly in any R & D effort, results are largely unpredictable, and many "contingencies" occur, leading to unanticipated changes in the work required and, of course, in the contractual obligations.

For example, suppose you are developing a computer system for a customer under a contract in which you have estimated the effort to achieve their original goal, as they expressed it in the RFP to which you responded with your proposal. Now, halfway through the project, the government's project manager comes to you with a change of some sort. It may have been the result of a dictum from on high, of a new Act of Congress, of a new acquisition of hardware, or of a problem occurring somewhere else, but it requires a drastic change in your effort. You agree to prepare an estimate of the added costs to the government to make the changes and amend the contract.

You submit this estimate to the contracting officer. He duly does all the paperwork, and your contract is amended—increased—to reflect the new and added work.

This can happen more than once during the life of the project. In fact, for some types of projects, it's a way of life, occurring regularly. This is especially true in technical work, developing new equipment or a new technology of some sort.

The costs for such changes are usually estimated first by the contractor, then negotiated with the contracting officer and the government's technical staff. There is no "competition" in such pricing because you already have the contract. There is only negotiation to arrive at a final figure agreeable to both parties.

That means that you do not have to "sharpen your pencil," as you did when you bid the job originally. The government will usually agree to pay you any reasonable amount for the added work.

Many companies base their price, in bidding—and even their decision on whether to bid or not—on the probability of such changes. If they are reasonably sure that there will be such changes, they will go in at a low price in their original bid—frequently even at or below their break-even point. They expect to make money on the changes. It's on the changes that they will be able to get the "right price," and they are willing to actually pay for the job by bidding in slightly below estimated cost. In the jargon, they are "buying in" or "buying the contract."

It's a successful and profitable subterfuge, if we can call it that, for those companies who do it successfully. Success depends on the accuracy with which they can gauge the probability of changes and the probable number of such changes. If they are mistaken, they will lose money in all probability.

That makes it a dangerous game for amateurs. It is played successfully only by experts, people who can almost unfailingly predict changes. It is definitely not recommended for beginners at government marketing or for others who have not yet acquired the experience and know-how required to play this game.

Many of the firms specializing in technical-publications work are experts at this game, for this reason: much of the technical-publications effort is based on the writers' abilities to analyze equipment and equipment needs from the engineering drawings. The engineering drawings are almost never up to date: you find yourself holding a drawing revision B, while trying to compare it with a piece of equipment that was built to drawing revision F! The drawing changes to reflect the engineering development that has gone into the equipment exist only as rough sketches, and it will be some time before a final drawing, revision F, is available.

If you bid the job from the drawing package available at the time of bidding, you were probably bidding on the basis of obsolete drawings and will have to expend much effort to get the technical documents up to date. Therefore, if you are preparing technical documents for a piece of equipment still under development, it is almost a sure bet that you will have many changes.

This is one kind of competition you will face in many bids and for which you must be prepared. But be sure you know exactly what you are doing before you attempt to play this game.

Still Another Price Strategy

A woman asked her grocer about the price of bananas one day.

"Seventy-nine cents a pound," he told her.

She was outraged. "You must be crazy. Who would pay seventy-nine cents for bananas?"

He shrugged. "They're high," he admitted. "If you want them, you have to pay the price."

"I can get them down at Joe's Market for thirty-nine a pound," she said.

Her grocer suggested, as tactfully as he could, that she get them there.

"Joe is out of bananas today," she lamented.

He grinned. "When I'm out of bananas, I sell'em for twenty-nine cents a pound. But only when I'm out of 'em."

Moral: It's easy to give away something you don't have. Or offer to give away something the customer doesn't want.

For several years, I won a contract for "editorial services" that included a "laundry list": editing, writing, drafting, illustrating, typing, proofreading, and photography. Each was to be quoted by the hour or by the page, as appropriate, and the government would decide who was the low bidder by a "bench test." Here's how that worked:

Since the contract was to be a "call contract" or Basic Ordering Agreement, under which the contractor would estimate each task assigned using the rates established in the contract, the government came up with a simulated task for which they estimated a given number of hours and/or pages in each category of services on the list. They then costed the task, using each bidder's proposed rates, to see who would have done the job at the lowest total figure. That was the low bid.

Since we had done our homework and learned that this agency never ordered photography under this contract (they had an extensive photo capability of their own, which they couldn't keep busy), we decided to give photography away. We bid photography at a ridiculously low rate, while maintaining our standard rates for everything else. Of course, we came up the low bidder in the bench test. And in four years of performing on that contract, we never were ordered to perform any photography.

And there is a variant of the same strategy:

Under all such contracts—Basic Ordering Agreements and similar call-contracts—the contract establishes the standard rates for all services through some sort of unit pricing, but each task is bid individually as the need arises. The government issues the task request. The contractor estimates the labor categories and hours required, ariving at total dollars by applying the contracted-for rates, and issues an estimate. If the government does not agree with the estimate, negotiation ensues until a figure is agreed upon.

That is the extent of the government's control once the contract is established—to agree or disagree with an estimate for a task in terms of the total dollars and to negotiate if there is a difference of opinion. And that's an important point, which must be made clear here: the government may not, under the law, tell the contractor how to manage the job.

That is, the government, having asked the contractor to estimate the task, cannot tell the contractor whom to assign to the task. If the contractor wishes to use a clerk as an engineer or a draftsman, and if the contractor produces work of acceptable quality and accuracy and charges only the clerk's rate, he may do so. He is required only to charge the agreed-upon rates for those actually working on the task and to produce an acceptable result. Succeeding in doing that, he may do pretty much as he pleases otherwise. This makes another cost strategy possible, one that has been used successfully for very large contracts: "giving away" certain classes of labor.

In many task-type contracts, such as those we have been discussing, the laundry list of labor categories becomes quite long, listing several levels of proficiency in each professional category. It might, for example, list Engineer I, Engineer II, Engineer III, etc. The government would have defined each level in terms of educational and experience requirements; that is, an Engineer I might be a recent graduate with less than two years' experience, whereas an Engineer III might be someone with at least five years' experience and a master's degree.

In studying the requirement and arriving at estimates of costs, you may have decided that the bulk of the work could be handled by an Engineer II, with only a relatively slight amount of work for the other levels. Now, having so decided, you might list your rates as follows:

Engineer I:	$4.75/hour
Engineer II:	8.90/hour
Engineer III:	14.50/hour

On a bench test, your bid is likely to come up low, of course, since no one expects to get even the new grad engineer at $4.75 per hour, much less to be able to add overhead and profit and bill at that rate. Now, how do you handle this problem when you actually have to produce your $4.75/hour engineer? You don't. No matter what task comes to you for estimate, you never include Engineer I hours in your estimate. All work is handled by the others, those for whom you have quoted rates you "can live with." Will the customer be unhappy with this? No, not as long as you manage to handle each task at some acceptable total price and you produce acceptable results in each task.

Is this a cynical way to do business? Unethical? Dishonest? That's a matter for your own conscience and code, but consider this: you have no intention of defrauding anyone. You expect to perform each task ably and at rates compatible with today's costs. Your sole purpose in using this strategem is to win the contract. And you are facing competitors who are not asleep either but are pursuing every strategy they know to win.

In one such case, we actually quoted one class of engineer at $1.00 per hour, raising a few eyebrows. But, after performing $250,000 worth of tasks for the customer, they were happy with us and selected us again the next year as their contractor. We never had the slightest difficulty with the contract, other than the normal technical problems.

Government solicitations for such types of contracts tend to request too many levels of labor in each category, in possible anticipation of future needs or because the requester in the government has simply copied an old listing out of another solicitation package. I have seen many solicitations that included three and even four levels of engineer, technical writer, draftsman, etc. But rarely have I seen tasks that required more than two levels to actually do the job—usually a journeyman, who leads the task, and some junior people who work under his direction.

Also solicitations often overstate the requirements and qualifications. What a solicitation describes as "light editing" is often within the capabilities of a good secretary; "engineering" tasks can often be performed by "designers" or even competent draftsmen, in many cases; etc.

Always consider, when preparing your proposal, how you would actually do the job (not necessarily how your proposal says you will do the job)—who would be assigned and what support he or she might need. In practice, in many large contracts, far too many competent design engineers spend far too much of their time at the drawing board making finished drawings, when they should be making rough sketches for a draftsman to convert to finished drawings. Cost-plus contracting has led many companies to become careless and inefficient in this manner, since the government is paying the bill for inefficiency and often encourages it deliberately.

Is Your Price Too Low?

Strangely enough, in many cases it is possible to come in with too low a price. If your price is far below the customer's own estimate, he may take this as an indication that you don't really understand the job and couldn't possibly perform adequately at the price quoted. He might characterize this as being "nonresponsive."

But there is another reason too low a price may be greeted with negative reactions. If you are bidding near the end of a fiscal year, the customer may have some specific amount of money that he has to spend before the fiscal year ends, and your low bid may actually represent a threat to him in that respect.

In our legislative and executive systems, there is such a thing as "full funding," which means that a program is authorized and funds are appropriated for the entire life of the program, although that may be for several years. In that case, the responsible agency can carry the money over, year after year, to the end of the program.

Full funding is the exception, not the rule. In most cases, even for a multiyear program, the agency must submit its estimate of required funds to Congress every year for approval and funding. And any funds unspent at the end of the government's fiscal year (September 30) are turned back to the Treasury.

Turning back unspent funds is a cardinal offense. It suggests, for one thing, that the agency did a bad estimating job when the budget was submitted. It also suggests to members of Congress that the agency does not need as much money for the new year as their budget estimate indicates. The agency runs the risk of having funds cut. Since the main business of government seems to be to spend money, that's a complete disaster.

Even the chief executive of our government is upset by such deficiencies in spending the money that Congress has authorized. For the past few years, almost every year has seen what the White House has come to call a "shortfall" in spending, usually of several billion dollars. Each year, as we approach the end of the fiscal year, government executives concerned with budgets and spending begin what has become a national pastime in such circles: estimating the year's probable shortfall in spending. And when executive actions taken to accelerate spending succeed in reducing the shortfall projected to a lower actual figure, this is hailed as a triumph of government management. This, then, is a factor to consider too, in pricing, especially in the third quarter of the fiscal year.

Sometimes it is possible to learn what the customer has to spend— even, in some cases, what he has actually estimated for the project. Any information you can get on this subject may be valuable.

In a recent case, the government solicited proposals to present a half-hour play, 12 times each day during the tourist season at an historic site in Yorktown, Virginia. In prior years, the playlet had been presented by an organization via a negotiated contract, negotiated without competitive bidding, at a cost to the government of $50,000 a year. This year, the agency found it necessary to solicit competitive bids for the job. This was one of the exceptions. The government provided its own estimate, which was somewhat less than the $50,000 they had been spending each year.

The low bid for the job was a little over $33,000, but the agency decided in favor of an organization who bid $39,000. Their stated reasoning? The $39,000 bidder proposed to pay the actors a bit more than the $33,000 bidder did. The agency concluded that the $39,000 bidder would probably hire slightly better actors than the $33,000 bidder would!

That's the agency's *stated* reason for selecting the higher bid, which is not necessarily their *true* reason. But even if it is, the selection was based purely on price, albeit in reverse of the usual price criterion.

In another case, a bidder was called in for dicussion of his proposal to initiate publication of a Job Corps newsletter. Reviewing his proposal, the customer finally requested a supplemental submission to expand on a few fine technical points about staff qualifications (as psychologists and sociologists, not as writers and editors!). The customer then turned to the bidder's costs. The customer expressed the opinion that the costs were far too low and that the bidder could not possibly do the job for the stated price. The bidder agreed to review his costs. He reestimated the entire job, using an entirely different estimating system than he had used to arrive at his original estimates. His figures came out almost exactly as they had in his original estimate. When he submitted the additional technical information requested, the bidder stated in his letter that he had reviewed his cost figures and wished to stand firm on his original figures.

The bidder was then called in for a second meeting; and this time, the customer wished to discuss costs only. He stated bluntly that he disagreed with the bidder's cost estimates and suggested quite strongly that if the costs were not raised, the proposal would be rejected as nonresponsive, failing to reflect understanding of the problem, etc. The bidder went back to his office and told his assistant: "Redo the cost proposal. Raise the figures about ten percent. That will make us just a bit higher than the company he *wants* to give the job to, and we'll lose on the basis of price. Then we'll protest and pin his ears back."

He was exactly right. His 10% price increase made his proposal just a bit higher than that of the next-lowest bidder, who was promptly—almost hurriedly—awarded the job. The first bidder decided not to protest for reasons of no concern here. But his strategy was probably wrong. He should probably have stuck with his price and lodged his protest as the low bidder if the agency still insisted on a "wire job." He would probably have been given the job, however, since he obviously had the highest-scoring technical proposal.

These are among the many factors and possible situations you must consider in preparing cost estimates and cost proposals. It is not always best to be low bidder. However, if and when you are bidding at what you know to be an unusually low price, be at pains to make clear that you know your price to be low and that it is not lack of understanding or underestimate but the result of superior planning or whatever factors enable you to come in so low. Prove your case in your costs, as you do in your technical plan. And be sure to include in your technical plan enough detail to support your contentions about costs.

Supporting Costs in the Technical Proposal

In almost every case of competitive procurement via the proposal route, you are cautioned in the RFP that your cost proposal must be a separate document (and sometimes the RFP stipulates even that it must be sealed in a separate envelope) and that no costs are to be revealed in your technical proposal. This, of course, is to prevent the technical evaluators from being influenced by knowledge of your cost estimates. They are supposed to make an entirely objective evaluation of your technical proposal on its technical merits, without regard to costs. Only when they have completed technical evaluations and assigned point scores to the technical proposals are they permitted to learn what the estimated costs are for each proposal.

The RFP often makes a point also of cautioning you not to reveal cost information of any kind in your technical proposal, for the same reason. This does not, however, prevent you from furnishing information that gives some indication of your estimated labor hours and other costs. And, in fact, it is desirable to provide some estimates by such things as man-loading charts, such as the example following.

In such a chart, you estimate the labor hours (or days) of the key staff: manager, engineers, mathematicians, scientists, writers, illustrators (if illustrating is a major function), and others whose efforts will represent the major portion of the labor costs. Usually, you do not list estimates for such general support as clerks and typists.

If you break this down suitably by tasks and subtasks, phases, and other pertinent subdivisions, you accomplish several things:

1. You substantiate your technical discussions and approach, and you demonstrate your understanding of the requirement.

2. You reinforce credibility by furnishing details and revealing that you can, even at this early stage of analysis and planning, plan the project in some detail.
3. You furnish yourself a basis for cost estimating and for discussing and/or defending your cost estimates, should that become necessary in negotiations.
4. You weaken the impact of any competitive proposals that have failed to provide such detailed information.
5. You give the reader (evaluator) a good "ball park" on the scope of the effort your propose, and he can arrive at a rough estimate, at least, of your probable costs, since he can ball-park the hourly rates for the people and your probable overhead.

And there is one other important consideration, which we'll defer for a moment.

If the effort is to result in a physical product of some sort—a manual, equipment, a training program, a report, or other—representing a significant part of the effort overall, there is a need to quantify, even though the customer may not have quantified.

If you have prepared a man-loading chart of some sort, you have already quantified most of the labor in the major categories. But if a manual or a training program of some kind is to be delivered—if, in fact, it is the production of such a product that will account for most of the required labor and effort—that, too, should be quantified: number of pages estimated, illustrations, slides, audio tapes, copies, bindings, etc.

Solicitations quite often do not furnish quantitative estimates from the customer, the implication being that you are the one to quantify estimates. And it is important that you do so for all the reasons already stated, but for this one also: to protect yourself against overruns and changes, for which you would otherwise have difficulty getting paid.

If you have failed to quantify both labor and product, the customer's technical or "program" personnel with whom you are working have a license to steal from you, to demand whatever occurs to them as desirable. And you have no defense.

Let us suppose that you agree to prepare a program to train junior naval officers in naval security regulations. You write a fine proposal for a thick training manual, with lots of good illustrations, and you estimate a round price of $30,000. But you fail to specify the 600-page manual you anticipate or the illustrations.

The government buys your proposal and awards you a contract. You work closely with the customer's staff, and you get along fine. They love what you're doing for them, and they're full of helpful suggestions and new ideas as they see the draft develop. You want to get along with it, of course, since there is other business there, so you "go along." Then one day you suddenly realize that you have overrun the contract and are losing money. You begin to analyze the problem, and you realize that you have produced a 1,000-page manual and a far greater number of illustrations than you had estimated originally. You mention this to the program people. They shrug. The contract doesn't say anything about number of pages or numbers and kinds of illustrations. Their inference is that you are contractually obligated to satisfy them, whatever it takes to do so.

You appeal to the contracting officer. He is sympathetic, but he is a contracting officer. His job is to administer the contract, which he now gets out of the file and reviews carefully. He finds no stipulation as to number of pages and illustrations.

He peers at you over his glasses. "What do you want me to do?" he shrugs. "How do we establish a cut-off point or a norm? How can anyone decide by what amount the project is overrun or if it's overrun at all?"

He's right, of course. You're dead. There is nothing to do but try to persuade the program people to be more understanding, if you can.

The above is an actual case, except that the proposal did specify the number of pages and illustrations, number of copies, bindings, etc. And when the project began to overrun, the contractor appealed to the contracting officer, who turned to the program people and asked, "Do you fellows have any more money? You'll have to pay if you want more than what's listed in the proposal you bought."

It's easy to fall into this trap, but it costs a great deal of money to learn this lesson the hard way. Always quantify, because usually your proposal is incorporated "by reference" into the contract. If you haven't quantified and your customer also hasn't quantified . . .

While on the subject of cost overruns—although this is a contract-management consideration—never overrun, even on a cost-plus, without a clear okay from the *contracting officer*. He is the *only* one who can approve a change that will cost the government more money. Usually, he will not give you a verbal okay either but will ask you to wait for a formal contract amendment. (Modifications change contract provisions that do not involve money. Amendments change contract provisions that do involve money.)

If you do work not authorized by contract, even on a cost-plus contract, there is a very good chance that you will not be paid for it. The government is not obligated, legally, to pay you for extra work not formally authorized by contract amendment. The contract includes this pre-cautionary information and instruction, and it's an important one. Techni-cal or program people often ask for things for which they cannot pay. If they cannot get the extra cost okayed—cannot give the contracting officer an official authorization to "obligate" the funds—you won't get paid. You can and should make money on "changes," but you must be sure that you get the official okay to bill the change.

How to Handle the Hard-to-Price Proposal

Many solicitations are issued by people who are not especially famil-iar with the work and are unable to specify the requirement adequately for bidding. The lack of quantity estimates is not the only area in which an RFP may be vague.

In one such case, the government asked for the development and production of a brochure that would be sort of an annual report of techni-cal accomplishment by their engineering R & D staff. The contractor was to develop the report and print it in 500 copies. The report was to be approximately 50 pages, with approximately 75 color photos. That may appear to be fairly specific. But we didn't find it so. We found these questions unanswered:

1. Copy typed or typeset? If typeset, ragged right or right justified?
2. What kind of paper stock for printing? Cover printing?
3. How many pages to have color photos? Cover in color?
4. Who supplies photos? Include photography in our costs?
5. What kind of binding?

Costs depend heavily on the answers to these questions, especially with color separations running to hundreds of dollars each, with paper costs varying daily, and with great variance also in binding costs, espe-cially in short runs, such as the 500 specified. The prople who prepared the solicitation package were engineers, not publications specialists, and the lack of such information reflected that. The question facing us was how to handle this best.

Now the "obvious" thing to do, for the uninitiated bidder, is simply to write or call the requester and ask the questions—the obvious and the wrong thing to do, in our opinion, because this is what would happen: the customer would get us some answers, even if he got them as a result of our suggestions, which he might well ask for. Having got those answers, he would feel obliged to make them available to everyone who had ordered a copy of the solicitation and was likely to submit a proposal. We would then have done two things wrong: we would have "educated" the customer *prematurely*, and we would have educated and alerted competitors, some of whom may not have been any more knowledgeable about the subject than we were.

Moreover, having a solicitation modification go out to all requesters of the solicitation might well increase the competition we would have to face, for this reason: an RFP with such deficiencies as this one tends to discourage many bidders from the vague and difficult-to-answer RFP. Providing more specifics makes it easier to write a proposal, especially if you are not very expert in the field, and usually highly specific RFPs produce more proposal responses than do vague ones.

So it did not appear to be in our interest at all to ask any questions, just as we tend to refrain from asking questions at pre-proposal conferences.

This is a case, however, where you've been handed a "lemon"—a difficult-to-respond-to (difficult-to-price) RFP. And for the alert marketer, when someone hands you a lemon, the right thing to do is to "make lemonade" with it, which is what we proceeded to do.

We estimated, although we did not know how correct we were until later, that the customer planned to spend something on the order of $25,000 or had budgeted that amount in making the customary in-house estimate. And while we didn't especially want to "leave money on the table" in submitting our price, neither did we want to price ourselves out of the game. At the same time, we knew that we had to provide those quantifying specifics that would protect us from exorbitant demands later by the customer's program people. We therefore resorted to the tactic of offering the customer several options. In our technical proposal, we explained the uncertainties created by the questions that had not been answered in the statement of work, and we suggested the minimum and maximum specifications that we believed would do a satisfactory job for the customer.

In our cost proposal, we again explained, from a cost viewpoint the three options, estimating first the product that we believed would represent the minimum (and cheapest) result compatible with the customer's needs. We prepared our Form 60 (government cost form) for the minimum option but explained and presented the two other options, along with their costs.

This brought us to the table immediately for a best-and-final session as we expected. Our formal submission brought us to the table not only as a highly knowledgeable bidder but as a low one. Yet, we did not shut the door on permitting the customer to spend a bit more, if he had it and wished to spend it, to get a little fancier final product. As it turned out, the customer accepted our highest option, which was still a shade under his budget maximum, and awarded us the contract.

This strategy of offering options is one way to handle such problems as the vague and hard-to-price proposal, and we have used it successfully in other cases. It gives you the best of all worlds in some ways, giving the customer a low price, if that's what he wants, but keeping the door open to spend more if he chooses to. And of course it avoids that delicate problem of asking questions that will benefit your competitors more than they do you.

It has one other benefit, too: it opens your customer's eyes to possible deficiencies in competing proposals. If competing proposals do not point our the uncertainties in the statement of work nor offer solutions, the customer must begin to have some doubts about those proposers!

That latter point is important to note. To make your own proposal more attractive at the expense of competing proposals, you can often find some problem areas to stress. If you prove your point and convince the reader that you have indeed put your finger on some critical questions and that competitors have not perceived these, you raise doubts about the quality of the competing proposals.

Safeguarding Proprietary Information

Occasionally you may wish to include information in your proposal that you regard as proprietary, for example, some special methodology of your own. You do not wish that information revealed or used for any purpose other than to help you win a contract. Certainly, you do not want it to be used to aid competitors. You can safeguard that information by suitable proprietary notices. There are at least two procedures you can employ:

1. Place a notice on the title page of your proposal specifying that the information contained in pages or paragraphs number so-and-so (listing the pages or paragraphs) is proprietary and not to be revealed or used anywhere except in evaluation of your proposal (but it will be made available to the government should you win a contract!).
2. Place a notice of this type on each such page.

To play safe, it is best to do both. Many RFPs contain instructions for safeguarding your proprietary information, if any. In that case, it is best, of course, to follow those instructions exactly.

If you fail to do this, you may get an unpleasant surprise: the agency may be so convinced that there is a better way to do the job that they will cancel the solicitation and rerelease it later, with your information specified as a requirement or a suggested way of attacking the problem! Such things have happened.

Bidding to a prime contractor for digital communications equipment to be known as data collection and distribution units (DCDUs) we found that the customer specified that each DCDU was to include a computer plus other, special digital units, all of which were to form a single configuration at each DCDU location.

We proceeded to develop our proposal, including suggested design approaches for the special digital equipment and specifying computers from the computer division of our own company. That division was charged with writing certain sections of the proposal dealing with the computer.

As the eleventh hour approached, we learned that our computer division had fallen down on the job and hadn't written anything at all. Consternation! We groaned and prepared to abandon our proposal, which was almost ready for final typing. But we had a hardy soul or two in the group who stubbornly refused to give up and but suggested an all-night session to study the problem further before giving it up.

Reviewing the specifications again, we discovered that the DCDU actually required the use of the arithmetic unit of the computer only and would actually not make use of the central processing unit or most other elements of the computer. We conceived the idea that we could actually do away with the computer entirely, simply adding a specially designed arithmetic unit, saving a great deal of money. Necessity-born invention— *desperation*-born invention.

We failed to consider the need for a proprietary notice to protect our new design idea, a disastrous mistake. The customer agreed so thoroughly with our analysis and design approach that he cancelled the RFP and re-issued it, incorporating our approach as a requirement!

14

Proposal-Writing Considerations

Sell the sizzle, not the steak.
—ELMER WHEELER

What Business Are You In?

Peter Drucker, the noted business management consultant and author, made it a major point of one of his books to establish that far too many business executives do not know what business they are in.

Another marketing authority points out that in the final analysis, *every* business is a service business.

And the marketing executives of the advertising world—"Madison Avenue"—preach and practice selling the benefits, not the product.

All are saying, each in his own way, the same thing: understand what and why your customers are buying, and cater to that motive.

Let's look at what "understanding what business you're in" means.

The railroads thought they were in the railroad business for many years, even after trucking companies and airlines began to make serious inroads into their business. In fact, they fought the trucking companies bitterly. But, faced with the realities of bankruptcies, they began to work with the trucking companies, and today some railroads derive important revenue from transporting loaded trailers across the country on flatbed cars, to be picked up at the other end by tractors. Had they recognized earlier that they were in the delivery business, there would probably have been fewer railroad bankruptcies, since the railroads would have changed their ways to accommodate modern standards and conditions.

I know the owner of a small offset printing shop. He's good at laying his customer's copy out for them and knows where to send them to get

typesetting, artwork, writing, and editing services. Almost all his customers rely on him to help them in that manner. In return for that, they give
him their printing work. But he still believes that he is in the printing
business.

On the other hand, the two gentlemen who own a cocktail lounge in
the basement of this building call their establishment the "Down Under
Club," although it isn't really a club at all, and it's incredibly successful.
Giving it a clubby atmosphere made it an "in" place, although there are
dozens of other bars, some much more plush, within easy walking
distance.

You can "find out what business you're in" only by identifying what
it is your customers are buying—not what you're selling. Why do they
buy from you? What does buying from you do for them? What are the
motivators? How are you different from your nearest competitors?

People who buy from my friend the printer can buy printing in
hundreds of small offset shops in this area. The people who patronize the
Down Under Club can get a drink, have a sandwich, listen to music in
dozens of places nearby. Why is this place so busy every day, when
another, quite similar place in the basement of a nearby office building
isn't busy at all?

The answer tells you what business you're in. And when you know
what business you're in, you're in a position to plan and market
intelligently.

What has all this to do with proposals? Just this: a proposal is a sales
presentation, a set of reasons for doing business with you rather than with
your competitors. You have to furnish your prospect with those reasons,
make him *want* to do business with you. Find the reasons he should be
doing business with you, if you want to sell him.

We are talking about persuasion, of course, which is what selling is
all about. The proposal is an exercise in written salesmanship.

The Art of Persuasive Writing

A proposal is a sales presentation. Its purpose—*your* purpose in
writing it—is to *sell* something, to persuade the reader to *buy* what you are
offering. Your main weapon in attempting to sell your proposal is language—words and the way you structure them, choose them, use them.
Words are not really accurate communication devices. Some words have
very restrictive meanings; others have very broad and general meanings.

Words have *denotation* (literal definitions) and *connotation* (implied
shades or nuances of meaning). "Determined" and "stubborn" are syn-

onyms, but you like to think that you are determined and the other fellow is just plain stubborn. You have courage, but the other guy has a lot of brass. You take calculated risks, but he is foolhardy. And so on.

To write persuasively, you must have some understanding of other people. *Psychology* is a stronger word than I want to use here, especially since it tends to sound a bit cynical in connection with selling. A good word is *empathy:* the ability to see the proposition through another's eyes, feel it through another's probable reactions.

Still, there are certain basics, especially in this Madison Avenue age, when we are bombarded with superlatives used to huckster the flood of products offered on TV and through the print media.

You can assume, when you offer a proposal, that the reader/evaluator is not naive. The readers of your proposal have developed an almost instinctive resistance to the superlatives, the overpowering adjectives, the sweeping claims. Using these is almost certain to bring a small, amused smile to your reader's lips.

Consider the following introduction used in many proposals:

> Our company, Black and Black Data Processing, is the largest in our industry, with hundreds of thousands of man hours' total experience, supporting virtually all agencies over the past quarter century.

Let's try it this way:

> Black and Black Data Processing employs 4,200 people in our 31 branch offices in the United States. Black and Black has been in business continuously since 1956. Past and current clients have included the U.S. Navy, the Department of Agriculture, HEW, and the Commerce Department, among others.

Which statement do you find more credible? Which more impressive? (And which more subdued?)

We all use hyperbole in everyday conversation: "I've seen that movie a hundred times. It's a million laughs. But they charged me an arm and a leg to get in." We thus tend to dismiss all sweeping, rounded-off numbers as ordinary overstatement, intended for emphasis rather than for accurate reporting.

On the other hand, we tend to believe what appear to be true quantitative statements. A listener might snort derisively when you say, "I must have read a million books in the last ten years." Try saying, "I read at least one book a week. That's at least five hundred books in the last ten years."

Once, when I presented a small proposal to the contracting officer of the Office of Economic Opportunity, he merely glanced at my cost estimate and said: "One hundred-fifty percent overhead. What a nice round number. Why didn't you make it one hundred forty-nine point seven percent? I wouldn't have questioned it at all. Now let's call it one hundred twenty-five percent, shall we?''

Of course we did.

Adjectives are deadly. They tend to make your proposal a set of claims, without proofs, without evidence. They tend to be emotional, opinionated, arrogant.

Nouns are different. They are quiet statements, self-confident, emotionally neutral, objective, dispassionate. They tend to be the evidence:

1. Our nickel–chrome–steel alloy was developed at great expense in our own laboratories and produces the toughest alloy in its class, pound for pound.
2. Our own nickel–chrome–steel alloy has been tested and shows an increase of 22% in Rockwell hardness, as compared with competing alloys.

The first statement is a claim with a self-appraisal. The second is merely a reporting of purported facts—and will usually be accepted as fact.

How can a reader evaluate the true meaning of such words as *greatest, best, largest, most modern, most advanced*? As a matter of fact, the mere use of such words suggests that the writer of the proposal "doth protest too much." Such words sound almost frantic, begging to be believed.

Persuasive writing must follow the rules laid down earlier. First, the reader must be aroused to interest and desire, by an appealing to the desire for benefits—for what the proposed project will *do*. The proposal must make the promised benefit *credible*, and that is what we have been discussing, in fact: how to be credible.

It is in establishing credibility that we must resort to logic. Logic does not create interest or the desire to buy. Rather, it provides the buyer with a rationalization for a decision to buy by making the sales argument believable.

The promise of benefits must be made "up front" in the proposal. The rest of the proposal must be devoted to logic and believability. The rest of the proposal must *prove the case*—persuade the reader that the benefit(s) will be delivered:

1. Logical base for the promised benefit: an understanding of the need, the knowledge/skills required to solve the problems and satisfy the need (right approach), with all the "technical argu-

ments'' required to demonstrate that this is the correct understanding and the correct approach.

2. Logical program (plan of action) to implement the approach successfully and carry the project out.
3. Logical base (evidence) to demonstrate that the proposer has a successful track record in the appropriate field (the right experience and prior accomplishments) and has all the necessary staff and other facilities to mount the effort and complete it.

Technical Argument

Technical argument is just another name for logical argument, to distinguish it from the use of *argument* which denotes a shouting match. Technical argument is building your case, brick by brick, cementing each one neatly in place. In the typical proposal, it is your own analysis, spelled out in orderly sequence, permitting—nay, aiding and guiding—the reader through your own thought processes, which led to your conclusions and plans for the project. Take the reader through every step, guide him across every crossroad, show him how to overcome every obstacle, as you did in developing your plan.

Show him each road down which you peered or along which you traveled for a few steps, and why you found it to be a dead end or a maze, causing you to back out and try another road, until you had finally mapped the whole trip.

If quantifying is one major tool in creating credibility, detail is another giant step along that path. Glossing details over, uttering vague assurances, asking a reader to accept premises on nothing more than the authority you assume—all are destroyers of credibility.

Whether we ''believe'' what we ''understand'' or ''understand'' what we ''believe'' is a philosophical question, and of little importance here. What is important, and true, is that finely detailed proposals are persuasive and vague ones are not.

When I order you to do as I say because I say it is the ''right'' way or the ''best'' way, I am not even trying to ''persuade'' you; I am trying to browbeat or con you. When I take you by the hand and lead you down the road, I *show* you where it leads, and I don't have to persuade you: you will persuade yourself. You have seen the road for yourself.

The main purpose of all that detail, then, is to *show* you, rather than *tell* you. I am virtually saying, ''Don't take my word for it. See for yourself.'' To do this, I must roll up my sleeves and show that I have nothing concealed. I lay it all out, sort it out, and let you see my whole hand.

I assume, when I write a discussion, that my reader is an intelligent adult, perhaps not quite as well versed in my field as I, but no neophyte either, I therefore explain not only what I have analyzed and how I have analyzed it, but why, as well. I attempt, in fact, to have my reader relive my entire analytical journey, to duplicate the learning experience I have undergone by making that journey.

I employ logic in my own thinking, and I present that logic in my discussion. I offer premises that reasonable people knowledgeable in our technical/professional field will accept, and I develop logical syllogisms from those premises.

Handling Innovations

There is a great deal of advantage in being different and in being innovative. At the same time, there are hazards.

Innovators always run the risk of being scoffed at, ridiculed—especially when they are defying conventional wisdom. Pasteur, Edison, Kettering, and even lesser lights had to endure jeers, accusations of being idiots, and sometimes even charges of being charlatans, simply because they were attempting something that was "different."

When Governor Earle of Pennsylvania created the first high-speed turnpike, he was jeered at by experts who "knew" that no automobile tire could withstand sustained speeds over 35 miles an hour. The skyscraper was a ridiculous idea, too, according to many established experts.

The proposal writer faces the same hazard in offering radically new and different ideas. Asking your customer to risk all on a new and untried idea is bound to cause him to withdraw a bit and reconsider. A great deal of salesmanship is needed here.

For one thing, you must follow the principle of evolution, not revolution. Change must come gradually, and you must venture on the new step with some caution, as you would along an untried mountain track, where you step forward cautiously to test the new foothold but hold on to some firm support until the new step has been tested and proved reliable.

You must give your new idea some respectability other than pure rhetoric and abstract logic. In offering a customer a new idea—failure-probability analysis, for example—I first pointed out that it was merely an inverse of an already accepted and thoroughly respectable discipline: reliability analysis. So failure-probability analysis wasn't a quantum leap after all, but merely a completely logical next step, with ample precedent for the basic idea.

Many proposal writers at such crossroads fall back on library research and pepper the bottom of each page with bibliographic shoring, citing vast numbers of authorities to support their viewpoints.

This, too, can quickly degenerate into a scholarly dissertation and not a proposal at all. It also renders your proposal difficult to read and follow, when overdone. Use this method with some caution.

In general, when you are offering an approach that depends on a rather new idea, you are going to have to work harder at being credible— at proving the viability of your idea—than if you had followed conventional approaches. This, however, is not an argument against new ideas. Quite the contrary, you should not offer a new idea unless you yourself have researched and thought it out thoroughly and are fully prepared to demonstrate its practicality. You must be convinced yourself before you try to convince your reader. And that's a general truth.

You must bear in mind that your proposal is going to be read by a number of people. You can get an indication of how many from the number of copies requested. Some of them will be your peers technically. They'll understand and follow arguments and explanations expressed in the technical terms of your profession, and they'll accept the technical premises upon which your arguments are based. But some are likely to be lay readers, as far as your profession is concerned, and they will not be able to follow your arguments unless you express the ideas in common language and explain your premises.

Even more of a difficulty is the reader who has some technical knowledge of your field, but far less than you have. This individual can be the most skeptical, the hardest to convince. This is especially true if your technical arguments are just a bit beyond his comprehension and experience.

That means that you must exercise extreme caution so that you are not talking over the head of *any* of your readers. At the risk of boring some readers who may be as experienced and knowledgeable as you are at whatever technical/professional field is involved, you must offer at least a perfunctory explanation/justification of your premises and arguments.

To illustrate this and to demonstrate the idea of different language for different audiences, the Postal Service Training and Development Institute furnishes a good example.

The Postal Service operates its PST & DI in Bethesda, Maryland,

and in Norman, Oklahoma. The Bethesda establishment is concerned with training Postal Service supervisors and managers at all levels—it was originally the Postal Service Management Institute—while the Norman facility handles all technical training, training maintenance personnel for the Postal Service (which has been undergoing automation over the past few years).

Consequently, the staff at Norman are primarily technical people— engineers, scientists, technicians—although they have a few people on staff who are professional educators and developers of training systems.

The Bethesda staff consists of people who have a great deal of experience in Postal Service operations—mail handling, mail transportation, contracting, administration, and management—but a substantial number of the Bethesda staff are experienced training technologists, rather than subject-matter experts. They deal in learning designs, usually along the lines of preliminary analyses and behavioral concepts.

This becomes quite clear when you examine the RFPs issued by the two institutions during the years when each was building courses and curriculum materials. To qualify your proposal with the Bethesda staff, it was important that your proposal reflect an understanding of behavioral technology as applied to training. On the other hand, to qualify your proposals to the Norman organization, it was important to reflect an in-depth knowledge of the subject matter and a detailed plan of development and organization.

Consequently, in proposing to both organizations successfully for a number of years and for a number of projects, my proposals to Bethseda were always heavy with initial analysis and planning and with learning design based on behaviorism, whereas my proposals to Norman concentrated in how the content would be developed and presented in terms of the subject-matter technology.

The differences between the two sets of proposals was primarily one of *language* and general impact or effect. In each case, my successful proposal presented an image or either (1) an experienced and able educational technologist who could cope with the subject matter adequately (for Bethesda) or (2) an experienced and able technical expert who could design an adequate program of instruction (for Norman).

A proposal always casts an image of the proposing organization. It's implied in the general approach, in the language the proposal employs, in the theme or main message, and in whom the proposal appears to be addressing.

Even when you do not deliberately attempt to create an image, you inevitably do so. The reader—your prospective customer—will infer an image of you from what you say and how you write. It's inevitable that a reader will "tag" you.

Some years ago, while with the Educational Science Division of U.S. Industries, I learned that one of our regular customers for our teaching-machine programs had let a substantial contract to another firm to write a "paper" program—one to be printed, rather than filmed for teaching-machine presentation.

When I questioned the firm as to why we had not been invited to bid for the job, their reaction was one of surprise: it hadn't occurred to them that we might be willing to prepare a program to be printed, despite our many earlier explanations that we customarily did both kinds of programs. They had tagged us as teaching-machine specialists rather than as training-development specialists.

Customers have a *need* to tag you, to file you away mentally in some single category for future reference. Unless you are indeed specialists in some narrow category, you must combat this human tendency.

Proposals also convey general messages that can be read between the lines—implicit, if not explicit. If you are generally vague and evasive about what you propose to do—a common failing of many proposals—the implied message is this: just give us the money we ask, and we'll do whatever it is you want done, because we can handle it. If you are highly detailed and explicit, the message implied is this: we have examined your proposition thoroughly and have developed a detailed plan, presented here, and we know exactly how to go about solving your problem or meeting your requirement.

In short, what applies to words and sentences—dictionary definitions versus connotations or shades of meaning—applies also to the proposal overall. It carries both an explicit message (what you have actually said) and an implicit message (what you have implied, or what the reader *believes* you have implied: his inferences).

You may protest at this point, "How can I control what a reader chooses to infer about my meanings?" That is a writer's problem. Effective writing—effective communication, to be more exact—requires *empathy,* that ability to examine the message from the typical reader's viewpoint.

Murphy's Law says that anything that can go wrong will. The analog of that should be one of the writer's laws: anything that can be misunderstood will be. Or, as one editor put it to me, "It is not enough to write so that you can be understood. You must write so that you cannot be misunderstood." That is an editor's function. The capable editor examines the writing for possible ambiguities, conflicting interpretations, implications, and other bars to clear understanding.

In one of my manuscripts, I stated that the following text would cover certain topics but that one special piece of equipment would be "dealt with" later. The editor remarked in the margin, "Sounds like a threat." Irrelevant? Maybe. But if "dealt with" meant that to the editor, it might mean that to others, and there was certainly no harm in changing the words to "explained later" or "discussed later."

Another editor, in another case, objected to my use of the word *epitomizes*, believing it to be an inappropriate term. The editor was wrong, as our dictionary consultation demonstrated swiftly enough. But checking with other writers and editors, I soon learned that few people, even writers and editors, knew the *precise* meaning of that word, and its effectiveness in my manuscript depended on precise understanding. Reluctantly, I changed it, because there was no other word quite as *right* for my purposes. But my objective was to be understood, not to be right.

Being right is not nearly as important as communicating accurately. As a writer, I have been a reader all my life as well, and I have developed a larger-then-average vocabulary. And that presents a difficulty, of course, when you are trying to find the words and constructions that most people will grasp quickly and easily.

In the Pentagon, it has become somewhat fashionable to refer to anyone responsible for a project or a function as the *cognizant officer.* Unless you happen to be aware of this misuse of the word, you may believe that *cognizant* means "aware of," rather than "responsible for."

Behavior has a special meaning to the the training technologist and the psychologist, from whose profession the meaning has come.

Every profession, trade, business, or craft develops special jargon of its own, terms that are usually totally unintelligible outside that field of users. In the case of developing users' manuals for the Remington-Rand LARC computer some years ago, it was found that a certain component in the system had been referred to by all the engineering staff as shmoo registers. This caused quite a problem. The publication staff objected violently to using this frivolous slang in official manuals being prepared for the customers, who numbered the U.S. Navy among them.

Ultimately, after a good bit of detective work, it was discovered that the registers had been so dubbed because the oscilloscope tests resulted in a display that resembled cartoonist Al Capp's imaginary creatures. In the manuals, the component was referred to as a "fast register," although the engineering staff never accepted the change.

Some of this jargon ultimately finds widespread acceptance and understanding, as in the case of the military vehicle known as the jeep (also named after a cartoonist's imaginary creature). Even here, acceptance was not immediate. During World War II, the birth date of the jeep, armored outfits insisted on calling the quarter-ton vehicle a *peep*, reserving the name *jeep* for what the Army officially called command and reconnaissance vehicles. If you ordered a jeep from the infantry, you got a different vehicle than if you ordered one from an armored division!

Jargon can therefore be dangerous, unless you are quite sure that you are using it correctly in the given case, that is, that your reader will understand your reference exactly.

The Proposal as a Sales Presentation

There are certain accepted "rules" of selling and advertising (which is simply written salesmanship). The first rule is *get attention*.

In the world at large today, many things are competing for attention. TV commercials are a good example, since we are all familiar with them, and great care goes into their development by the Madison Avenue experts. A well-designed commercial starts with something novel or dramatic, or it uses some other characteristic to make you notice it. Unless your attention is gained in some manner, the message cannot be delivered, of course. Consequently, the dramatic chases, the impelling musical themes, the cartoon characters, etc.

The real purpose of getting attention is the next step: *arouse interest*. Your attention won't last long if you are not given a reason to continue watching and listening. Getting the prospect involved is a matter of appealing to his or her interest, that is, persuading the viewer/reader to see his or her own fortunes at stake: presenting motivators.

Promises and fears are used: the promise of security; being loved or at least admired; having fun; avoiding embarrassment; avoiding insecurity; making money; keeping up with the times or with the Joneses; avoiding work; having life easier; self esteem. The appeals are *emotional:* you are not offered beer, but you're offered good times with your friends; not cologne, but love; not hair curlers, but high fashion or sex appeal.

These are promises of what the products will do for you, because that's what you buy: not things, but what things *do*. You buy a paperback book if you want only to have the pleasure of reading the book and talking to your friends about it. You buy the hard-cover edition if you want also the pleasure of seeing a good collection of books in your home.

Arousing one's interest is primarily a matter of linking the prospect's well-being and fortunes with what your product or service will do for the prospect. It's a promise of results: Be beautiful. Attract women. Have fun. Be respected. Be secure. Be fashionable. Be loved. Be admired. Be envied. Be the first to own one. Be a leader. Avoid embarrassment. Avoid trouble. Avoid hard work. Get a good job. Protect your children. Ensure your future. Etc., etc., etc.

Now that the advertiser has got the prospect's attention for long enough to make the promise, it's time to do two other things: expand that beginning interest into a full-blown desire to buy and prove that buying will indeed produce the promised result—the benefit. And that's where the real selling begins.

Obviously, it takes a great deal more effort to sell a $10,000 automobile than it does a $5 bottle of cologne or a 75¢ can of beer. If you are selling beer on TV, you "order" your viewers to rush right out to the market and pick up a six-pack immediately. If you are selling a refrigerator or an automobile, you urge the viewer to hasten down to the showroom first thing tomorrow morning, where the salesman on the floor can take up the battle to close the sale.

Your first message is a promise of *benefits* to result. Your next effort is to establish credibility, to make your claims believable. This is where you begin to use logic for the first time. Your customer–prospect must be persuaded that you—your product and/or service—can and will deliver the benefit.

In commercial advertising, you might use a "white jacket" (representation of a doctor) to sell pharmaceuticals or tooth paste, a laboratory scene to sell a household product or motor oil, a test sequence to sell automobiles, or other devices to give your promises some prestigious backup, depending on your appeal and promise. You must somehow support the claim, whether it's Rosie selling paper towels or Professor Wisdom selling encyclopedias. Some of these supporting presentations are emotional (e.g., "ask someone who knows"), while others are pure logic and/or physical evidence, such as laboratory and test results. But all are used for the same purpose: to convince the prospect that the claims are more than empty promises, that the promised benefits will result from the purchase.

The analogy—the comparison of commercial advertising to proposal writing—is not as farfetched as one might think. In fact, it is an excellent analogy.

I once became well acquainted with a man who had once chosen a competing proposal over my own for a project that subsequently gave him many problems and disappointments in the firm to whom he had made the award. One day, I mentioned the matter to him. He immediately went to his files and dug out my proposal. He sat down and read my proposal through thoroughly.

"It's every bit as good as the one I selected," he told me. "I don't know why I didn't call you in for discussion. But I had a great response to that solicitation, and I probably read your proposal at five o'clock, when I was pooped and not paying much attention."

Later, you'll read of cases of the opposite kind—cases where I did something special to get attention and won the contract in almost every case!

Your proposal may be competing with only a few others, but in most cases, it's competing with many others. It's not at all unusual for an agency to receive 20–50 proposals, and there are cases where over 100 proposals are received. Your proposal is competing for attention. That's the first of several competitions it will have to survive if you are to win finally.

There are a number of ways to gain that attention, many of which will be offered in a later chapter. They all have to do with being *different* in some respect. And it is advantageous to be different in *several* respects.

You can be different in some physical considerations of your proposal package, in *what* you say in your proposal, in *how* you say it, and in how you organize it.

At first glance, you might have difficulty perceiving the appropriateness of emotional appeals in a proposal to a government agency, since it is purely a business matter rather than a personal one, and proposals are supposedly evaluated on a purely objective basis.

There is no escaping the fact that proposals are evaluated by humans; the government is an organization of people—individuals, with all the biases and emotional prejudices of people at large. Those human frailties cannot help coloring and influencing the judgments of those who apply the "objective" ratings. Every word in your proposal must be interpreted —words are mere *symbols* of meaning—to determine how well they respond to the requirements and the evaluation criteria.

The individual in the government who has requested the proposals and who is usually the most influential individual in choosing a winner wants your service or product to do something for him: solve a problem, improve a system, take over part of the workload, help implement a new program, provide special capabilities, etc. But that's not all. The individual's personal characteristics come into the equation.

Some executives are busy and self-confident. They want a contractor to take over and run the project with a minimum of demand on the executive's time and attention. Others are fearful of being responsible for projects in which they are not totally involved, totally in control. They want contractors who will stay in touch constantly, keep the executive informed, get approvals for every proposed step, provide a wealth of "documentation."

The customer may want your specialized knowledge and experience, or he may want only your hands and feet. He may want to be deeply involved in initial planning, or he may want a plan presented for approval, with little personal involvement prior to that. He may welcome or fear take-charge people. He may favor big companies, or he may prefer small ones. He may or may not be influenced by the proximity of the company facilities to his own office. He may prefer a distant company and opportunities for frequent visits to the company's facility. He may like complex, grandiose projects, or he may prefer simple concepts. He may be a secure or an insecure person. He may be influenced by appeals to his own ego, or he may be repelled by them. He may be easygoing, or he may be a hard driver.

I know two government executives who have a prejudice about good and bad writing. A badly written proposal will usually get a turndown, no matter how sound the plan it presents.

Another executive is highly antagonistic to "75¢ words." Use the simplest language possible, if you want to win his heart. He also turns off to what comes across to him as braggadocio, and he hates pompous and elaborate company names and job titles. "*The* bigger the name (title), the smaller the company," he mutters. And he definitely favors small companies, but he hates small companies that try to appear to be big companies through what they believe to be impressive names and titles.

I was lucky when I first met him and sold him. I came across to him as self-confident but not arrogant. Had I been smug and assured him I knew all the answers and could do "anything," he would have politely ushered me out, as he later told me. And he would have done the same had I tried to trade on some mutual acquaintances we discovered in our conversations or otherwise tried to use anything but open discussion of how I might be able to help him, to win his approval and his business.

These are all emotional reactions, based on individual characteristics, and they are definite factors in how your proposal is received and evaluated. You must consider them in shaping your sales appeal.

(Consider this too. Elaborate and pompous language; words that send the reader to Webster's unabridged; buzz words; technical jargon; superlatives applied to your own self, company, or proposal; and other such writing offends and adversely impresses many readers who will evaluate your proposal, creating skepticism—and even contempt in some cases. On the other hand, simple, straightforward expression, factual statements, and a subdued tone generally in your proposal will offend no one, nor will they cause any reader to doubt your professionalism and capabilities. Why risk it?)

The important thing is to determine what the emotional appeal should be. What does the customer really want?

In general commercial advertising, the appeal is made to everyone, with the knowledge that those to whom the appeal has significance will listen and be influenced. The problem is simply to decide which is the most universal appeal, which will touch the greatest number of viewers or readers.

The proposal is different in this respect. There are only a small number of readers, and there is a leader whose judgment and reactions will probably be decisive. The appeal must be right for that individual. The RFP analysis and other gathering of intelligence on the project must be directed toward making an accurate judgment of the right appeals. Your proposal must promise the one thing that the customer wants above all else: a requirement he can safely turn over to you and not be bothered with personally, a project he can personally direct and be closely associated with, a supply of qualified personnel to help him get his job done, a solution to a vexing problem, the promise of becoming a hero in his organization, a technological breakthrough he can get credit for, a set of prestigious reports he can generate, an easing of his own everyday workload, a freedom from dependence on his own in-house staff, or any of many other possibilities.

A Case in Point

Where there is an incumbent contractor already doing the job for which you are bidding, there is always the problem that the customer is reluctant to make a change, if the incumbent is doing a satisfactory job. Consequently, the RFP usually asks proposers to present a phase-in plan, describing how they would take over the work without disruption or delay in the services. This is usually a key consideration and requires careful attention.

In one recent case, involving registration of pesticides and data processing on-site at an EPA facility, the existing project was to be enlarged and expanded through combining two services being provided by incumbents and adding an additional service not previously provided.

The successful proposer, an ambitious and hard-driving minority firm, came up with an excellent strategy. Their proposal pointed this out: The new project would require a transition or phase-in, no matter who won the contract, because at least one of the incumbents must be terminated to make a single project of all the work now being provided. The proposal went on to present a carefully designed phase-in program.

However, it went even a step further than that in thinking out problems by developing and presenting a simplified flow chart showing how all the various areas of activity related to each other. These relationships were far from being self-evident, and probably the customer had never really thought about interrelationships of the many functions and tasks.

These two items were the two main strategic points, demonstrating clearly that the proposer had studied the requirement closely and had developed a true, in-depth grasp of the complex project.

The Role of Logic and Reason

Once you have identified the key result the customer wants and have somehow made the promise of delivering that result, you have to prove your case—establish credibility. This is where you begin to resort to reason, to logic.

Be clear in your mind about it. This is not what creates the buying desire. Not at all. You created that by emotional appeals, by promising benefits the customer wants. Now you must convince him that you can and will deliver those benefits.

He has already made his buying decision, tentatively. He wants to believe you because you are promising him what he wants. But he has the problem of being well aware that you have, to this point, made only a promise, a claim. He needs to become convinced that you can back that claim up with facts.

Actually, he has still another problem: he must justify that buying decision, even if he himself is already convinced. He may be the most influential voice in the final decision, but he is not alone. Usually, there are other members of an evaluation team (or source selection board, as it is often called), and there is a contracting officer who will be heard also.

Recognize, first of all, that the values of the technical evaluators and the contracting officer are not necessarily the same. The evaluators are concerned primarily with the program and/or services you offer—that is, their quality—while the contracting officer is concerned with value. He will often be prejudiced in your favor if yours is the lowest bid and is technically satisfactory, even if not the top-scoring proposal technically. In most cases, he will not even attempt to judge the worthiness of your program but will accept the evaluators' judgments in that area. If you believe that his is a commanding voice—and it is in some cases, but not in all—try to demonstrate the best value in terms of dollars per unit product/ service delivered.

To deliver compelling logic to technical evaluators, bear in mind always that the more innovative your plans or the more extreme your promises of benefits, the more evidence you will have to provide. That is, if you can offer 50% more result for 20% fewer dollars than others can, you are going to have to provide some pretty solid proofs of that to make the promise credible.

In one such case, the leader of the evaluation team insisted that we could not deliver the project results we promised for the price we quoted. However, the contracting officer brought a site-inspection team to our facility to survey our operating capabilities, while he investigated our pricing and financial capabilities. We managed to satsify him that our estimates were based on sound analyses, and that we were capable of funding the effort. This was the information he needed to back up his pressure for awarding us the contract—and he succeeded.

So the logical, reasonable proofs you are now about to present have one or more of at least three objectives:

1. To turn interest into desire to buy by supporting and reinforcing the appeals—to turn interest into conviction.
2. To enable the readers to rationalize the buying decision already made, so they can justify to themselves the decision to buy on logical grounds.
3. To give the readers the "tools" they need to support a buying decision.

From this point on, you must demonstrate—logically—your understanding of the problem or requirement, your technical analysis, your approach, your specific proposed program, and your qualifications—your resources and professional capability, including experience.

However, in doing this, don't lose sight of that emotional appeal, those benefits you promised: you must reinforce those promises and never let the customer lose sight of them. Point out, as your dicussions, arguments, and proposed actions progress, how they relate to delivery of the promised benefits. Be aware of hazards, as you do this. It's all too easy to go overboard in your enthusiasm.

In one case, bidding to the training department of the Bureau of Naval Personnel, our proposal stressed continuous reporting to and communication with the technical staff of the department, especially, of course, with the department's project manager.

That nearly undid us, because we went a bit too far with it. In a best-and-final presentation and negotiation, the contracting officer, an able and perceptive individual, reviewed these provisions of our proposal aloud.

"Are you saying that we should help you make the decisions, do the planning, and hold your hand?" he demanded of me.

I hastened to assure him that we merely meant to keep the technical staff fully advised and informed, with ample opportunities for review and approval as work progressed. But it was a close thing. We had nearly convinced him that we were unsure of our own abilities and wanted lots of help from the bureau's staff!

Incidentally, to make a case for saying things in plain English rather than technical/professional jargon, my experiences with the above customer are interesting:

Each time we bid to this customer—and we won four out of seven bids here—we spent at least two or three hours at the table in discussions before negotiating the acutal contract, despite the fact that we were obviously going to sign a contract that day.

Our conversations were with the professional staff, of whom several were Ph.D.'s in psychology, and they ranged over the entire subject of training, well beyond the questions of the particular project we had proposed on.

One day I asked about these conversations, stating that I found the sessions most enjoyable but was curious about them.

To my surprise, I learned that this professional staff who had always communicated among themselves and thought in terms of the jargon of their calling were "fascinated"—their word—by our ability to translate that jargon into easy-to-follow, everyday language. They were themselves gaining new and better insights into their own disciplines and professions!

It turned out that this was no small influence in their rather frequent decisions to award us the contracts, even with the big-league opposition we faced each time.

Consider this. Expressing concepts in technical jargon or idiom is no demonstration of understanding, particularly if you are parroting the accepted technical cliches. Anyone can get these out of a reference text, for one thing. For another thing, such technical idiom often tends to express very broad concepts, and its use does not provide evidence of understanding the concept. The ability to state and/or explain the concept in everyday, lay language is excellent evidence of understanding.

All scientists who deal with the evolution of species (Darwinism) use the technical idiom *adaptation.* This has led many dilettantes in that field to believe that environmental conditions actually cause a direct change— mutations. *Adaptation* is a technical idiom—an expression whose meaning is not to be taken literally but that refers to a lengthy chain of evolutionary events so well understood by the professionals that it is tiresome to repeat it. So the idiom *adaptation* was invented to refer to it. In actuality, *adaptation* means this: When some change—climate, natural enemies, food supply, etc.—threatens the survival of a species, genetic changes (mutations) that aid the species in surviving are perpetuated, while the original members of the species die off. The species is then said to have ''adapted,'' because it so appears, in retrospect over thousands of years.

If you use the idiom *adapted* to a scientist who fully understands the meaning of the term, you have communicated. But if you use it to someone who does not understand the term, you have failed to communicate because the other party either does not understand and is puzzled or misinterprets and is thus misinformed.

That is the hazard in using buzz words, jargon, and other language that is not intended to be taken literally or has no literal definition but is a special symbol.

Bear in mind at all times that (as the general semanticists say) words are not the things they represent but are mere symbols. The purpose of the word is to invoke an image or idea in the reader's (listener's) mind. The communication is effective only to the extent that the reader (listener) gets the same image or idea that the writer (speaker) had in mind when using the term.

When you converse, you get immediate feedback. You know, almost immediately, whether you are getting through or not, and you can embark on simplifications, ancillary information, and other arguments if you are not being followed as you wish to be.

In writing, you do not have that opportunity. If you fail to make your point, the misunderstanding or lack of understanding persists. You have only one shot at making the point. Moreover, you do not have the help of gesture, raised eyebrow, sardonic look, or other aids to meaning that you use, often unconsciously, when you are speaking. The printed words must convey *all* the meanings—every shade, every nuance. *Unless you can find some other devices to help.*

The greatest mistake you can make as a writer, perhaps, is to assume that you are entirely dependent on words and that words and word constructions are your sole medium. The fact is that a writer of fiction ordinarily deals almost entirely in words, although there are a few exceptions. (For example, some mystery writers have used diagrams in their novels to help the readers visualize certain key scenes.)

In proposal writing, as in technical writing, we do not have such a stricture. We can and should use graphics freely. Our function as writers is to convey images and ideas as effectively and as accurately as we can. And there are many images that are all but impossible to communicate in words alone. How, for example, could you teach PERT or critical path method (CPM) charting with words alone? How would you demonstrate a mechanical design or a circuit idea without a drawing?

These are such obvious cases that they are no problem. The problem arises in more subtle cases, where it has not occurred to the writer that the time spent in developing a sketch of the idea is time well invested.

The point is—and mark this well—that you do not use graphics (illustrations) to support text, nor do you search the text for either opportunities or needs for graphic illustrations. Quite the contrary, you identify the concepts and images you want to paint and decide whether you can paint them more effectively and efficiently with words or illustrations. Illustrations should never be used to support and reinforce text. The reverse is true: most illustrations require some text. The illustration should be the main medium of communication, and language the supporting element.

At the same time, you should not have to *explain* the illustration but only to add some details that may be important and difficult to incorporate in the illustration. The more text you need to support an illustration, the less useful the illustration is. Carry this far enough, and there is no need at all for the illustration!

Want an example of a good illustration? Take the photo of the Marines raising the flag on a peak in Iwo Jima. How much text—how much explanation—does that require? Really, next to none, of course. It tells its own story as plainly as can be. That's what makes it a great picture—not the drama portrayed nor the emotionalism of the times, but the fact that it does not need a single word of explanation, except to someone who is, for some reason, unable to identify the uniforms and the era. In some future time, when the present generation has departed, it will be necessary to use a caption explaining the picture. But not until then.

Great paintings in a museum are another set of examples. The really great paintings need no language. They tell the whole story themselves.

Don't be a writer; be a *communicator.* Use whatever you need to get your message across clearly—to ensure that your reader gets your own image, exactly as it exists in your own mind. Don't describe a parallelogram or a vector; SHOW IT.

Some readers may be impressed by the sheer bulk and weight of your proposal. There's no denying that. But at least one contracting officer told us that he would welcome the thinnest possible proposal that would demonstrate our plans and intentions. And we suspect that there are many others who feel the same way.

There is a way to have your cake and eat it, in that respect. You can use appendices and achieve both ends, if you use appendices properly (which few people do). Use an appendix when you have information (e.g., detailed treatises) that is likely to interest *some* but not *all* of your readers. Some of your readers, perhaps, want to read all the painstaking technical detail, while others do not. In that case, you should supply that detail as an appendix.

Use tabular formats, too, whenever possible, to conserve pages and words. Here, too, many writers appear uncertain as to when, why, and how to organize tabular data. Two principles may help:

1. When you are making comparisons of one thing with another, especially when you are comparing parameters, it is wise to consider developing a table.
2. When you have a great deal of repetitive information, again it is wise to consider using a table.

A table is not necessarily devoted to figures—numerals, that is. A table may be used effectively when all the information in the table is text (words). Or even symbols.

Suppose an RFP requests that I furnish detailed information about past government contracts covering various publication functions performed, and I have 10 such contracts to present. It would undoubtedly require several pages of text to furnish all the information in normal

Table 2. Prior Publications Contracts

Agency	Services				
	Writing	Editing	Typesetting	Illustrating	Duplication
USDA	X	X		X	
Army	X	X	X	X	
Navy	X	X	X		
GSA	X	X			
DOT	X	X	X		X
Labor	X	X			X
Commerce	X	X		X	X
Postal Service	X	X	X	X	
DOE	X	X			
Interior	X	X	X	X	

narrative. Consider how much text it would require to convert Table 2 into narrative.

Of course, the customer finds this kind of presentation a handy reference, as well as a convenient way of gaining a broad picture almost at a glance. And that brings up another point, which has to do with persuasive writing and strategies. In many cases, you can use a table to stress and highlight your own qualifications. If you were able to list 40 or 50 contracts, with qualifying experience and responsibilities in all, you'd never get your reader to wade through a lengthy text description of each. But he wouldn't really have to "read" a tabular presentation of that set of qualifications: a glance at such a table would be impressive enough, wouldn't it? Obviously you'd deliberately structure the table—select the items— for maximum visual impact, too.

How and Where to Use the "Heavy Weapons"

The thing we want to do with our proposal include the following:

1. Get attention.
2. Arouse interest.
3. Create desire (to buy).
4. Generate credibility.

These things we have been discussing have more than one edge. Graphics and tables, for example, are good communicators: they help you get your message across, persuade the reader to see the proposition as you see it, or at least understand your mental processes in arriving at your conclusions and recommendations.

They can be used to arouse interest simply because they get a coherent message across fast, before the reader's interest lags. They can be used to generate credibility.

If you find that one of the tools you have developed for use well into the proposal—in the qualifications and experience section, for example—turns out to be dynamite, you may want to consider moving it up front as an "assault weapon" to generate interest immediately.

Suppose that you developed a table showing an enormous amount of qualifying experience and acheivement in a single page—so enormous, that it causes you yourself to let out a long, low whistle of astonishment at your own track record. (That does happen.)

It way well be a good tactic to open your proposal by saying something such as the following:

> While details of Black & Black Corporation will be presented later, in our chapter
> on corporate experience and qualifications, a quick overview of Black & Black
> experience may be gained from the following table.

You then introduce the table on the next page and thereby take a long step toward gaining attention and arousing interest immediately (if the table is as impressive as you believe it to be). And that favorable first impression is highly beneficial in this respect: a typical reader will approach your proposal with one of the following attitudes:

1. Never heard of you, but I don't like your name or the fact that you're a stranger to us. You're going to have to show me.
2. You're entitled to your day in court. I'll read what you have to say, and I hope it's good.
3. Ho-hum, hope this one isn't as dull as the last one.
4. I know this outfit, and they're pretty good. This ought to be a good proposal.
5. Hmmm! This looks like a pretty strong outfit. This ought to be a good one.

Obviously, after the first page or two, the reader is skeptical, adversely impressed, stubbornly determined to be as objective and fair as possible, or well impressed.

If the reader is adversely impressed, the proposal will probably get the worst interpretation possible. Every time the reader comes across something startling, new, different, or controversial, he is likely to mumble something such as "What are they talking about! I don't believe it!"

If favorably impressed, he may say, "That's a new one! Never heard of that before, but they seem to know what they're talking about. Let's read that again."

A favorable first impression does definitely help, which is why big companies send marketing people out to meet the customer and be just as nice as possible. It's far better if the reader knows who you are when he sees your name on the cover of your proposal.

When we talk about presentation techniques and strategies, we'll get into this subject of grabbing attention and making strong and favorable first impressions again. But the main concept and objective here is to condition the reader's mind in any way you can to *expect* the best. People will read into things what they expect (or want) to find there.

Make a customer like you and think well of you, and he'll rationalize all slipups in your favor: you're too nice and too good an outfit to do shoddy work, of course. Therefore, factors beyond your control were responsible. But make a bad impression, and the customer can find a million things to complain about and to condemn you for. And in both cases, the customer will truly believe what he's thinking because he wants to believe it.

That unsuccessful proposal writer who was fond of showing his understanding of all Postal Service RFPs by a speech about "gloom of night and heat of day" (mentioned earlier) always got off to a bad start this way, of course, since the reader was occupied with getting his computer program straightened out or debugging his training program.

You are writing to the people who are responsible for the projects that will be undertaken. It is those program people who read and evaluate proposals. They are the buyers, although the contracting officer signs the contract in their behalf. If they are having trouble getting accurate reports out of their computer, they are concerned with your ability to solve the problem and make the system work properly—and that's all they care about.

Must You Agree with the Customer?

Disagreeing with the customer is a way of commanding attention. Admittedly, there is a certain risk in it. However, it sometimes turns out successfully.

In one case, the Postal Service solicited bidders to provide a set of computer management services—services to develop computer programs, that is. The solicitation called for a wide variety of computer-related skills, with a variety of people knowing different computer languages and people familiar with different computer models. The statement of work made it clear that the customer expected the contractor to have an on-hand staff among whom could be found any combination of these skills and this knowledge, on demand, whenever the customer had a task to be performed. It would obviously call for a very large staff. We were left with the alternatives of submitting a no-bid or taking issue with the stated requirement (running the risk of being nonresponsive). In short, this requirement was a lemon for us. But after we debated it a while, we decided to try to make lemonade from it.

We therefore told the customer, in our proposal, that we fully understood the requirement and how he thought it should be filled by having such a staff on hand. But, we said, perversely enough (by Murphy's law), even if we had such a wide diversity of talent on permanent staff, inevitably the person we wanted to handle a task would be unavailable for one reason or another.

Therefore, we said, the requirement should properly be interpreted not as having such people always at hand but rather as being able to *provide* such people whenever the Postal Service needed them. The ability to "reach out" and recruit talents upon demand was a specialty of ours, which we could document. And we went on to present the evidence that we could do this. It was a good try, and we had nothing to lose, since we were dead anyway if we tried to pursue any other course. It worked, fortunately. We were persuasive enough to get the customer to agree with us, and we won a substantial contract.

Note that we not only exercised a great deal of tact, but we assured the customer that we did not misunderstand his end intent, even though we disagreed with how he proposed to satisfy it. In fact, we simply interpeted his statement of the requirement a bit differently than he suggested and so were not really nonresponsive at all! Doing this successfully calls for great writing skill, perhaps, even great powers of persuasion. But there is something even more significant that should be detected here: reasoning.

The Real Difference between "Good" and "Bad" Writing

Over the years, especially during those periods when it has been my job to be an editor and reviewer of other people's writing, I have become more and more convinced that most cases of really bad writing are not truly that at all: they seem to be, usually, cases of bad thinking. That is, given a normal education and the ability to construct a simple, reasonably grammatical sentence, there is no reason for anyone not to express clearly what he or she has in mind. And when he or she fails to express an idea with reasonable clarity, it is probably becuase he or she does not have a clear idea to express! You can write only what you have formulated mentally, what is in your mind. (What else could you write?)

I believe I have proved that often enough to serve well as a premise, especially during stints I served as an editor in technical-publications groups. When a technical writer who appeared to be adequately educated and intelligent brought me a bad piece of writing—and I mean "bad" in the sense of being vague, obfuscatory, rambling, poorly organized, etc, rather than having a few faults of grammar or spelling and punctuation—I had a sure fix: I took the piece away and ordered the writer to discontinue writing for a day or two and devote the time to restudy of the drawings or other source material.

I told the writer very clearly, in those cases, that it was my conviction that he simply did not understand the equipment or the concept well enough. The result was almost always an immediate protestation that I was wrong. But when the writer did as I bade, he almost always came up with a far better piece of writing.

I believe that in most cases when an individual writes badly, in the sense of poor organization, unclear statements, etc., the problem is one of either trying to wing it without adequate information or a simple lack of enough study and analysis. Defective mechanics—grammar, rhetoric, punctuation, spelling, and the like—are not poor writing. In fact, they are relatively easy for a competent editor to repair. But poor organization, unclear ideas, non sequiturs, pointless rambling—these are poor writing. These are faults that no amount of editing can repair.

So, far more important than writing is thinking. Clear thinking is essential to produce clear writing, and poor thinking must inevitably produce poor writing.

The Evolution of Bad Writing

A Harvard professor, William Leavitt, remarked that if you don't know where you are going, any road will get you there. That's doubly true for writing. Bad writing is writing that doesn't know where it is going. But it doesn't get there at all. Where it gets is nowhere.

Every piece of writing has to have an objective, a point. Your proposal, overall, must have a point (e. g., "commonality"). It must have a theme that characterizes it, and it must have some goal, some point to be reached, some idea to be argued and proved.

A chapter must have a point. In your proposal, you may have a chapter designed to present your detailed program, another to present your credentials as qualified contractor, another to present and prove your technical arguments.

A paragraph must have a point. (We call it a *topic sentence.*) The paragraph must be about something, and the first sentence should tell the reader what it's about. If it starts off introducing an oscillator, it shouldn't go on to discuss an amplifier. Even a sentence must have a point. It's a statement.

Here's an example taken from a published program on solar energy, and it refers to the sun, which was mentioned in concluding the previous paragraph:

> This amount of potentially useful energy is staggering, but logical. Since all forms of energy originate from the sun, the basic source is, by necessity, a reservoir of almost unimaginable size.

The first sentence of this paragraph is a non sequitur. It's none too clear what the author was trying to say, and it's anything but logical in construction. The second sentence of the paragraph may be arguable, but it's almost unclear in its meaning as is the first sentence. For example, "the basic source" is undoubtedly an appositive for "the sun," but that's my inference. It isn't (grammatically) in apposition to "the sun."

I believe that what the author was trying to say was this:

> The sun is a basic source of energy, from which all energy available on Earth originates. That makes it a reservoir of staggering capacity.

Even worse is an effort to introduce and explain the heat pump:

> A heat pump is correctly identified as a refrigerant machine that can extract useable (sic) heat from a source that is at a temperature too low for *direct* comfort applications.

Eventually, this paragraph makes its point that a large *quantity* of heat at a low temperature can be converted to a smaller quantity of heat at a higher temperature, after explaining that temperature is heat *intensity*, while calories or BTUs are heat *quantity.* A heat pump is a device that can trade the two. The entire section was misconceived. It should have introduced the concepts first and the device after the concepts and principles were explained.

As it was, the entire section never did finally make the closure between the two ideas and make clear that the heat pump was, in fact, a device for making such conversions.

This is a common fault in the writings of technical and professional people. They often fail to make *closures*—sum up and explain the *essence* of what they are saying. In failing to do so, they often fail to make the essential point of the entire piece.

I am sure that many who read the section just quoted from, unless they are already somewhat familiar with the subject, will never grasp the entire point of the discussion. They will be exposed to a set of facts and ideas, but it will be left to the readers to gather them together and draw conclusions from them.

Properly, that section could have started out in either of two ways:

1. "The heat pump is a device for converting quantities of low-temperature heat to smaller quantities of higher-temperature heat." And then the writer should go to the basic principles of why and how this is possible and to the mechanics of how the heat pump does this.
2. The writer could start with basic scientific principles, explaining heat characteristics, explaining the possibility of conversions from quantity to intensity, and then, finally, introducing the heat pump as a practical device that can do this.

Somehow, the author managed to fail to do either, choosing the worst possible course.

The writing reads as though the author sat down with his pen or typewriter and proceeded to wander down the road at random, jotting down whatever occurred to him about the subject. And that's probably exactly what he did, creating a collection of sentences and thoughts related to each other but not arranged in any orderly fashion or pattern, without a central theme, without a *unity.*

Bad writing comes about when you start to write before you are ready to write—before you have thought your subject out, done your research and your planning. You can imagine the results if you tried to build a house or design a system of any kind that way—just letting things happen instead of making them happen.

Here is my own law: only the bad things happen themselves, without help. You have to make the good things happen.

One writers' cliché is that all good writing is rewriting. Many professional writers start with a generalized plan and start writing (but rarely without a plan of some kind). They set down all thoughts and ideas as they occur, following the general outline of their plan. They write until they have said everything they can think of to say or until they have set down all the information they believe necessary about the subject. And then they start over. Then they begin to analyze what they have written, chapter by chapter, page by page, paragraph by paragraph, sentence by sentence. They analyze, criticize, go over the original plan, modify it, sharpen it, add detail. And then they rewrite. They rewrite the entire piece, to be sure that it does the job well.

That's not entirely practical for a proposal. The time element alone usually prohibits extensive rewriting. There's a draft stage, heavy editing, review, and some rewriting, but there is a time constraint on most proposal efforts. It means that the proposal must be done right the first time, or at least close enough to right so that complete rewriting is not necessary. That means planning. And the author's planning is an outline, sufficiently detailed to get it right the first time.

One well-known author considers the use of long and unusual words and the other elements of bad writing to be a conscious or unconscious effort to cover up ineptitude. He's undoubtedly right, if you consider ineptitude equivalent to having nothing to say or having only vague ideas about what you should say.

If good writing is clear communication, then bad writing must be the total lack of communication or a deliberate effort to confound communication. Behavioral psychologists tell us that people reveal their real attitudes and intents by body language. When a person holds his hand over his mouth while speaking, it's supposedly a sign that the person really wants to evade speaking, would rather not say what he is saying, is reluctant to say it at all.

Here's an excerpt from a government document:

> The ratio (or amplification factor) of private sector activity to federal activity can be characterized by the ratio of the number of privately financed to federally financed solar heating and cooling systems installed annually.

What this says (I believe!) is that the ratio of private-sector activity to federal activity in solar heating is the ratio of private-sector financing to federal financing of solar heating systems. Which, of course, says absolutely nothing, except that the ratio is the ratio. What it apparently means to say is that the source of financing for solar heating and cooling plants is the clue to federal versus private solar heating development. But that, of course, is such an obvious fact that it's better not said. Apparently the author thought so too, or he would have said it more plainly.

Here is another gem:

> The following objectives provide qualitative and quantitative milestones toward which the program can strive.
>
> MEANING: The program should try to reach the following objectives.

This example suggests that the writer was hesitant to say what he did, reluctant to take a firm position, so he *wrote* hesitantly, revealing that he was not sure of his position. He was preparing an escape route, a means for retreating, should anyone challenge his statement of objectives as valid and worthy.

All writing has *connotative* meaning as well as denotative or literal meaning. All writing *suggests* a meaning or a shade of meaning beyond what appears on the surface of the language. And inevitably, all writing suggests the mental set of the writer. The style, the choice of words, the organization of the language tell the discerning reader, most clearly, whether the writer really believes what he says, whether he is confident, hesitant, fearful, uncertain, etc.

Many research reports will say: "The data gathered in the study, upon close analysis, tend to indicate the possibility that under certain circumstances . . . ." What clearer indication do you need that the writer has drawn no real conclusions and is extremely cautious about saying anything at all, perhaps nothing more than could have been said without the benefit of the research? How could he expect any reader to have any confidence in what he is saying?

Communication Is Not the Only Casualty of Bad Writing

The point was made earlier that you cannot expect to sell a customer anything he does not understand; that is, if you fail to communicate, to make the customer understand your proposed program, products, services, approaches, etc., you can hardly expect him to buy.

The point was further made that to achieve credibility, you must help the customer to understand your arguments. You must communicate your rationale in sufficient detail and with sufficient logical argument to put his mind at ease and to persuade him that you have made a proper analysis and a proper plan.

But now we come to another aspect of achieving credibility: your own enthusiasm and confidence, as revealed in your writing. Will the customer believe in you and your proposal if you evidently do not believe in yourself and your proposal?

Write badly enough—vaguely, evasively, cautiously—and your customer cannot but conclude that you are yourself doubtful and hesitant and are quite possibly writing with your tongue in your cheek and both index fingers crossed over their neighboring fingers.

In the world of salesmanship, enthusiasm and confidence are deemed to be essential qualities. The prospect must be aware that you (the salesman) believe in what you are offering and are completely turned on about it.

A single, casual call on a gentleman in OSHA (Labor Department) led me into a string of contracts worth a great deal of money. Later, when I had done a good bit of work for this gentleman and had become rather well acquainted with him, he told me that my initial approach had been exactly right for him: I hadn't come on "too strong," as he put it, but had approached him with apparently genuine interest in his problems and needs and, most important, confidence in and enthusiasm for the services I could offer to help him. Anything less and he would have shaken my hand, thanked me for my time, and advised me, "Don't call me; I'll call you." But I would, of course, have never heard further from him.

Proposals must reflect that same confidence and enthusiasm. You can't really expect an executive to commit hundreds of thousands—perhaps millions—of dollars to a program in which even you apparently do not have great confidence. There, credibility becomes a casualty of faltering and uncertain expression, as an emotional impact of the style. Make no mistake about it: the true intent of the writer always shows through the style, just as you can read between the lines of most statements of work and detect the implications.

Proposal writers often have the notion that by being vague and general in what they say in their pages, they encourage the reader to place the best possible interpretation on the language and to read the right things into the gaps. It doesn't happen. The reader wrinkles a brow, looks perplexed, then shrugs and casually drops the proposal into what some evaluators have called the "so what? file."

How to Avoid the Problem

Far better to avoid than to attempt to correct the problem. Avoidance —prevention—is far easier than correction. And that involves just two major considerations:

1. Thorough research, research to the point where you are sure of your conclusions, opinions, what you wish to offer the customer, what you wish to say—exactly—about each topic.
2. Thorough planning, to the point of outlining before you write.

There is at least one other consideration, which is highly important—so important that it merits its own paragraph and discussion.

Self-editing. The ability to edit one's own work is a sure preventive. But by *self-editing,* I do not mean reviewing and correcting for grammar, punctuation, and the like. What I do mean is this: develop the ability to recognize when your writing is beginning to slip into vague generalities and to depart from specifics.

It is not at all uncommon for a writer to rationalize his own vague writing as being the best way to "say it," rather than facing up to the probable truth: he really doesn't know what he's talking about (writing about, that is) and is simply trying to wing it.

When you find that you have written something that is evasive and general and fails to make positive, direct statements, to summarize, to interpret, to capsulize, take it as an all but certain indication that you need to go back and do either more research or more thinking about the subject —perhaps both.

To an editor, the signs are plain enough: where the writing is highly detailed and specific, the writer was in familar, well-known territory. Where the writing becomes general and skips superficially through the topic, the writer was on unfamiliar ground, feeling the way gingerly. The writer should learn to recognize these signs before the editor gets to see the manuscript and to recognize what they mean—and then take the appropriate action: scrap the manuscript and rethink the subject, doing additional research, if necessary.

Outlining and Planning

Outlining presents special problems, and one in particular, Here is the way far too many outlines read:

Maintenance considerations
    Preventive maintenance
    Corrective maintenance
    Overhaul and repair

Chided that this is a bit skimpy, the writer may then proceed to amplify the outline in this manner:

Maintenance
    Preventive
        Inspection
        Replacement of worn parts

> Lubrication
> Cleaning
> Corrective
> Troubleshooting
> Fault isolation
> Replacement
> Overhaul and repair
> Disassembly
> Replacement
> Reassembly

That is an improvement, of course, but still not nearly enough. It's fault is not only in the fact that it's still somewhat skimpy and incomplete but is a common fault of most outlines: it lists what the writer proposes to talk about but not what he will say about each topic. Therefore, it's a generalized outline that might be applied to any writing effort rather than being specific to the writing effort at hand. It describes what will be covered but not how the subjects will be covered. Nor does it give any idea of the depth of detail into which the writer will go in his proposal.

Fortunately, most RFPs and statements of work tell you what depth of detail the customer wishes to see by furnishing lists of specifications and indicating what "responsiveness" means, in the given case. In the next chapter, we'll offer a suggested means for ensuring responsiveness, which will also furnish a checklist to aid you in planning and outlining.

A Suggested Aid to Good Writing

In the case cited earlier, where a writer presented a rather confused explanation of a heat pump, the point was that the writer should have summarized the essence of heat pump operation and principle immediately, or at least he should have led up to it by laying the groundwork first. But at some point, the explanation should have identified the key characteristic of the heat pump—that it "pumps" heat by converting heat quantity to heat intensity.

The ability to summarize a complex concept is a key to clear writing —a key to true understanding, which is a vital prerequisite to clear writing, as we have pointed out before.

You should, as a writer, be able to do this for every concept: organize the idea and present it in lay language, in a nutshell that captures the essence of the idea. Unless you can do this, you probably do not have a true understanding of the concept. And you can interpret any inability to express a concept in lay language as probable imperfection in your understanding.

For example, educational technologists use the word *behavior* in a special sense, and they stress that a training program should not be undertaken without first developing a set of "behavioral objectives." They go on to explain that a behavioral objective is a statement of what the student should be able to *do* (e.g., solve a quadratic equation or solder an electrical connection) as a result of the training.

Confronted with a proposal that expressed a set of behavioral objectives but did not define them as such, a senior staff psychologist demanded to know where the behavioral objectives were. He failed to recognize them because they weren't labeled. And that's a pretty good indication that he was dealing in techhnical jargon rather than in concepts and ideas—in what the jargon *meant*.

There's an aspect of the syndrome that leads to much bad writing— dealing in jargon rather than in meanings. It seems to be a common failing of technical and professional specialists of all kinds.

When transistors first began to appear in widespread use, engineers and technicians who were unfamiliar with them were flooded with technical literature which explained that, although vacuum tubes are voltage devices, transistors are current devices and that that factor was an absolutely critical requirement to comprehend, if one wanted to understand transistors.

Eventually, that turned out to be sheer nonsense, at least as far as practical application and understanding were concerned. Transistors are turned on and off by voltage differentials, just as vacuum tubes are, and the amount of the voltage differential (within the operating limits of the device) controls the amount of current flow through a transistor, just as it does through a vacuum tube.

To argue otherwise was sheer pedantry, serving absolutely no good purpose in proliferating knowledge and applications theory. Certainly, it only made it more difficult for the engineer and technician to understand the transistor, since operation was based on a new and different theory, whereas it would have been every bit as valid to employ explanations similar to those used in training engineers and technicians in vacuum tube theory. It was an exercise in hairsplitting, serving more to confuse than to enlighten the reader.

Unfortunately, some professional people write proposals in the same way, splitting hairs over fine points and thereby missing the main point and the opportunities to impress the discerning reader that they really do have a deep understanding of the proposition, since they can express it in simple terms that anyone can follow. And this ability is far more impressive to many readers than the ability to hunt up rare and difficult words found only in the unabridged Webster's.

One wise writer has made the observation that he always visualizes himself explaining a proposition to his young daughter, and he structures his language and ideas as though he were. That's a good way to do it. Even though you may believe that you are writing for the edification of another expert or specialist in your field, deliberately assume that you are writing also to managerial people who are laymen in your specialized field and that you must make them understand your concepts.

This can be done with the most complex ideas, if you use a little imagination, truly think about it, and truly understand it. Georges Gamow managed it with Einsteinian physics and relativity, written for the layman (*1, 2, 3 Infinity*) and Lancelot Hogben managed it with mathematics (*Mathematics for the Millions*).

Here are some examples of bad writing and how they can be improved.

From a Labor Department monograph of job analysis:

> A review and analysis of job content data can illuminate situations in which employees with given levels of expertise are performing work significantly above or below those levels or have been given duties which are essentially unrelated to the primary content of their jobs.

It takes a few minutes' study, but it soon becomes obvious from such study that what this writer was laboring mightily to say was simply this:

> People are often assigned work either above or below their technical capability or unrelated to that capability. Analysis reveals this.

Or from a Labor Department monograph on apprenticeship programs:

> Central to a successful redesign of apprenticeship training is systematized followup information gleaned from studies of completers and dropouts enrolled in programs during the recent past. Is the education apprentices receive while participating in the process adequate and useful to the degree that they remain in the occupation for which they were trained? Does serving an apprenticehood provide completers with greater occupational and upward mobility than their less formally trained counterparts? What factors are likely to cause apprentices to become dropouts? And, if training is terminated before completion, does it still have some value to the individual in terms of providing him with a marketable skill?

Which says:

> What happens to graduates and dropouts of apprenticeship programs will tell us how to redesign the programs. We need to know how many enter into and remain

in the trades they were trained for; whether graduates of such programs are more successful in related employment than others who didn't undergo such formal training; what causes dropping out; and whether dropouts have learned enough to get a job.

Few are better at obfuscation than the framers of our laws. Here is a single sentence from the Consumer Product Safety Act. You figure this one out and how it could have been said more simply and directly:

Except as provided by paragraph (2) of this subsection, not less than 30 days prior to its public disclosure of any information obtained under this Act, or to be disclosed to the public in connection therewith (unless the Commission finds out that the public health and safety requires a lesser period of notice), the Commission shall, to the extent practicable, notify, and provide a summary of the information to, each manufacturer or private labeler of any consumer product to which such information pertains, if the manner in which such consumer product is to be designated or described in such information will permit the public to ascertain readily the identity of such manufacturer or private labeler, and shall provide such manufacturer or private labeler with a reasonable opportunity to submit comments to the Commission in regard to such information.

Give up? All this says is that if some manufacturer's or private labeler's product is going to be criticized (e.g., pronounced unsafe) publicly by the commission, and the public criticism will clearly identify the product to the public, the manufacturer or private labeler must know about the intended disclosure at least 30 days before it happens, so as to have a chance to respond and rebut. The exceptions are those cases where the commission decides that public health and safety are so threatened that faster action is needed to protect the public and is unwilling to hold up the disclosure a full 30 days, the other exception explained in another paragraph.

It is almost impossible to write a sentence as long as the one reproduced here and achieve clarity. Few individuals can retain the original thought throughout a sentence of that length. The reader must stop and analyze the sentence. And if he is under no compulsion to do so, he probably won't. He may even discard your proposal with a weary sigh if he faces that situation. Especially if he has many others to read.

On the other hand, the simple act of chopping long sentences into several short ones, while it may help in many cases, is not necessarily the answer either. There is such a thing as getting thoughts into some logical sequence—"logical," that is, in terms of reader comprehension, not *your* comprehension. You're writing from the vantage point of having some idea, even if only half-formed, whereas your reader has no idea what you are getting at until he reads what you have written. He needs help.

This goes back to the point made earlier, that of summarizing the main idea at the beginning, letting the reader get an idea of what is coming. Take that lengthy sentence we just read, for example. It started out with one exception, mentioned the 30 days required, went on to mention information to be disclosed to the public, stipulated that this applied to those cases where the public would be able to identify product by label or manufacturer, and only then got to the real point of the entire thing— giving the manufacturer/labeler a chance to defend his product or answer the information.

It should have started with that latter thought, or at least it should have made the point early enough so that the reader could see where the sentence was going. The reader may be able to retain quite a lot of information while battling through a verbose sentence or paragraph, if the information has some clear point made early or if there is a sequential, related string of ideas building to a main point.

"Telegraph" when you write. Use the old-fashioned dictum: "Tell 'em what you're going to tell 'em, tell 'em, then tell 'em what you told 'em."

Ideally, the statement should have started with something such as "A manufacturer or private labeler shall know at least 30 days in advance what information is to be released publicly about his product, if the information identifies his product." Etc. From this point on, the reader can relate. He knows what the idea is, what it's all about.

15

Proposal Formats and Packaging

Only bad things happen all by themselves. Good things happen only when they are MADE TO HAPPEN.

—Holtz's Law

The "River Raft"

The typical proposal—and *typical* means "average," or not very good— follows a river-raft philosophy: it simply rambles along, following the general course of the river and the random currents. It's an uncontrolled presentation, just as a river raft is an uncontrolled conveyance—or, at least, the modicum of control consists simply of maneuvering among the random currents, spontaneously, as the need appears.

Successful proposals are rarely written that way. The successful proposal is planned carefully and steered carefully, according to the plan, its ultimate destination. It doesn't arrive there by accident, and it doesn't detour along the way. It is navigated, piloted through the shoals and deep water and across the finish line.

A proposal has a beginning, a middle, and an end, as does any organized piece of writing. They should be readily distinguishable from each other. Overall, the proposal should follow this general logic:

I. Introduce yourself—briefly (with promise of details to appear later in proposal)—presenting your general qualifications.

II. Recapitulation of the requirement, in terms that do not parrot the customer's language but make it abundantly clear that you fully understand what is wanted.

III. Discussions, to expand on your understanding, to add to the customers's understanding, to demonstrate your complete competence in the field, to present technical arguments and develop a reasoned approach, so presented as to persuade the customer that it is the best approach.

IV. Your specific program, which implements the approach you have just sold the customer and serves as a firm promise of the desired results. It's a firm commitment, a pledge to deliver the goods.

V. The remainining credibility factors: your qualifications as an organization, your staff résumés, and their qualifications. You must present *all* qualifications—staff, physical facilities, experience, and any other important resources.

Formatting and packaging this information is important. It must flow smoothly, permitting the reader to progress through the text without confusion; it must be overall a logical presentation; it must stress the more important points; and it must aid the reader in evaluating it.

It's a basic rule of salesmanship that the sale is closed more easily when the salesman makes it easier for the customer to say yes than to say no. That's why a smart salesman asks you whether you want delivery Monday or Tuesday, whether you prefer, red or green, etc. That's why a mail-order sales package often includes a return envelope, postage-paid, and an order form that requires only your name and address. In proposals, you can make it easy for the reader to give you a high technical-point score—easier than finding reasons to give you a low one.

A General Approach

Each proposal is inherently an individual effort because ordinarily the proposal is a design for a custom service or a custom-built product—that is why you have been invited to submit a proposal and enter into technical competition rather than mere price competition. At the same time, there is a general approach to writing most proposals, and a generalized framework can be used as a basis for organizing and developing your proposal. (See the following suggested outline.)

There are cases where the RFP/SOW dictates a given format and structure for proposals, and this may differ widely from your organization's usual practice. Obviously, you can't—or shouldn't—fight the customer on this: follow the requested format, by all means, if one has been stipulated.

More commonly, the RFP spells out the kind of information required without stipulating any particular format for it. In this case, the choice is yours, of course.

Here are a few basic considerations about format, order of presentation, etc.:

1. The presentation should be such as to present the reader with minimum difficulties in following the writer's train of thought.
2. The classic method of presentation, and the one most of us find easiest to assimilate, is to proceed from the general to the particular.
3. Deductive logic is much easier for most of us than inductive logic. Deductive logic is the result of applying known principles or premises to a set of facts. Inductive reasoning is deriving principles from the study of facts.
4. All writing, if it is to be orderly and organized, must have a beginning, a middle, and an end. That means an introduction, a body, and a conclusion. Or, in classic advice, "Tell them what you're going to tell them, tell them, then tell them what you told them."
5. A proposal, when it is written and offered to a customer, is a sales presentation. It may become a "contractual document" later— you hope it will—but during its generation and at all times prior to its acceptance, it is a sales presentation. It should follow the known principles of success in selling.
6. The basic, accepted principles in selling are to get attention, to arouse interest, to develop credibility, and to ask for action. Some authorities add to create desire. Desire to buy already exists, in this case—you've been invited to bid, and the customer will buy one of the proposals. And you don't have to ask for action here, either, because the customer has announced that he will buy. But he does have to come to believe that you can and will perform, as promised—that's the "credibility."

One thing we know about buyers' motivation is that no one ever buys a thing or a service; they buy results, benefits, what the thing or service *does.* If your prospective customer asks you to develop a computer program, it's not because he wants a computer program *per se* but because he has a problem or need that the computer program will solve or satisfy. That's the result he seeks—the "benefit." In that sense, all businesses are service businesses: customers are always buying a service—what your product or effort produces as a result.

Bear this in mind as you develop your sales arguments in your proposal. The customer wants some benefit, some result—and that's all he wants. As you analyze his need and what you can offer to satisfy it, always think in terms of the final result the customer is after—the benefit of your service.

In all your presentations, in every way possible concentrate on making the customer perceive the result or benefit. As you examine alternatives, explain how one produces better *results* than the other. And "better" can mean less costly, more reliable, faster, easier, etc.

Make the front part of your proposal primarily an explanation of the results the customer wants—make sure you understand what results he wants and that he knows that you know what results he wants—and a pledge to produce those results. Stress this aspect as early in the proposal as possible and as frequently throughout the proposal as possible.

Suggested General Proposal Outline

Front Matter

> Copy of transmittal letter
> Title page
> Foreword or preface (optional)
> Table of contents
> Proposal response matrix
> Executive summary

Chapter I: Introduction

1. *About the offeror*
   Brief introduction to the proposer, general qualifications, indication that details will be presented later in proposal.
2. *Appraisal of the requirement* (or problem, as appropriate)
   State customer's requirement/problem, in your own words, stressing element(s) you consider most significant.

Chapter II: Discussion

Pick up where Chapter I stopped, expand into generalized discussion of requirement, problems, state of the art, etc., leading reader through your own analyses, study of various alternatives, reasons for selecting chosen approach. This must include all relevant technical arguments and prove the case. Topics (which should get sideheads) may include, but are not necessarily restricted to:

- The essential need (problem)
- The state of the art
- The various alternatives
- Comparison of alternatives
- Selection of the best alternative
- Appreciation of contractor skills and resources needed (may work in plugs for yourself here by referring to past projects!)

The selection of the demonstrated best alternative is your approach, and this should be made clear by having a sidehead that says *approach* and is sprung directly from that set of alternative examinations and technical arguments.

Chapter III: Proposed Program

Here is where you present the specific proposal itself—what you actually now offer to do. What has gone before was intended to lead up to this and to show that this is *the* way to go—the best way. Conversely, having proved your approach, as you should have, this section must demonstrate clearly that you have the detailed plan, the resources, and the will to implement that approach properly, for this *is* the implementation plan. You must cross every *t* and dot every *i* here. Following are some of the topics and sideheads that should appear in this section, with possible others in some cases. The RFP/SOW should guide you in this and in how much importance (relatively) each of these topics should assume.

1. *Project organization and staff*
   Explain how the project will be organized, staffed, housed, and supported. Indicate a clearly thought-out, detailed plan, including responsibilities, reporting, direction, liaison with customer. (Key résumés may go here.)
2. *Tasks, subtasks, phases, man loading*
   Ideal for tabular and/or graphic presentations, listing main phases and tasks/subtasks, indicating how and to whom (functionally)

assigned, estimates of man hours/days required for each, projected elapsed times for functions to be completed.

3. *Management*

Discuss project management (use management chart) and control; explain management controls, reporting, other details to give reader complete understanding of management plan. Make clear that a *plan* is involved.

4. *Quality control*

Explain how you will ensure quality performance/products. Should tie in with management plan and other procedures/controls. Make clear that you have a quality control system, which will be followed.

5. *Special provisions*

How you will take care of contingencies—unexpected emergencies of any kind—staff illnesses, uncontrollable schedule slippages, other problems, especially those difficult to anticipate.

6. *Deliverables*

List specific items to be delivered—reports, manuals, prototypes, illustrations—whatever they are. Include all.

7. *Schedules*

Make firm commitments on schedules—*when* you will deliver an item or complete a task. Must tie in with what you have said about handling problems.

Chapter IV: Experience and Qualifications

This is your "company résumé"—an accounting of successful projects and the capabilities you offer the customer. Describe your organization generally, with charts. Show top management and reporting orders. Describe management systems and controls. Describe and list specific physical resources—offices, shops, laboratories, equipment, materials, purchasing, administrative staff, subsidiaries—whatever is appropriate to the requirement.

Résumés may have appeared in a prior section, but you may offer additional résumés here, to demonstrate backup capabilities for staff and capabilities of top management and contract administrators, cost control, etc.

You may choose, on the other hand, to include all résumés here and provide only thumbnail sketches of key (proposed) project staff in the prior chapter. Both methods work satisfactorily, but the customer should be able to find the résumés without difficulty, and he should be able to identify those individuals proposed for the project.

Some of the topics and sideheads that may appear here include the following:

- The ——— Corporation: A General Description
- Corporate structure and management
- Physical assets: offices, equipment, shops, laboratories
- Relevant past projects
- Current projects
- Support staff
- General management controls
- Subcontracts and purchasing procedures
- Cost control systems
- Consultants available
- Letters of commendation/testimonials
- Honors and awards
- Specific contract information
- References

Chapter V: Highlights of Proposal

This is optional. You may think it unnecessary if you have included an executive summary in the front matter. However, it is somewhat different in its coverage than the executive summary is in that it is not merely an abstract of the proposal—and indeed is not an abstract at all—but is a recapitulation of only those points you believe to be your most important selling points. It is a reminder to the reader of the reasons for awarding you the contract. (Companies have sometimes called this "Reasons for Awarding This Contract to the XYZ Corporation.")

Relate this to the suggested general outline enclosed here. Where is the first place you can suggest the benefits of what you propose? In the transmittal letter, of course. Although that is addressed to the contracting officer, it is a common practice to enclose a copy of it in the proposal itself, immediately inside the cover.

If you use a foreword or preface, you can devote this almost entirely to why the customer should buy from you. You can do it again in the executive summary. And you can do it still again in the introduction.

If you have handled this properly, you should have thoroughly whetted the customer's appetite by now. He should be panting to start turning pages to see how you will accomplish these promised great results for him.

If he is not already interested, you are already in trouble. Every page of your proposal should be designed specifically to persuade the reader to turn to the next page, to want to see what is on the next page.

In fiction writing, this is known as a *narrative hook,* which refers to "hooking" the reader. Note how they do it on TV: even before they announce the title of the program or launch into the opening commercial, they give you a brief preview—something comical, intriguing, exciting— anything that will (hopefully) hook you into wanting to see what it's all about.

Narrative Hooks in Proposals

The proposal is not fiction (or shouldn't be). Yet there are ways to hook readers of proposals, too. For one thing, find the most startling thing you have to say in your proposal and telegraph it up front. Suppose, for example, that you have cleverly thought up some method for effecting a 20% cost reduction. Mention this early:

In the following pages, Zilch Electronics will reveal a technique we have developed especially for the proposed project, which will cut the cost of annealing the floogie bar by 19.5% through a revolutionary new annealing process, resulting from tests we conducted in Kobe for the Japanese Navy.

Or:

In a project similar to this, Zilch Electronics developed a special system for production-line testing that resulted in an average failure rate of 0.005%, with an average failure-free operating cycle of nearly four years. We believe that this method may be applied to the proposed project, and we shall discuss it later in this proposal.

The hook may be on almost any subject. Perhaps you have managed to recruit the world's most outstanding scientist in celestial mechanics or have got a consulting agreement signed with the most prominent authority in heart-valve repair. Of course, the idea must relate to the project and better results for the customer.

Perhaps your company has some outstanding new piece of equipment—the most advanced computer or an electron microscope.

In many cases, I've found an obscure but important problem that will probably not be mentioned by anyone else. I've turned such things into hooks by dramatizing them up front in the proposal and promising to

reveal a solution for this most difficult problem, which should be anticipated by any competent contractor (thereby suggesting that any proposal
that fails to recognize and identify this problem is of questionable quality). I've found this approach to work quite well when I could identify
such a potential problem.

Bear in mind, as you seek out such items, that the customer may not
be particularly expert in the field and that you may have to educate him so
that he will be able to recognize the seriousness or the importance of what
you are saying. That is, perhaps a failure rate of 0.005% doesn't mean
much to him. You may have to explain that this compares with a typical
failure rate, for such equipment, of 0.1%, or whatever the usual failure
rate is. You have to be sure, in short, that you make the point clearly
enough.

Statistics (simplified) can be very useful. If you can promise that
your design will result in a search radar that can detect, track, and monitor 150 hostile missiles while continuing high and low search scans, you
should be able to make your point that your proposal is worth reading!

The most unforgivable sin of a writer, like that of an actor, is boring
the reader. Perhaps a proposal is not the kind of literature you'd like to
while away an evening with, but it does not have to be stultifying.

If you have not detected it yet, you should begin to realize now that
you can write the front part of your proposal only after you have written
the middle and the end! You can hardly select the most interesting facets
without having examined them all. My personal preference is to write a
"dummy" introduction as a lead. I then write the rest of the proposal and
come back and completely rewrite the introduction. That's a personal
work habit and not necessarily the best way for you. But you must never
try to finalize the introductory material before you have written the whole
proposal.

In any case, do not waste time in the introduction describing your
organization and your general qualifications. Introduce yourself, describe
your broad qualifications as briefly as possible and in such terms as to be
at least superficially credible (e.g., name a few prominent customers for
whom you have done work), and hasten to refer the reader to the detailed
qualifications section that will appear later. Focus attention on whatever
appears to be a critical point—the excellence of your staff, your physical
facilities, your extensive experience, the low cost, or whatever the RFP
has led you to believe is uppermost in the customer's mind as the most
important factor(s).

Of course, you should try to relate whatever hook you use to that
customer-perceived most-important factor. Here are examples of how an

introduction to an organization might be written in a variety of ways, to stress any of several possible major appeals or themes:

> Zilch Electronics is pleased to offer the U.S. Navy an extraordinary design for an advanced voice scrambler, based on a completely revolutionary approach. After many years of supplying U.S. military organizations with secure communications equipment, Zilch has developed a concept under which even should the device fall into the hands of an enemy, it will be of no value to them and will not endanger U.S. Navy security.

> Zilch Electronics has been pleased to employ the services of Dr. John A. Mac-Gowan, a well-known authority in secure communications concepts, to aid in the analysis of the need described in the subject RFP. Dr. MacGowan has signed a consulting agreement with Zilch and will be an active, full-time consultant and technical director on the proposed project. Zilch has assembled an outstanding team of specialists for the project, representing the most authoritative knowledge in the field of secure communications, all with extensive experience in military design programs.

> After careful analysis of the need described in the subject RFP, the special Zilch Electronics team assembled for the study has developed a remarkable design. The design proposed in these pages is based entirely on Zilch's past successful experience in developing military communications equipment. But at the same time, past successful designs have been so simplified that the proposed design will result in a voice communicator of such light weight and low cost that it may be used as individual equipment, to be issued freely and deemed expendable, drastically simplifying maintenance problems.

Of course, many other variants are possible, but you can see that it is possible to write a hook in the opening sentence.

The Executive Summary

Most proposals are read, studied, reviewed, and evaluated by a team of government people, although there may be one dominant executive who leads the review and is largely responsible for the final determination. Presumably, the top managerial executives of the agency will not study your proposal in all its details but will want a brief review of your general approach, plans, and qualifications. They want only an abstract of your proposal, leaving it to their staffs to make the detailed review and evaluation. They may read your introduction, may even skim through your proposal—or they may not.

For the benefit of top management in the agency, it is customary and advisable, in a proposal for a project of any substantial size, to provide an abstract usually called an *executive summary*. And while this is presumably intended for the executives, everyone who reads the proposal will usually read the summary first.

The executive summary, which is normally part of the front matter (but may be provided as a separate document, particularly when the proposal is quite large), should be written with this use in mind. Describe your proposal in its essence, but be sure to get in your major selling points. This was done in the following example of an executive summary in a proposal that wound up as Number 1 in technical evaluation. It was accompanied by an overall chart of the project, presented at "high level" (simplified and generalized).

SECTION I. EXECUTIVE SUMMARY

THE OFFEROR:

The offeror of this proposal is a partnership between two firms. One represents experience in, and knowledge of, logistics management, government, military organizations, and international operations management. The other represents knowledge, experience, and existing resources in international shipping and shipping management, especially in Saudi Arabia.

————is able to offer the U.S. Corps of Engineers the following set of advantages:

1. A DEDICATED ORGANIZATION, TAILORED FOR THE JOB. LOGOPS was designed especially for the proposed project.

2. RESOURCES IN BEING. LOGOPS has 1,400 people and ample quantities of trucks, barges, cranes, and offices in Saudi Arabia at this moment, ready to be placed in the service of the Corps. LOGOPS also has committed complete warehousing and shipping facilities in CONUS, including vehicles and handling equipment.

3. STAFF IN BEING. LOGOPS' top- and intermediate-level executives and functional managers are already "on board," alerted to the project requirements and ready to be assigned to it immediately.

4. A CONCENTRATION OF STRENGTH. LOGOPS offers both organization and staff capability. One proposed executive is a former Deputy Assistant Secretary of Defense, with extensive experience in logistics and military supply planning and management on a worldwide scale; another has spent many years in Saudi Arabia in logistics management functions; all represent many years of relevant experience and capability.

5. THOROUGHNESS OF PLANNING AND PREPARATION. LOGOPS has spent a year planning for this project. We have conducted studies and investigations, here and in Saudi Arabia, and have developed detailed plans for the proposed project. Unlike most proposal efforts, this has not been a hasty improvisation but has been carefully assembled, as these pages will show.

6. A CAPABILITY FOR IMMEDIATE MOBILIZATION. Because of all these assets—year-long preparation; in-being human and material resources, here and in Saudi Arabia; and detailed arrangements already

made for start-up—LOGOPS offers the U.S. Corps of Engineers an unprecedented rapid mobilization capability. LOGOPS can be in initial operation immediately and in full-scale operation in a much shorter time than that stipulated in the RFP.

7. ARTICULATED FOR RESPONSE. LOGOPS recognizes that the project will be characterized by problems, by changes, and by unanticipated and sudden requirements. LOGOPS has therefore been designed to be responsive to the Corps under a widely varying set of conditions. The organization's structure is designed for mobility of support to functional managers, to back them up with both planning and administrative support, permitting line managers to concentrate on their missions. At the same time, LOGOPS managers have been chosen for more than technical skills: they have been chosen for managerial competence—the ability to make decisions and take actions as situations require. They have been made completely familiar with this project and will be indoctrinated regularly, not only on the need for responsiveness to the Corps, but for exercising the managerial initiative to meet the needs of the Corps.

8. TECHNICAL APPROACHES AND PLANS TAILORED FOR THE PROJECT. LOGOPS proposes conventional technical approaches for "normal" situations but recognizes that situations may rarely be "normal." Our approaches therefore include an extensive and well-thought-out set of procedures for emergencies—delayed shipments, changed RDDs, sudden requirements, mechanical breakdowns, etc. We have also made preparations to establish safety and training programs to begin on Day 1. Further, we have selected a proposed CONUS site which is at dockside and will thereby eliminate time and cost of drayage from the CONUS warehouse to the dock. Also, anticipating the probability of widely varying peaks and valleys of activity, LOGOPS proposes to staff minimally at the outset. Below the level of functional managers and functional specialists, LOGOPS will employ part-time and temporary help and will shift its personnel and physical resources, as the situation demands.

9. COMMUNICATIONS AND INFORMATION FOR MANAGEMENT CONTROL. LOGOPS proposes to ensure rapid communications and a complete flow of information, both internally and between the Corps and LOGOPS as part of the overall ADP system. This system will function to provide reports, other documentation, and support of cost control systems for both LOGOPS and the Corps of Engineers.

10. OTHER LOGOPS RESOURCES. LOGOPS has guaranteed access to, and control of, shipping offices throughout Europe and other parts of the world. These are available to be placed in the service of the project to aid in shipping material from non-U.S. sources, for assistance in recruitment of managers and specialists outside the United States, and for any other needed purpose. A shipping office in Houston, Texas, is also affiliated and available for such assistance as LOGOPS may require.

LOGOPS recognizes as the main mission of this project an integrated support system of logistics management and material movement. The efficiency of execution depends on management support—planning, information, problem solving, reporting, administration, and communications.

Title Page

The title page (Figure 21) is simply a convention. It has no real value, perhaps, but it is customary to use one. Ordinarily, it is simply a reproduction of the proposal cover, with the addition of a date. However, it

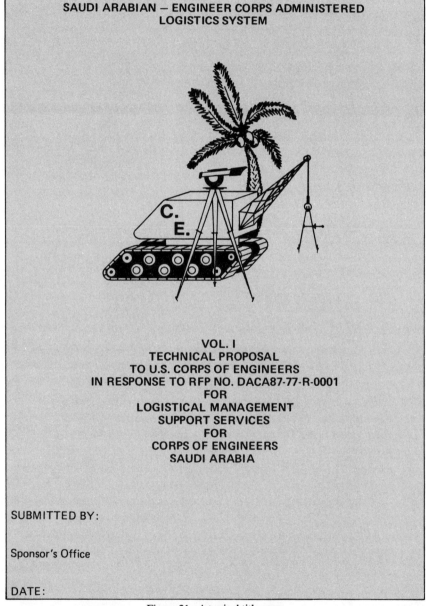

Figure 21. A typical title page.

should carry the RFP number and the RFP title and specify that it is a technical proposal in response to that RFP. The information may or may not appear on the cover. My personal preference is to use the cover in some imaginative way to command attention. An example or two of how to do that will be given presently.

Response Matrix

The response matrix, which may be called by other names in other places, can be one of your most powerful tools for winning maximum technical points. It develops as one of the first actions following a decision to bid—to write a proposal. Its value is twofold: (1) it virtually ensures that you will not allow anything to fall between the cracks if you have prepared it properly (you will have listed every possible item to which you must make a specific response) and (2) it guides the proposal evaluators in scoring your proposal technically, against their missing your response to specific points.

It is not at all unusual for those evaluating the usual river-raft proposal to miss points in your response, especially since your proposal probably does not follow the sequence of checkpoints that the customer has in front of him as he reads and reviews.

To develop such a matrix, you begin by studying the RFP and listing every item called out in it to which a response is requested. (The sample that appears here (Table 3) is page 1 of 17 pages that made up the complete matrix.) In the format shown as a sample, the location of the specification in the RFP/SOW is first identified; then a brief summary of the proposal's response is entered, followed by detailed identification of where the response may be found.

Note that the proposal references often have multiple listings for RFP items called out. This is normal because you may have to address the same item in several places, for example; under both technical discussion and specific proposed program, and perhaps again under management discussions, deliverable items, schedules, past experience, etc.

Once the draft response-matrix is completed, it forms an excellent basis for outlining, strategy formulation, flowchart development, and general writing. It is also valuable as a check list for editors and reviewers, to ensure that every point has been responded to, even fill-in forms.

It is particularly important that you have included all evaluation items that were brought to your attention in the RFP. Evaluation items deserve your special attention, of course, and should be always in mind as

Table 3.   Proposal Response Matrix

		RFP Address and References
Sec.	Para. No.	Summary
Part 1, D	1	Information to offerors
	2a.	Failure to submit requested data
	2b.	Compliance statement
	2c.	Completeness, cross-reference, and index
	2d.	Data submitted does not relieve submission of contract data
	2e(1)(a)	Content of technical section, Volume I
	2e(1)(b)	Time-phasing for Saudi material
	2e(1)(c)	Objectives and understanding of problems
	2e(1)(d)*1a*	Current and proposed organization
	2e(1)(d)*1b*	Extent and type of subcontracting and use of subsidiaries
	2e(1)(d)*1c*	Personnel mixture proposed (US/TCN/Saudi Arabians)
	2e(1)(d)*2a*	Identify personnel contributors (writers), including subcontractors
	2e(1)(d)*2b*	Résumés of key personnel
	2e(1)(d)*2c*	Level of contractor representation for postaward meeting.

you develop the response matrix, the executive summary, the highlights, and all other key areas.

The use of such a matrix follows the principle of making it easier for the customer. While the RFP will usually give you a general idea of specific evaluation items and their relative weighting, in practice the evaluators usually have a somewhat more detailed set of criteria and weighting factors. In the normal course of their review, they will read your proposal first, then go back through it again to make specific judgments

Table 3. (Continued)

CDL No.	DD Form	Volume	Sec./Chap.	Page
			Proposal Address	
		Acknowledged		
		Acknowledged		
		I	Statement of compli- ance	ii
		I	Proposal response matrix	
		II	Proposal response matrix	
		Acknowledged		
		I	II/2	7
			II/3	1,4
			II/4	5,6
			II/5	1,2
			III/1	12,13
			III/2	8
			III/3	8,9
		I	II/5	22
		I	II,III	All
		I	II/1	1,4,5,8
		I	II/1	33
		I	II/1	37
		I	II/1	38
		I	II/1	38
		I	II/1	58

and point awards. The response matrix aids them in looking things up and making judgments.

Résumés

In almost every case, you are required to provide résumés of the key personnel whom you propose to use on the proposed project. The résumés may easily be the single most important part of your entire proposal. In many cases, the agency is most concerned with the caliber of the proposed staff and scrutinizes the résumés with great care and interest. Résumés should be selected and prepared with the greatest care.

Devices That Help the Reader

It used to be a practice, in printing technical books and textbooks generally, to leave a rather wide outside margin on each page and to print there, opposite each paragraph, a short phrase indicating what the paragraph is about. This was called a *gloss*. It's a most helpful device for the reader, giving him both a preview of what appears on the page and a convenient means to track down desired information.

Another, somewhat similar device, is the *blurb*. The blurb is a brief teaser statement, appearing under the title of a magazine article or a short story. It also presents the essence of information and is intended to lure the reader into the piece.

Both of these can be employed to good advantage in proposals. In one system used by a large aerospace company, the proposal is arranged so that each page is an entity unto itself, with a headline, a blurb, and text, with each page covering one topic only.

In a requirement that has a number of specifications, a page might be devoted to each specification, for example. The specification would be identified at the head of the page. A blurb, summarizing the contents of the page, would follow. The details would then be presented in the rest of the page.

These devices help the reader, and they help the writer. The reader may use these as a general guide, and the writer may use them as selling tools—to point out and highlight critical items.

Figure 22 shows how both blurbs and glosses can be used to good advantage to accomplish both aids to understanding and aids to selling most important points.

An approach used by one major aerospace/defense contractor with great success follows this idea closely. However, they make an effort to make each page a new entity of its own—i.e., they try to use one page and one page only for each item. Each page then, begins with a sidehead, a blurb, and a description with glosses in the margin.

Obviously, there are some cases where you cannot express the entire idea in a single page. It is far more effective, however, to start a new topic, with its sidehead and blurb, on a new page, rather than at the middle of a page already given over to another topic.

```
MODERN APPROACHES TO LEARNING
```

*An old, ill-regarded concept, "teaching to the examination,"
has value when used properly, according to modern educational
theory and principles.*

"Teaching to the examination" is sometimes regarded as a
shallow and faulty method of loading the scales in favor of
the instructor--it presumably makes it easy for the students
to score well and reflects favorably on the competence of the
instructor. It is therefore regarded with some distaste, by
many, as an invalid approach. However, it can be a perfectly
valid approach to training if the examination that is being
"taught to" <u>covers all the desired behaviors.</u>* Then mastery
of the examination is mastery of the subject!

*Teaching to the
examination can
be an effective
means for teaching.*

In a sense, this describes modern educational principles.
Learning is defined today in terms of the behaviors that will
demonstrate achievement of the desired learning. Causing the
learner to display these behaviors, no matter how it is brought
about, is a valid goal and a valid achievement by the instructor
or learning system. This concept is formalized in such educational principles as operant conditioning, reinforcement, mathematics, etc.

*Modern educational
principle involves
the idea of
"behaviors."*

Operant conditioning is a principle that describes the process of conditioning a learner to respond to a specific stimulus.
Properly trained, the learner always makes the desired response
to the specified stimulus.

*Operant conditioning
is one principle
describing how to
achieve a behavior.*

*Behavior, in the educational sense, is the means of describing
learning in terms of what the student will <u>do</u> to demonstrate
that the learning has taken place--e.g., soldering a connection,
dividing 81 by 9, etc.

Figure 22. Using blurbs and glosses.

Other Format Matters

Most proposals are typed, of course, although some organizations go
to the great and unnecessary expense of having proposals typeset. The
question arises, in many organizations, of whether to type the proposal
double-spaced or single-spaced. This may not seem to be a momentous
question, and indeed it is not, but many proposal managers appear to
agonize over the question. On the one hand, they feel, double-spaced
copy is easier to read. On the other hand, double-spacing also doubles the
sheer bulk of the proposal and the duplicating and labor costs.

The fact is that, as many tests have indicated, it is probably not easier
to read double-spaced copy for a simple reason: we are conditioned to
read single-spaced copy all our lives, and it is actually an extra effort to
scan double-spaced copy. Personally, I favor single-spaced copy, for
several reasons.

If your typewriters are equipped with a half-space ratchet (IBM can so equip their typewriters, on special order), you might compromise and use 1½ spaces between lines. In many cases, I have found this to be highly suitable and even attractive.

Titling Illustrations

Almost no one ever titles an illustration to best advantage in a proposal. This is because they lose sight of the fact, which we have tried to stress as often as possible here, that a proposal is a sales presentation and should be making maximum use of sales psychology at all times, taking advantage of every opportunity to SELL.

Consider the organization chart (Figure 23) for example. It has a simple title, "Proposed Organization," which is an entirely accurate description. And that's all it is—accurate.

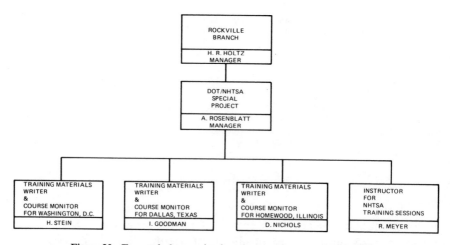

Figure 23. Even a drab organization chart can have a selling caption.

The title could have been used to help sell the proposal. It might have been titled something such as "Proposed Organization, Tailored for Results." That is, the titles of illustrations ought to concentrate on what benefits are shown by them.

A title such as "Proposed Circuit Design" becomes "Circuit Designed for Ultra-High Reliability" or "Design for Low Cost at High Quality." A proposed floor plan titled "Proposed Facility" could become "Dedicated Facility for a Dedicated Project." "The Zilch Development Laboratory" becomes "Latest Laboratory Facilities to Be Made Available for Project."

In short, the philosophy is to remind the customer, continually, that you are *offering* things to him, things that will *benefit* him.

The Philosophy of the Proposal

Too many job seekers write their résumés and go to interviews hat in hand—as beseeching supplicants, that is, looking for a handout, humbly asking—instead of making an offer. In actuality, a résumé is an *offer*. You offer to exchange your services, your talent, your training, your experience, your abilities for—what? You may demand a certain salary and other conditions, or you may solicit an offer from the prospective employer. But in either case, it's an exchange. You give something of value, and you get something of value in exchange. It's not a handout or a favor; it's a negotiation.

You should approach proposal writing in the same manner. You are not asking for favors or rewards for being a good writer. Quite the contrary, you are making an offer, and so far, the other party has all the best of it because he is already getting the benefit of what you have come up with, after analyzing his need, and you are giving him a great deal for nothing simply by writing the proposal and presenting it to him.

The proposal is your *offer*. And in making this offer, you stipulate a price (in your cost proposal). Obviously, you would like him to accept your offer, or you wouldn't go to the expense and trouble of working it up. But it is an offer, and it has to be made as attractive as possible. You have not only to present and explain the offer but to present all the arguments for accepting your offer. You have to explain to him and remind him as often as possible of the reasons for accepting your offer.

You must never assume that the customer will make the mental transitions, that he will translate the unemotional terms of an objective description into the benefits they are the harbingers of. You must write on the premise that the customer knows only what you tell him, neither more nor less. He may or may not understand the power-saving benefits of solid-state components. He may or may not realize that digital computers offer certain specific advantages over analog computers. He may or may not perceive the sophistication and the benefits of your management plans.

You must assume that he does not and, therefore, explain them. If he is already as expert as you, he will skim quickly over your explanations but will grasp them. If he is less expert, he will study them, and he may go to his own experts for verification. But he will have been made aware, at least, that you claim special benefits for your plans. Lose no opportunity to *sell*.

Achieving Credibility

The promise of benefits is designed to arouse both interest and desire. If you have perceived correctly the results—benefits—the customer wants, you cannot but help arouse his interest when you make specific pledges to secure those results for him.

The desire to secure these benefits, however, is not the same as the desire to buy what you are offering. The customer will develop the desire to take you up on your offer only when he has come to believe in your offer . . . when you have established credibility. The customer must be convinced, somehow, that you can and will deliver the promised results.

This is why you must demonstrate an accurate understanding of his needs, the technical competence to satisfy them, the facilities and resources to carry out the project, and a sufficiently detailed plan so that he does not feel he is buying a pig in a poke. In short, your proposal must say:

1. I understand your requirements. Here is what they are.
2. I know how to satisfy such needs. Here are my ideas and how I will go about satisfying your needs and furnishing the desired results.
3. Here is my specific program and the resources available to me, with my pledge of phases, functions, and deliveries.
4. Here is the evidence that I have done similar work in the past, successfully, and satisfied other customers' requirements of a similar nature.

If you study the various proposal sections suggested in the outline, you will see that every section and every topic listed as an aspect of coverage in the section addresses one or more of these four points: understanding, desired end-results, credibility, and pledges. Every successful proposal addresses these points successfully—it must, to win an award.

By far, the larger proportion of your proposal addresses credibility. It is relatively easy to demonstrate understanding (although a surprisingly large number of proposals fail to do so). It does not take a great deal of time and text to arouse customer interest, since he already wishes to buy something. The biggest uncertainty factor, usually in both his own mind and the bidders' minds, *is whom?* From whom will he buy?

Some Tips on Credibility

In the most general of terms, the specific, detailed proposal is far more believable than the vague, generalized proposal. The reasons are rather obvious: anyone can write a vague and general proposal, but you have to know what you are doing—have the technical competence, for example—to develop a detailed plan. And the detailed plan is its own evidence that you have done the necessary homework.

Many proposers have the notion that the sheer bulk of a proposal contributes in direct measure to favorable evaluation and award. There is good evidence that this is so, despite customer protestations to the contrary. (Some bid packages even limit the number of text pages you are permitted to submit.) Somehow a thick proposal is far more persuasive than a thin one. ("Thick" and "thin" are in relation to the size of the job and the competing proposals.)

In my own experience, I have known some customers to complain mildly about having a thick, heavily detailed proposal submitted to them when (they say) it was not necessary to provide such lengthy arguments and detailed plans. However, I have never known anyone to lose because of an excessively large proposal, although I have known the reverse to be true in many cases.

There is a way to have your cake and eat it too: use appendices, following the final chapter or section. And here is the right way and wrong way to use such appendices to your proposal.

An appendix should contain information that is of probable interest to some, but not all, readers. The information is there for those of the readers who wish to read the entire paper to which you have made frequent references or who wish to see your highly detailed plan or outline. But the reader who is not interested in such detail does not have to wade through it or find the end of it so he can skip it.

Typical Appendices. In bidding for a Job Corps center, we referred to lengthy lists of training "resource materials" that we would have access to for possible application: films, filmstrips, slides, textbooks, and many other aids. There were, literally, thousands of such items. We cited a few typical ones in the body of the proposal and advised the reader that a complete listing would be found in an appendix.

We have used appendices to provide copies of testimonials and letters of commendation; bibliographic notes; lists of materials; detailed outlines; drawings, especially those of other projects listed as qualifying experience; reproductions of papers and/or other documents cited; background information about the parent organization; examples of illustrations and/or written products produced in other projects; samples of products we anticipate producing in the proposed project.

It is possible, in this manner, to produce a relatively small proposal proper, yet have a rather substantial proposal overall. And when you believe the situation warrants it, you can produce a multivolume proposal, making a separate volume of the appendix or appendices, as we have done successfully in a number of cases.

Exhibits

Another device we have resorted to successfully, which is somewhat closely related to the appendix, is the exhibit. This is something separate from the proposal itself, yet a part of it.

An exhibit is something that does not, for one reason or another, fit properly into the proposal itself, not even in an appendix. It might be audio tapes, slides, original art, bulky drawings, a model, photographs, or almost anything else not part of the proposal presentation *per se.*

We have extended this idea, on occasion, to "beat the rules" or to help make our presentation something distinctive, something commanding attention.

For example, where the customer has restricted you to some given number of pages and you feel that you need more to make your case properly, you may be able to slide in some extra pages as an appendix or exhibit, particularly if separated physically from the proposal proper.

Be careful when you do so that your proposal is still a complete document, satisfying all requirements, without the appendix or exhibits. An appendix (or exhibit) should not ordinarily contain anything that is essentially part of the proposal, particularly not when there is a size restriction imposed on the proposal.

In one case, we developed some sample illustrations whose original sizes were approximately 3×4 feet each, reducing them for inclusion in the proposal as samples of what we proposed to develop. But, having no legitimate use for the original art samples and believing them to be attractive, we were struck with the idea of incorporating them in the package overall as exhibits. We thereupon delivered a 3×4-foot proposal! This caused no little comment and attention and, we believe, contributed to winning the contract.

These are attention-getting ideas. (Remember that first rule: Get attention.) Another we used successfully was a foldout cover.

Frequently drawings are too large to fit into an $8^{1}/_{2} \times 11$-inch format without reducing them to the point of illegibility. The usual device in such cases is to make foldouts of them—they must be folded out of the proposal or manual.

In one case where we had developed an overall chart that we believed to be especially attractive and well thought out, we decided to use it on the cover. But it was just a bit too large for the cover, even after reduction. We therefore folded that portion beyond the $8^1/2$-inch horizontal dimension underneath, producing an $8^1/2 \times 11$-inch cover that folded out! It too was a good attention getter and helped greatly to make our proposal command some special attention.

In still another case, our proposal included a rather good program-control chart; that is, the chart that we developed to explain the program was complete with major milestones and target dates, organized so that the project manager could use it conveniently to track and monitor the work as well as keep a convenient status or progress check by making a few marks on it. When we perceived that such was the case, we covered the original—about 2×3 feet—with transparent acetate and delivered it as an exhibit. The government's project manager got the message all right: he perceived that we were making him a gift of a control chart, and he liked it very well, mounting it on his wall immediately. (As soon as we saw this, we had a pretty good idea of where the contract award would go!)

Getting attention doesn't win contracts. But it does help to make the evaluators highly conscious of your proposal. And this is especially valuable when a large number of proposals have been submitted and your company is not particularly well known to the customer. (On at least one occasion that I now know of, we lost principally because our proposal was one of a large number and didn't get much attention. The customer admitted later, in our follow-up, that ours was easily as good as the one that got the award. He freely admitted that he simply had become surfeited with reading the large number of proposals.)

Letter of Transmittal

It is customary, although not a contractual or response obligation, to submit a letter of transmittal with your proposal. Theoretically, the letter is a separate document, addressed to the contracting officer and enclosed in a separate envelope. In practice, many bidders send the original to the contracting officer, in a separate envelope, but reproduce the letter as the first page inside the cover of the proposals (technical and cost).

Some bidders regard the letter of transmittal as a routine and say little or nothing of significance in it. Others regard the transmittal letter as a most important part of the submission. And at least one successful bidder I know believes that his transmittal letter is the most important part of his submission.

Even reaching a compromise among these conflicting views, the letter of transmittal should not be dismissed lightly. It can be quite important, as at least one bidder reports. He says that in many of his proposals,

```
                                        April 18, 1978
                                        Ref:  Proposal response to
                                              RFP 003A-H-79-006


        U.S. Dept of Labor
        Division of Procurement
        Washington, D.C. 20210


        Attention:  Contracting Officer

        Gentlemen:


        Behaviors, Inc., is pleased to offer a unique program for the
        training of handicapped workers in response to the referenced
        RFP.  Under the concept offered here, handicapped workers will
        be assigned to cooperating employers for on-the-job training
        at special work stations, designed by Behaviors, Inc., and will
        become gainfully employed and productive within a few days after
        initial assignment.  Behaviors has made arrangements with several
        major corporations to participate in the project, and the results
        are expected to become a model for widespread proliferation.

        The project, as proposed here, will result in a detailed methodology
        for analyzing the handicapped workers' individual skills and handi-
        caps and will provide a detailed and definitive methodology for identi-
        fying the proper match of handicaps-skills-required behaviors nec-
        essary to make the work assignments.

        This new approach to an old problem will revolutionize the treatment
        of the problem by bringing about an order-of-magnitude decrease in
        the cost of creating gainful employment for the handicapped, while
        adding substantially to the labor pool in several areas that are
        almost critically short of properly skilled labor.

        The signer of this letter is authorized by Behaviors, Inc.,
        to make this offer in behalf of the corporation and to
        stipulate that the offer is firm for a period of 120 days from
        this date.

        The signer and Behaviors, Inc., wish to make clear to the Depart-
        ment of Labor that our full corporate resources are pledged to
        the success of the proposed project, and no effort will be spared
        to ensure complete and unqualified success.

        Should further information be desired, either informally or by
        formal presentation, please feel free to request same from the
        signer of this letter.


                                        Very truly yours,



                                        For Behaviors, Inc.
                                        Hiram G. Watthour, Ph.D.
                                        Executive Vice-President
```

Figure 24. A typical transmittal letter.

there is little to choose from among most of the bidders, who are all pretty much equal in capabilities, qualifications, and proposal quality. He insists that the evaluators, in these cases, make their determination principally upon the letter of transmittal and pay scant attention to what the proposal itself says!

In any case, the transmittal letter should summarize the main selling point, theme, or approach of the proposal (ideally, they will be the same), specify that the signer is authorized to make the offer, spell out the term of the offer, pledge the offeror's best efforts and complete conformance, and invite the customer to request further or additional information, if required.

If the letter is to be enclosed in the technical proposal, it must not reveal the price. It may, however, indicate the estimated effort—so many man days or man months, etc.

It might follow the general lines of Figure 24. In that example, the basic idea underlying the proposal is sketched in swiftly, with careful delineation of its special characteristics and clear suggestions of ultimate benefits—a breakthrough in solving the problem effectively.

The purpose is to create a favorable climate for consideration of the proposal—conditioning the reader to expect something new and different and arousing immediate interest.

One thing to keep in mind when writing a transmittal letter is that it may be the only vehicle through which you can communicate directly to the contracting officer, since he will probably not read your proposal. Therefore, you should try to include in your transmittal letter any points you wish to make to the contracting officer to enlist his support—e.g., cost-reduction plans or promised low program costs (although you will not reveal dollar figures here).

16

Production and Packaging the Proposal

The package is often as important as the contents, as far as customer reaction is concerned. At least, proper packaging adds appeal and creates favorable first impressions.

Composition and Artwork

Most proposal requests today carry a notice cautioning the bidder against submitting proposals "unnecessarily elaborate" and costly, since that may be taken as a sign that the bidder is lacking in proper cost-consciousness. Translating this caution into end results poses a problem for many. They are not sure just what it means.

It refers to the practices of many large firms, in bidding for large projects, of going to the extremes of binding proposals in morocco leather, with fancy spines, gold lettering, etc. It does not refer to having the proposal typeset, printed, and bound by any of the usual office methods, such as spiral plastic binders. Nor is it an injuction against having a well-printed cover and professional artwork. In fact, your proposal should be highly presentable and "professional-looking." It simply should not go to extremes.

Typewriter composition—IBM Selectric or Executive (or their equivalent)—is perfectly acceptable. However, if your organization happens to have an IBM Composer or other typesetter, certainly you can gain a great deal in appearance and general impact by using it to compose your proposals and title your drawings. And, of course, such typesetting is especially useful for preparing headings, blurbs, and glosses and making life a bit easier for that unfortunate soul who must read a mountain of proposals and evaluate each. For that reason, too, it's advantageous to allow generous margins for readers' notations.

It is desirable that illustrations—including charts, graphs, maps, etc. —be as professional in appearance as possible. If you happen to have a staff artist, by all means use him. (In most cases, a competent draftsman can do the job well.) However, with the various art aids available from any good art-supply shop today, almost anyone can do a professional-looking job of charts and graphs. Most modern art-supply stores have transfer types, paste-up forms, templates, and sundry other aids that enable the amateur draftsman to make up a presentable chart.

Production Considerations

Most offices today are equipped with a xerographic copying machine of some sort, and most of these today are far better in the quality of copies they can produce than were the copiers of a decade ago. And since you usually need a rather small number of copies for submitting to the customer, it is rarely necessary to go to the expense and experience the usual delay of having copies printed by offset.

Offset printing is cheaper than office copies if you are producing 100 or more copies. For smaller numbers—10, 20, or thereabouts—it is often less expensive to do them by office copier, unless your office labor is especially high-priced.

A problem arises for many organizations in reproducing drawings, especially when they are greater than 17 inches wide, since few office copiers handle anything larger than that, and many will not go beyond 12-inch widths. Also, if you have had a professional illustrator prepare an original piece of art, the original may be 30 or more inches wide, with the expectation of being reduced for final reproduction and binding in the proposal.

Many organizations therefore go to the printer with the oversized pages—for example, drawings—only, having the printer produce the required number of copies at the final size desired. For drawings not greater than 11 × 17 inches, this is usually quite feasible. However, for extra-long drawings—and they can easily become several feet long, even in final size —this can be quite an expense. Negatives and printing plates for long drawings can easily mount up, as does the cost of running them on a large press.

The easy way around this dilemma is the ozalid process. If the original is at the final size and done on a translucent medium, such as Mylar or tracing paper, it is easy to reproduce the original at low cost by the ammonia process. And even if it is oversized or done on an opaque medium, the typical ozalid (blueprint) shop can make a negative and reproduce from that at low cost. (Moreover, a blueprint shop will often do the job for you much more rapidly than a printer.)

Production includes binding. The 18- or 19-hole punch and spiral plastic binder are quite popular, and such equipment is in common use today. However, if such equipment is not available, there is absolutely nothing wrong with "side-stitching" the proposal with a heavy-duty stapler.

In the final analysis, such matters have little to do with the final outcome—the failure or the success of the proposal—as long as the proposal is clean, neat, well-written, and properly edited and tells its story well. On one occasion, I submitted five proposals for five projects to the same customer, all typed on a portable, illustrated by yours truly (no artist, for sure!), reproduced on a not-especially-good office copier, side-stitched with a stapler, and covered in ordinary paper rather than proper cover stock.

Three of the five proposals produced contracts, totaling some $127,000, much to the fury of competitors who had gone to great pains to produce typeset, printed proposals with attractive covers and professional drawings.

Exceptions

There are some exceptions to the rule. For one, if you are bidding for a project requiring professional publications, with artwork, etc., it is advisable to use only professionally drawn illustrations to exemplify the quality of your proposed work. And if you are offering to write and/or edit something for a customer, careless grammar, incorrect spellings, and other such faults are going to be fatal faults—of course!

Similarly, if you are bidding for an engineering task, your engineering drawings had best be done by a draftsman and look as though they had been prepared by a professional, with great care.

There are other special cases. When we bid—successfully—for a Jobs Corps center, we required only 20 copies of the proposal. However, we went to the printer because for one thing, we did not have a very good copier in house, and for another, the boss insisted on it for appearances'-sake! Learning how small the cost difference was between 50 copies and 250 copies, he opted to have 250 copies printed. It turned out to be a blessing because the proposal was so detailed that it served us well as an operating and procedures manual for the first year of the project. And we have known of other cases where the proposal was required in large quantities to help run the project after award.

A Few Other Considerations

In a large proposal, it is often highly advisable to use page dividers and tabs to help evaluators find information they are looking for. Here again, making life a bit easier for the readers will endear you to them somewhat. At the least, they will know that you have been thoughtful in developing your proposal.

Remember that the technical proposal and the cost proposal are almost always separate volumes and should be clearly marked on the outside cover.

Typically proposals wind up in a frantic, last-minute panic, no matter how early they are started or how leisurely the effort begins. And at least once in a while, you find yourself making a frantic, last-minute dash to get your proposal package delivered on time.

There are other cases when you have finished comfortably ahead of schedule—or think you have. The temptation to deliver several days early is great: no last-minute panic this time. *Don't.* Invariably, in those cases, a day or two before the deadline—and after you have delivered your proposal—you get an extension or a modification, giving you two more weeks and changing the ground rules somewhat. That means picking up your proposal and making the changes, then redelivering it. Finish your proposal, package it, and get it ready for delivery if you wish to, but don't deliver too far ahead.

A Few Cautions

The cost proposal usually has at least two forms that must be signed by an individual who can bind your organization. These signatures are musts. (I lost one contract by neglecting to sign it before it left the office.) However, you will note that the instructions often call for marking one copy *Original.* Presumably, that copy and that copy only requires an original signature, and the rest may be duplicated in the copying process. Unfortunately, in many cases, only copies go out, and the originals (the true originals) are stored in your organization's files. The government procurement official may—or may not—be willing to accept a duplicated signature as an original. (This problem, too, cost us one award.) To play safe, it has long been my practice to affix an *original signature to every copy* of the forms requiring signature. It's a bit of trouble, but it ensures you against this particular slipup.

You should stipulate—and the transmittal letter is one place you can do this—for what period of time your offer is valid. (Remember, you are making an offer.) In some cases, the RFP will say that an assumption of time is made, if you do not stipulate otherwise. However, it is wise to specify—90 days, 120 days, or whatever time you wish to offer.

Bear in mind, in doing this, that you must allow the government enough time to carry out all the functions required to execute a contract— 90 days or more, depending primarily on the size of the procurement.

17

The Special Case of Architects and Engineers

Architecture is primarily art, and engineering is primarily science. The two are married in "A & E" work, and special procurement procedures are used to award design commissions.

Category R in the *Commerce Business Daily* calls for architect–engineer services. All Category R requirements are filled through certain special procedures of prequalification and preselection of potential bidders, utilizing two special forms, Standard Forms 254 and 255.

SF 254 is a general (and complex) form that needs to be filed only once a year but must be filed with every agency to which the bidder wishes to propose. SF 255 is a form filed in applying for consideration for each specific requirement.

From a review of SF 254, a number of firms are selected and invited to submit SF 255 (although any A & E firm may file of their own volition). A "public advisory panel," made up of architects and engineers considered distinguished in their field, reviews the aspirants' qualifications and selects a number of firms for interviews and presentations.

Each selected firm is invited to make a formal presentation before the panel and to answer questions put to them. Following this presentation, the panel makes its selections of the three top-rated firms, in their rank order, and reports these results to the agency. The agency then invites the top-rated firm to submit its proposal, primarily price information, and enters into negotiations with the firm. Should the agency fail to reach agreement with the firm for the job, the next firm on the list is selected, and the process is repeated. Should the agency fail to reach agreement with any of the three firms, three more firms will be selected from the original list, and the proposal–negotiation process will be repeated.

Presumably, this procedure is followed principally because art is a prime consideration in architecture, and the panel acts as a sort of art commission, to ensure good architecture.

Unfortunately, even this procedure results in buildings that art critics and others denounce as ugly and unbefitting the majesty of the United States government. The new FBI building in Washington, D.C., has been heavily criticized, and the new Department of Labor building has not met with universal approval of its architecture either. And there have been many criticisms leveled at the architectural features of many other government buildings.

Much worse, in this writer's opinion, is the fact that this procedure is followed for many procurements where architecture and art are not at all involved and the requirement is really not an A & E requirement at all. A & E firms are asked to be safety experts, geologists, historians, biographers, and many other things not related to architecture and civil engineering, except by some tortuous chain of illogic. Under this procedure, designed to ensure good architecture and supposedly meant to procure the services of A & E firms, some of the following procurements have been made:

1. Design of an energy control system awarded to a large firm otherwise devoted to data processing and management consulting
2. Archeological-conservation study, to an Indian research institute
3. "Cultural resource salvage," to a university anthropology laboratory
4. A "mineral appraisal report," to a "mineral enterprises" company
5. "Systems technical support services" for U.S. Army tanks, to one of the "big three" automobile manufacturers
6. Environmental assessments, to a firm of environmental consultants
7. Weapons design, to an engineering research firm

From this list, you can see that it is not necessary to be an A & E firm *per se* to qualify for some of these tasks, nor should you skip over these listings and contract potentials because you are not an A & E firm. By far, the bulk of the requirements listed for A & E firms involve no architectural design at all but are engineering jobs (and not necessarily civil engineering): straight construction contracts; surveying; mapping; environ-

mental studies; safety inspections or studies; geological surveys; histori-
cal-site surveys; and many other nondesign tasks. Logically, many of
these could have been listed under any of several other CBD categories
and could have followed the usual procurement procedures. However,
things being what they are, it is good practice to scan these requirements
also, as possibilities for contracts.

18

Negotiations

All contracts awarded via the proposal route are "negotiated" contracts. However, the reason that word is in quotes is that actual negotiation may or may not take place. The fine print in every RFP solicitation advises you that after reading the proposals, the government may proceed to make a contract award without further discussion or negotiation. It exhorts you, therefore, to make your initial offer your best offer.

For many small contracts, and especially where the time is so short as to make negotiations difficult to schedule, the contract is, in fact, awarded without further ado after the proposals are evaluated. For large contracts—and in many cases, for small contracts—some degree of "negotiation" does take place.

The simplest form of "negotiation" is the request for best-and-final offer. This request may be made by telephone call, by telegram, by letter, or in a meeting. It usually permits the bidder to modify his technical proposal, as well as his cost proposal.

There are contracting officials who insist that every award be preceded by a request for best-and-final offer. There are those who ask for best-and-final offers from everyone who has bid—at least, from everyone whose proposal has been judged technically passable. There are others who request best and finals from only those whose proposals are "deemed to be in the competitive range," both technically and in price. And there are those who insist on full-blown negotiations, often extending over several weeks. This is especially true when a large and important contract is at stake.

Full-blown negotiations are most likely when the contract is rather sizable, when the work is especially important to the agency and they want to be especially cautious in selecting a contractor, and when the contract is to be some form of cost-reimbursement (e.g., cost-plus) agreement.

The first step is generally a call for a meeting and discussion. The proposer is usually invited to make a formal presentation, if he desires to. If he chooses to, his presentation is generally the first item on the meeting agenda.

Practices vary widely in making such presentations, depending generally on the size of the contract. For a small- to medium-sized contract, the presenters will probably offer a verbal presentation only, possibly with a chart or two. For large and important contracts, some companies will prepare full sound-and-sight presentations: slides, tapes, filmstrips, charts, handouts, etc.

The government people will then ask questions about the proposer's offer, questions related directly to what the proposal has said—or hasn't said, in many cases. (Perhaps *deliberately* hasn't stated!)

The government people—and the government team ordinarily includes people from the "program" side and the procurement officials— are generally rather circumspect in how they handle the discussion and what they say. If they want to do business with you and there are some problems in the way, they will try, as discreetly as possible, to give you hints of what they want you to do: reduce your price, modify your approach, change your management plan, etc. They cannot tell you plainly without running risks of violating procurement regulations and affording competitors sound legal grounds for protesting their loss of the competition. (Losers may charge that the winner gained unfair advantage or was unduly favored.)

In one case, where a supplier of "contract" technical writers had been almost a fixture on the premises of a NASA facility, the government (NASA, that is) decided that the on-site operation was, in fact, illegal. NASA thereupon issued an RFP for off-site technical-publications support.

The firm that had been doing the work on site had obvious advantages and submitted what should have been the winning proposal. They had one serious problem, however: obtuseness. The man who was to be the government's project manager—they called him the COTR, or contracting officer's technical representative, in this case—had serious objections to the individual the company proposed as their project manager.

In subsequent negotiations, the COTR-to-be tried in every way he could to impart this information to the proposer. When the message failed to get through to them, he turned to the next bidder, who also had serious problems but was open-minded and eager enough to accommodate the offer to NASA's wishes.

That latter company won the contract and kept it for six years. And then they became infected with the same disease of obtuseness and failed to accommodate their offer to a clearly expressed objection to price, whereupon they lost to a bidder who was listening more carefully and thinking more clearly.

In both cases, the problem stemmed primarily from having a team headed by someone who had become deliberately obtuse, for one reason or another, and refused to listen to either the government's people or his own staff. In negotiations, it is important, of course, to have your organization represented by a leader who knows how to negotiate but whose personal career and fate are bound up in the award. Your proposed project manager may well be the worst possible person to represent you—at least, to head the negotiating team—especially if he headed the proposal writing. He may find himself in the position of defending his own proposal or his own managerial strengths, in which case he is likely to rationalize the things he hears at the negotiation and report back to his company what he interprets rather than what was said!

Bear in mind, in such negotiations, that the government may be holding such discussions with others as well as with you. Even though you are in negotiation, you are not necessarily out of the competitive stage. You could be in several possible basic positions:

- Much stronger technically than others, but much higher in price too
- Weaker technically, but attractive in the price aspect
- About equal technically, but higher in price
- Out front both technically and in price
- Already selected as the probable winner, but going through a negotiation as a matter of fixed policy to get the best possible deal for the government
- Not seriously considered, but technically entitled to make your case and try to negotiate a contract

Many bidders, when they get to the negotiating stage, worry about "leaving money on the table," that is, lowering their price when they could have gotten a better price. That's a matter for your own conscience and business judgment. Following the philosophy of sticking to your price will probably make the contracts you win more profitable, but it will probably also cost you some contracts that you could have won.

Cost-reimbursement contracts are especially interesting cases. In some ways, they leave you more room for negotiating flexibility because you are, supposedly, entitled to recover all your costs. However, the government protects its own interests, too, and you are not going to be given a "license" to spend freely as a result of winning a cost-reimbursement contract. You may go in with a provisional overhead, subject to adjustment on audit, but you will probably have a ceiling placed on that overhead. If you allow your overhead to exceed the ceiling, you are going to have to "eat" the excess.

The same consideration will apply to direct costs. In cost-reimbursement contracts, you are often required to bill labor at what it actually costs you, plus overhead and G & A. But again, there will usually be ceilings on the rates you can charge for each class or category of labor. Other cost items—travel, for example—will be similarly controlled by ceilings or maximums. It may be advantageous, therefore, to lower your provisional overhead, if you can get the government to agree to a high enough ceiling to protect you from serious miscalculations.

If you are setting up a separate facility or division of your company to handle the contract, it may be advantageous to allow that separate entity its own overhead and/or G & A rate rather than burdening them with the overhead rate of the company overall.

You can usually negotiate matters such as accounting methods and systems, subject to the contracting officer's approval of your accounting system, but once you reach agreement, you will not be able to change the system without the contracting officer's approval.

Bear in mind, too, during negotiations, that the staff you offer is often the most important matter to the program people. Be flexible in this, too, trying to sense any particular objection to an individual proposed for the project.

You'll get clues even when the government team is trying to be objective and avoid giving you hints. Anything about which you are closely questioned or cross-examined is something you should be concerned about. If you are cross-examined about the qualifications of your proposed project manager, it may mean that the government has some doubts about that individual's ability to hire the right people quickly enough, especially if you have proposed to staff largely with new hires.

Prior to going into negotiations, you should have studied your proposal and your position closely, identifying those areas in which you believe yourself to be weak. This is no time to practice self-deceit. You should know whether you are weak in staff, facilities, price, experience, or other matters. Having identified those areas, you should prepare yourself to be cross-examined about them and to make strong representations.

This kind of consideration should influence your choice of members for your negotiating team, too. Bring along your best salesman. If you are proposing to hire many new people for the project, bring along your personnel manager or someone who can discuss that problem and present convincing solutions in a convincing manner.

In one "negotiation" (it was not really a negotiation, but a visit from a technical review team to assess the organization's technical capability), the organization came off badly as far as company experience was concerned. However, two consultants were present who were personally knowledgeable in the two areas and could discuss them capably. As soon as the meeting ended, the two consultants went to work and prepared an information package, presenting plans and credentials in those areas. The package was sent off to the agency within 48 hours. The gambit proved successful, and the company did win the contract, thanks to their foresight in identifying their weaknesses and bringing in two consultants to help them through the presentation and discussions.

Another company, one engaged in computer software development, was going after a large contract that required extensive documentation—a technical-publications department but had improvised and used an occasional free-lance writer editor when they had had to produce a manual.

In preparation for their bid, the company raided a competitor with a well-developed technical-publications division, hiring away several key people and setting up a technical-publications department that had no work to do! However, when negotiating time came around, they could produce a technical-publications manager at the table, and he could discuss the publications needs of the contract. (They of course did not mention how new the publications department was!) They were successful, too, owing to some foresight and preparation.

Unlike negotiations in the commercial world, negotiations with a government agency does not mean that you have necessarily been selected as the probable winner (subject to negotiating successfully), nor does it necessarily mean that the contract terms are the sole subject to be negotiated. Negotiations may concern any facet of your try for the job and are often nothing more or less than an extension (and part of) your proposal effort. You must therefore apply to them all the same strategies and techniques you used in developing your proposal, but staffing *this* team with people who have the right qualities; they should be likeable; good presenters; good sales people; knowledgeable about the company, the project, and the procurement procedures; and good negotiators. They have to be people who handle themselves well in face-to-face exchanges, for the government's final decisions may rest entirely on how well those "negotiations" go.

19

A Few Final Words and Some Useful Information

Having just a bit more knowledge than your competitors have may make the difference.

In business, as in most things, the object is to win. For many important government contracts, proposalmanship is the most vital ingredient in the formula of success. However, there are many kinds of government purchases made through other means. In the pages you have sweated through, you learned about IFBs, or "formally advertised" and competitive procurements, and RFPs, or negotiated procurements. But the government buys in many ways and through many different kinds of procedures. And frequently the chief difference between the business that succeeds "big" and the one which just "gets by," laboriously, is *knowledge.*

For that reason, and for no other, the dry, tabulated material listed in the Appendix to this book is just as important in winning government business as the fascinating subject of developing successful proposals.

You'll find listed in the Appendix some useful information on how to pursue the billions that the General Services Administration spends every year to buy and stock some 4½ million items used by the federal establishment. You'll find listings of names and addresses of many field offices of government agencies that offer help of many kinds to the business person.

If you are not already an expert at doing business with the government, you can benefit greatly from visiting these agencies, talking to their personnel, reading their publications, and letting them tell you about the many programs they offer. (You read about a few of them earlier in this opus.)

The Department of Commerce, for example, can help you break into foreign markets, both export and import, through a variety of programs they operate for the purpose.

GSA Business Service Centers can also offer help and provide you with literature, some of which is suggested as being especially helpful in the Appendix.

There are publications, also, some published by the government and some by commercial publishers, that will help you find your way around the federal establishment. And that's an important matter. An executive of the San Francisco office of OMBE (Office of Minority Enterprise, Department of Commerce) recently confided in me that this was one of the most difficult-to-comply-with requests made of him by the minority entrepreneurs his office is supposed to help. The federal establishment has become so great and complex that even government employees of many years' standing often cannot find their way around it!

The former chief of the printing section of the Agency for International Development, part of the State Department, told me before he retired, "The secret of finding business in the government is finding the doors. I always have trouble getting printers to come in to ask for the work I have for contracting out. They don't know we're here, and I have to use the Yellow Pages and go looking for them. There's hardly a day of the week I couldn't hand a job across the counter to any printer who walked in here."

And I know of other cases where a government agency had to go to the Yellow Pages to find someone in a hurry for a job that had to be done.

Appendix

Other Useful Publications

There are many publications—some government, some commercial—that are of value to the government contractor or prospective contractor. Here are a few:

Guides to Government Organizations and to Washington, D.C. (Revised annually).

United States Government Manual, Government Printing Office, Washington, D.C. 20402.

Washington Information Directory, The New York Times Book Co., New York, N.Y. 10022.

Braddock's Federal–State–Local Government Directory, Braddock Publications, Washington, D.C. 20036.

The Businessman's Guide to Washington, Collier Books, Macmillan Publishing Co., New York, N.Y. 10022.

Information for Marketing: Books and Reports

Directory of Federal Environmental Research and Development Programs, Government R & D Report, MIT Branch, Cambridge, Mass. 02139.

Federal Information Sources and Systems, PAD-77-71, Government Printing Office, Washington, D.C. 20402.

Anyone Can Do Business with the Government, Government Marketing News, Inc., Washington, D.C. 20036.

Directory of U.S. Government Buyers, Government Marketing News, Inc., Washington, D.C. 20036.

Directory of U.S. Government Audiovisual Personnel, National Audiovisual Center, GSA, Washington, D.C. 20409.

Guide to Federal Assistance Programs for Minority Business Enterprises, Department of Commerce (OMBE),Washington, D.C. 20230.

Periodicals

Federal Grants Reporter, basic text, bimonthly supplements, Federal Grants Information Center, Washington, D.C. 20037.

Federal Contracts Report, weekly, Bureau of National Affairs, Washington, D.C. 20037.

Contract Appeals Decisions, biweekly, Commerce Clearing House, Chicago, Ill. 60646.

Commerce Business Daily, daily, Government Printing Office, Washington, D.C. 20402.

Government Marketing News, monthly, Government Marketing News, Inc., Washington, D.C. 20036.

The Government Contractor, Federal Publications, Inc., Washington, D.C. 20006.

Federal Register, Government Printing Office, Washington, D.C. 20402.

Addresses and Other Key Information

How to Order the Commerce Business Daily

The *Commerce Business Daily* is currently $80.00 a year for regular second-class mailing, but since the mail service has slipped so badly and so many subscribers are complaining about getting it late, you can have it mailed first-class for $105.00 a year. (Ordinarily, it is supposed to reach you on the date of issue, having been mailed the day before, but it's a rare occurrence today to get any but the Monday issue, mailed the previous Friday, on the date of issue. And even the Monday issue doesn't always reach the subscriber on Monday.) It comes out of Chicago, although you order from Washington, D.C., so it isn't your location that slows deliveries down. Whichever you choose, you can order it by sending your order and a check to:

Superintendent of Documents
U.S. Government Printing Office
Washington, D.C. 20402

The Government Printing Office asks you to allow "at least 30 days" for delivery to begin, but it's been most subscribers' experience that it takes approximately 60 days—and sometimes even more—before you receive your first issues.

GSA (General Services Administration) Offices

The GSA Regional Offices are as follows:

Region 1: 620 Post Office and Courthouse
Boston, Mass. 02109

Region 2: 26 Federal Plaza
New York, N.Y. 10007

Region 3: 7th & D Streets, SW
Washington, D.C. 20407

Region 4: 1776 Peachtree St, NW
Atlanta, Ga. 30309

Region 5: 219 S. Dearborn Street
Chicago, Ill. 60604

Region 6:   1500 E. Bannister Rd.
            Kansas City, Mo. 64131
Region 7:   819 Taylor Street
            Ft. Worth, Tex. 76102
Region 8:   Denver Federal Center
            Denver, Colo. 80225
Region 9:   49 4th Street
            San Francisco, CA. 94103
Region 10: GSA Center
            Auburn, Wash. 98002

GSA business service centers are at the same addresses, with a few exceptions:

Region 1:   (Boston, Mass.):
            John F. Kennedy Federal Building
            Boston, Mass. 02203
Region 9:   Center at the San Franciso address, plus another at Los Angeles:
            300 N. Los Angeles
            Los Angeles, Calif. 90012
Region 10: The business service center is as follows:
            909 1st Ave.
            Seattle, Wash. 98104

The central office of GSA, headquarters for the administration, is as follows:

> General Services Administration
> Eighteenth and F Streets, NW
> Washington, D.C. 20405

Small Business Administration (SBA)

The Small Business Administration is headquartered in Washington, D.C., as follows:

> 1441 L Street, NW
> Washington, D.C. 20416

The SBA maintains a large number of field offices, in addition to having a central office within each federal region. The following list indicates the regional office and the field offices within each of the Regions:

Region 1:	150 Causeway Street	Boston, Mass. 02203
	326 Appleton St.	Holyoke, Mass. 01040
	40 Western Ave.	Augusta, Maine 04330
	55 Pleasant St.	Concord, N.H. 03301
	450 Main St.	Hartford, Conn. 06103
	87 State St.	Montpelier, Vt. 05602
	57 Eddyt St.	Providence, R.I. 02903
Region 2:	26 Federal Plaza	New York, N.Y. 10007
	Federal Building	Buffalo, N.Y. 14202
	225 Ponce De Leon Ave.	Hato Rey, P.R. 00919
	970 Broad St.	Newark, N.J. 07102
	Fayette and Salina Sts.	Syracuse, N.Y. 13202
	N.Y.S. Dept of Commerce	Albany, N.Y. 12207
	55 St. Paul St.	Rochester, N.Y. 14604

Region 3:	1 Decker Sq.	Bala Cynwyd, Pa. 19004
	7800 York Rd.	Baltimore, Md. 21201
	Charleston National Plaza	Charleston, W. Va. 25301
	109 N. 3d St.	Clarksburg, W. Va. 26301
	1000 Liberty Ave.	Pittsburgh, Pa. 15222
	400 N. 8th St.	Richmond, Va. 23240
	1310 L St., NW	Washington, D.C. 20417
	901 Market St.	Wilmington, Del. 19801
Region 4:	1401 Peachtree St., NE	Atlanta, Ga. 30309
	908 S. 20th St.	Birmingham, Ala. 35205
	222 So. Church St.	Charlotte, N.C. 28202
	1801 Assembly St.	Columbia, S.C. 29201
	Security Savings & Loan Bldg.	Gulfport, Miss. 39501
	Petroleum Building	Jackson, Miss. 39205
	400 W. Bay St.	Jacksonville, Fla. 32202
	502 S. Gay St.	Knoxville, Tenn. 37902
	600 Federal Place	Louisville, Ky. 40202
	51 SW First Ave.	Miami, Fla. 33130
	1303 W. Shore Blvd. N.	Tampa, Fla. 33607
	500 Union St.	Nashville, Tenn. 37219
	211 Federal Office Building	Memphis, Tenn. 38103
Region 5:	219 S. Dearborn St.	Chicago, Ill. 60604
	Federal Building	Cincinnati, Oh. 45202
	1240 E. 9th St.	Cleveland, Oh. 44199
	34 N. High St.	Columbus, Oh. 43215
	1249 Washington Blvd.	Detroit, Mich. 48226
	36 S. Pennsylvania St.	Indianapolis, Ind. 46204
	122 W. Washington Ave.	Madison, Wis. 53703
	Federal Office Building	Eau Claire, Wis. 54701
	201 McClellan St.	Milwaukee, Wis. 53233
	12 S. 6th St.	Minneapolis, Minn. 55402
	502 E. Monroe St.	Springfield, Ill. 62701
Region 6:	100 Commerce St.	Dallas, Tex. 75202
	500 Marble Ave. NE	Albuquerque, N.M. 87110
	First Natl. Bank Tower	Las Cruces, N.M. 88001
	109 N. Oregon St.	El Paso, Tex. 79901
	808 Travis St.	Houston, Tex. 77002
	600 W. Capital Ave.	Little Rock, Ark. 72201
	219 E. Jackson St.	Lower Rio Grande Valley Harlingen, Tex. 78550
	3105 Leopard St.	Corpus Christi, Tex. 78408
	1205 Texas Ave.	Lubbock, Tex. 79408
	505 E. Travis St.	Marshall, Tex. 75670
	1001 Howard Ave.	New Orleans, La. 70113
	30 N. Hudson	Oklahoma City, Okla. 73102
	301 Broadway	San Antonio, Tex. 78205
Region 7:	911 Walnut St.	Kansas City, Mo. 64106
	210 Walnut St.	Des Moines, Ia. 50309
	215 N. 17th St.	Omaha, Neb. 68102
	210 N. 12th St.	St. Louis, Mo. 63101
	120 S. Market St.	Wichita, Kansas 67202

Region 8:	721 19th St.	Denver, Colo. 80202
	100 E. B St.	Casper, Wyo. 82601
	653 Second Ave N.	Fargo, N. Dak. 58102
	Main and 6th Ave.	Helena, Mont. 59601
	125 S. State St.	Salt Lake City, Utah 84111
	Eighth and Maine Ave.	Sioux Falls, S. Dak. 57102
Region 9:	450 Golden Gate Ave.	San Francisco, Calif. 94102
	1130 O St.	Fresno, Calif. 93721
	Ada Plaza Center Building	Agana, Guam 96910
	1149 Bethel St.	Honolulu, Hawaii 96813
	300 Las Vegas Rd.	Las Vegas, Nev. 89101
	849 S. Broadway	Los Angeles, Calif. 90014
	112 N. Central Ave.	Phoenix, Ariz. 85004
	110 W. C St.	San Diego, Calif. 92101
Region 10:	710 Second Ave.	Seattle, Wash. 98104
	1016 W. 6th Ave.	Anchorage, Alaska 99501
	216 N. 8th St.	Boise, Idaho 83701
	504 3rd Ave.	Fairbanks, Alaska 99701
	700 Pittock Block	Portland, Oregon 97205
	651 U.S.Courthouse	Spokane, Wash. 99210

Federal Supply Service

The Federal Supply Service is part of GSA. Its headquarters office is at:

> 1941 Jefferson Davis Highway
> Arlington, Va.

The mailing address is Washington, D.C. 20408. Information about selling to the Federal Supply Service may be obtained at any of the GSA regional offices listed earlier.

Government Printing Office

The Government Printing Office (GPO) is located at:

> North Capitol and H Streets, NW
> Washington, D.C. 20401

The GPO maintains regional offices in several cities. Exact addresses are listed in telephone directories for those cities. The cities in which regional GPO offices are maintained are as follows:

Atlanta, Ga.	Boston, Mass.	Chicago, Ill.
Columbus, Ohio	Dallas, Tex.	Denver, Colorado
Hampton, Va.	Los Angeles, Calif.	New York, N.Y.
St. Louis, Mo.	Philadelphia, Pa.	San Francisco, Calif.
Seattle, Wash.		

Suppliers of papers, inks, and printing equipment must address their inquiries to the Director of Materials Management, Government Printing Office, Washington, D.C. 20401.

The Federal Regions

In general, the United States is divided into 10 federal regions. Most major agencies of the government maintain regional offices in at least some of the Regions, but not necessarily all. The Bureau of Indian Affairs, for example, maintains offices in areas where there is a reasonably large population of Indians; the Department of Agriculture tends to maintain its regional offices in rural, farming states, etc.

All about Federal Supply Schedules

Why Federal Supply Schedules?

Federal Supply schedules, issued by the Federal Supply Services (General Services Administration), are used to buy services and supplies that are required on a regular, routine basis, throughout the year, by various agencies or for stock in GSA stores. To minimize and simplify the amount of contracting and negotiation required to feed the military and keep all the routine machinery of government going, GSA maintains what it refers to as Basic Ordering Agreements with several thousand suppliers.

There are over 300 schedules in some 65 "groups" of items of supply and a number of them calling for services of many types. In fact, the GSA Form 1382, List of *Commodities and Services,* lists over 20 pages of such supplies and services, since many of the schedules call for many different supplies and services.

If your product or service is accepted for inclusion on a schedule, you are issued a Basic Ordering Agreement. This is not a contract. But under this agreement, you have negotiated a price and a discount schedule, if any, for a year, and government agencies may now order from you through the simple expedient of issuing a purchase order. The latter is the "contractual document." Nevertheless you must respond to an Invitation to Bid, as though you were bidding directly for a contract!

The government's position is that an award is predicted on whether or not "tangible benefits will result to the Government from an acceptance of the offer, it being considered that if an award would not afford advantages over procurement in the open market it would not be justified."

This means, essentially, that you must offer the government discounts "equal to or better than those offered your most favored customer." And the government reserves the right to negotiate with you to reach that point. This in no way compromises your right to bid individual government procurements, bid by bid, in addition to or in place of procurements made via such schedules. But you have obvious advantages, since individual procurements are not going to be made by competitive bids for anything that can be conveniently purchased via the schedules.

The schedules are also a way to sell your own proprietary items to government agencies, especially publications of various sorts, for which the government maintains a rather fat set of schedules.

There is another benefit: many state and local governments and their bureaus—libraries, schools, prisons, etc.—are authorized to buy via the GSA schedules through the same convenient purchase-order system, thereby avoiding the delay and the laborious paperwork of competitive bidding. Therefore, getting on the schedules helps open doors in many other places.

The following are the groups and "classes" of suppliers for which many schedules are maintained. The first two digits of the number appearing under "Class" are the numbers by which the schedules are commonly referred to.

The following is a list of the latest Federal Supply schedules in effect, as reported in the GSA Program Guide. The GSA Program Guide is a new publication, available from the

Government Printing Office for $3.00 as Stock No. 022–005–0012–0. It is to be issued at regular intervals to report changes in the Schedules, which are subject to sudden change.

One recent change has been to add certain items which had been procured by other means.

The inclusion of the items means that the GSA/Federal Supply Service has "management" responsibility for the items—i.e., buys them for the government at large. Responsibility for many items, formerly managed by GSA, has been turned over to other centralized procurement, notably the Veterans Administration and the Defense Supply Service.

Schedule	Title/Description
NIIS	New Item Introductory Schedule
19	Small Craft and Marine Equipment/boats, motors, accessories
23	Wheel and Track Vehicles—snowmobiles, trailers, golf carts, trail bikes
25 I	Vehicular Equipment Components—tire chains and clutch facings
25, 28, 29	Parts and Accessories—automotive, construction, excavating, mining, highway maintenance, and material handling equipment
38, & 39	
26 II	Pneumatic Tires and Inner Tubes—highway, off-highway, industrial, pursuit/emergency, high speed passenger, and agricultural
26 IV A	Tires—industrial, solid and cushion
29 I A	Engine Accessories—spark plugs, oil filters and elements, engine preheaters
30	Power Transmission Equipment—V-belts
32 & 34	Woodworking and Metalworking Machinery and Equipment—electric
35 II	Trash Compactors and Balers—industrial, institutional, and for truck mounting
35 IV A	Appliances—household and commercial washing machines and drying tumblers, electric
36 II A & B	Special Industry Machinery—lithographic printing plates (masters) and solutions; printing, duplicating, and bookbinding equipment; and pulverizing, pulping, and shredding machines
36 II C	Special Industry Machinery—security shredding machines
36 IV	Special Industry Machinery—copying equipment, supplies, services
36 V	Special Industry Machinery—chain saws
37 I A	Argricultural Equipment—cattleguards
37 II A	Lawn and Garden Equipment—lawn mowers, mowers, shredders, edgers, trimmers, roto-tillers, broadcast spreaders, sprayers, vacuums, sweepers, tractors, and accessories
38 I A	Clearing and Cleaning Equipment—rider-or walker-operated equipment, self-propelled
39 II A	Materials Handling Equipment—conveyors, hand-lift trucks, towveyor trucks and carts, warehouse trucks and tractors
41 I A	Air Conditioning Equipment—domestic use window units
41 I B	Air Conditioning Equipment—central air and export use window units
41 III A	Appliances—household refrigerators
41 III B	Refrigeration Equipment—drinking water dispensers
42 I	Firefighting Equipment and Supplies—fire extinguishers, accessories and firehoses
42 II	Safety and Rescue Equipment—breathing apparatus, safety climbing equipment, and welder's and general use protective equipment

42 III	Safety Equipment—shoe decontamination equipment
42 IV A	Safety Equipment—nonprescription safety glasses and goggles
44 I A	Air Treatment and Conditioning Equipment—air cleaners, portable humidifiers and dehumidifiers, heat pumps
45 IV A	Sanitation Equipment—industrial incinerators
45 VII A	Plumbing and Heating Equipment—domestic water heaters, gas and electric
45 VIII A	Plumbing and Sanitation Equipment—household garbage disposers
46 I A	Water Purification Equipment—water stills, storage tanks, purity conductivity meters and reverse osmosis systems
47	Pipe—culvert: steel and aluminum
47 II A	Pipe—plastic
49 I A	Maintenance and Repair Shop Equipment—hydraulic jacks, heat guns, and auger machines
49 I B	Maintenance and Repair Shop Equipment—motor vehicle and miscellaneous maintenance and specialized repair shop equipment
49 II	Maintenance and Repair Shop Equipment—ultrasonic cleaning systems and accessories
51 I A	Hand and Power Tools—pneumatic, hydraulic, powder actuated, gasoline engine and special purpose drill bits
51 II A	Hand and Power Tools—electric
52	Measuring Tools—measuring tapes
54 I A	Prefabricated Structures—buildings, enclosures, and sound-controlled rooms
54 II A	Scaffolding, Shoring, Work and Service Platforms and Steps—portable
56 III A	Construction and Building Materials—solar control film and screens
58 I	Communication Equipment—record pressing
58 II	Communication Equipment—message-and-data transmitting equipment and background music systems
58 III A	Communication Equipment—semiprofessional audio recording equipment
58 III B	Communication Equipment—professional audio and video recording equipment
58 V A	Communication Supplies—*audio magnetic tape*: reels and cartridges; *video magnetic tape*: reels, cartridges, and cassettes; *digital magnetic tape*: cassettes and cartridges; *word processing*: magnetic tape cartridges and magnetic data recording cards (double-sided only)
58 V C	Communication Supplies—instrumentation recording tape, standard and high resolution, and empty precision reels
58 V D	Communication Supplies—*recording tapes*: $1/4''$ audio, audio cassettes, $1/2''$ video (helical scan) and $2''$ video (quadruplex), and reels and hubs
58 VI	Communication Equipment—telephone, intercommunication and public address (wireless transmission/wired or cabled equipment), and telephone answering equipment
58 VII	Communication Equipment—radio transmitting/receiving equipment, tone/voice paging systems, and antennas
58 IX	Communication Equipment—telemetry, laser, radio navigation, radar, underwater sound, visible and invisible light, and recorder/reproducer set, signal data (multiapplication)
59 III	Electronic Components—microelectronic circuit devices

61 I	Batteries—6- or 12-volt lead-acid automotive storage
61 II	Batteries—heavy duty, electric storage
61 III	Batteries—dry cell
61 IV A	Batteries—automotive storage, wet charged
61 V A	Power and Distribution Equipment—portable generators
61 V B	Power and Distribution Equipment—nonrotating battery chargers
61 VII A	Transformers—for refrigerators
62 I	Lighting Fixtures and Lamps—household and quarters use
62 II	Lighting Fixtures and Lamps—*light sets*: emergency and auxiliary
62 III	Lighting Fixtures and Lamps—fluorescent and incandescent
62 & 67	Lamps—electrical and photographic
63	Alarm and Signal Systems—transit and traffic signals, and miscellaneous alarms and signals
65 I A & 65 I B	Drugs and Pharmaceutical Products
65 II B	Medical and Veterinary Equipment—surgical instruments and supplies
65 II C	Dental Equipment and Supplies—operatory and laboratory
65 II D	Medical and Dental Equipment—monitoring, electronic, medical and physiotherapy equipment, patient aids, tables, electrosurgical units, and audiometers
65 III	Medical and Dental Supplies—*gloves*: medical and surgical
65 IV	Medical and Dental Supplies—prescription opthalmic lenses and safety glasses
65 V A	Medical and Dental Supplies—*film*: medical X-ray, 90-second processing
65 V B & C	Medical and Dental Supplies—*X-ray film*: medical and dental
65 VI	Medical and Dental Supplies—antibacterial deodorant soap
66 I A	Instruments and Laboratory Equipment—measuring and drafting instruments
66 I B	Instruments and Laboratory Equipment—magnifiers and reducing glasses, lettering sets, and electronic distance measuring equipment
66 II B	Instruments and Laboratory Supplies—glass, plastic, and metal laboratory ware; laboratory distillation and demineralizing systems; vena puncture products for blood specimen collection; and prescription bottles
66 II C	Instruments and Laboratory Equipment—microscopes, contrifuges, pH meters, microtomes, stirrers, shakers, stereoscopes, binoculars/monoculars, and titrators/titration systems
66 II D	Instruments and Laboratory Supplies—industrial radiographic X-ray film, paper, and processing equipment
66 II E	Instruments and Laboratory Equipment—analytical balances and precision laboratory scales
66 II F	Instruments and Laboratory Equipment—*amplifiers*: low frequency, power, pulse, RF, and microwave
66 II G	Instruments and Laboratory Equipment—graphic recording instruments
66 II H	Instruments and Laboratory Equipment—measuring and test instruments
66 II I & J	Instruments and Laboratory Equipment—microwave and low frequency instruments, and RF components
66 II K	Instruments and Laboratory Equipment—data acquisition systems
66 II L	Instruments and Laboratory Equipment—power supplies, transducers, and servomechanisms and components

66 II M	Instruments and Laboratory Equipment—spectrophotometers, densitometers, liquid scintillation systems, multichannel pulse height analyzers, spectrometers, photometers, and polarograph analysis equipment
66 II N	Instruments and Laboratory Equipment—analyzers, chromatographs, colony counters, blood analysis systems, dilutors, pipetters, electrophoresis equipment, and image analysis systems
66 II O	Instruments and Laboratory Equipment—laboratory apparatus, laboratory and pharmacy furniture, and laboratory and clinical refrigerators and freezers
66 II Q	Instruments and Laboratory Equipment—oceanographic, environmental, and weather
66 III	Instruments and Laboratory Equipment—time recorders, date and time stamps, and card racks
66 V A	Instruments and Laboratory Equipment—solar and wind energy systems, subsystems, and components
66 VI A	Laboratory Equipment—glassware and supplies
67 II B	Photographic Supplies—film, chemicals, and photographic paper
67 III B	Photographic Equipment—cameras, projectors, and developing and finishing equipment
67 IV A	Microphotographic Supplies and Mobile Projection Stands—direct-positive and thermal developing duplicating film and mobile projection stands
67 IV B	Microphotographic Equipment and Supplies—cameras, projectors, printers, developing and duplicating equipment, computer output microfilmer, and chemicals, film, and paper
68 I A	Chemicals and Chemical Products—bulk sodium chloride
68 I B	Chemicals and Chemical Products—calcium chloride
68 I C	Chemicals and Chemical Products—bleach, laundry and household (sodium hypochlorite; calcium hypochlorite)
68 II A	Chemicals and Chemical Products—herbicides
68 III A	Chemicals and Chemical Products—medical gases
68 III C	Chemicals and Chemical Products—dry ice
68 III D	Chemicals and Chemical Products—liquefied petroleum gases
68 III E & F	Chemicals and Chemical Products—refrigerant fluorocarbons and sulfur hexafluoride
68 III G	Chemicals and Chemical Products—helium
68 III H	Chemicals and Chemical Products—fire extinguishing fluorocarbons
68 III K	Chemicals and Chemical Products—*oxygen*: aviator's breathing
68 III L	Chemicals and Chemical Products—industrial gases in high-pressure cylinders
68 III M	Chemicals and Chemical Products—industrial gases, liquid, in bulk and in low-pressure cylinders
68 V	Chemicals and Chemical Products—boiler feedwater and air conditioning compounds and polyphosphate glass
68 VI	Chemicals and Chemical Products—sanitizers, deodorants, and disinfectant cleaners
69	Training Courses, Aids, and Devices—teaching, reading, and test scoring machines, tachistoscopes, multimedia programmers, programmed learning materials, rear screen projectors, and training programs

70 X	Data Processing Storage and Related Equipment—storage, handling, and transport equipment for data processing supplies, and sound reduction equipment
70 XI	Data Processing Supplies—edp 1/2'' tape, 1600 6250 bpi, and wraparound tape reel bands
71 I A	Household Furniture—ranch style
71 I B	Household Furniture—early American and eighteenth century English and American reproductions
71 II A	Household Furniture—upholstered living room
71 II B	Household Furniture—modular multiple and individual seating units
71 III	Household Furniture—Danish, traditional, and modern styles
71 V A	Office Furniture—table (72'' × 30'') with folding legs and chairs, folding, wood and metal
71 V B	Office Furniture—bulletin boards and key cabinets
71 V C	Office Furniture—steel vertical blueprint filing cabinets, roll drawing files, and high-density movable shelf filing cabinet systems
71 V D	Office and Field Furniture—*office furniture*: map and plan filing cabinets and folding tables; *modular steel field office furniture*: filing cabinet, desk top, and end folding table
71 V E	Office Furniture—contemporary steel filing cabinets, shelf files, card files, and insulated files
71 V F	Office Furniture—freestanding partitions
71 VI A	Office Furniture—executive traditional wood
71 VII A	Household Furniture—metal indoor-outdoor, recreation room, lobby and reception room
71 VII B	Household Furniture—metal frame dormitory furniture for quarters use
71 VIII A	Office Furniture—executive unitized wood
71 X A & B	Furniture—special purpose and classroom; auditorium seating; and cafeteria and conference tables
71 XI A & B	Office Furniture—security filing cabinets, safes, vault doors, and map and plan files
71 XII A	Office Furniture—executive modern, wood, and metal
71 XIII A & B	Library Furniture—wood or metal
71 XIV A	Shop Furniture—desks, benches, and tables
71 XV	Household Furniture—traditional wood, and dinette table and chair
71 XVI B	Household Furniture—motel type and sofa beds
71 XVII	Hospital Furniture—patient room
71 XIX	Furniture—contemporary wall units for office use
71 XX	Household Furniture—contemporary oak furniture
71 XXI	Office Furniture—acoustical partitions
71 XXII	Furniture—lounge and reception room, and recliners
71 XXIII	Household and Office Accessories—artificial plants, planters, urns, and wall art
71 XXV	Furniture—storage cabinets
71 XXVI A	Casual Style and Household Furniture—rattan, plastic, and outdoor metal casual furniture, and dinette furniture
71 XXVII A	Furniture—office and household, centurion by federal prison industries
71 XXVII B	Office Furniture—contemporary centurion by federal prison industries
71 XXVIII A	Office Furniture—lateral files, special sizes and uses

71 XXIX A	Office Furniture—storage and sorting cabinets, and plastic storage bins
71 XXX A	Office Furniture—cabinets and desks, card punch and programmers
71 XXXI A	Furniture—directory boards
72 I A	Household and Commercial Furnishings—carpets, rugs, carpet tiles, and carpet cushions
72 I B	Household and Commercial Furnishings—*floor coverings*: tile, linoleum, and vinyl sheet
72 I C	Household and Commercial Furnishings—entranceway carpet mats and mattings
72 I D	Household and Commercial Furnishings—special purpose carpet
72 II	Household and Commercial Furnishings—*window shades*: cloth, vinyl, and fiberglass
72 III A	Commercial Furnishings—shopping handcarts (nesting)
72 V	Household and Commercial Furnishings—draperies and coordinating bedspreads, drapery hardware; cubicle curtains and matching shower curtains, cubicle hardware; and hospital mattresses
72 VI A	Household and Commercial Furnishings—venetian blinds
72 VII A	Household and Commercial Furnishings—plastic trash receptacles
73 III	Food Service, Handling, Refrigeration, Storage, and Cleaning Equipment—cabinet/showcase (nonrefrigerant/nonheating), cooking equipment, dishwashing equipment, food preparation equipment, food serving equipment, laundry equipment, refrigerant equipment, and other miscellaneous items
73 IV A	Appliances—household gas ranges
73 IV B	Appliances—commercial and household electric ranges
73 V A	Appliances—household dishwashing machines
74 I	Office Machines—electric typewriters (nonportable), composing, photocomposing, and word processing machines
74 II & III	Office Machines—adding, calculating, dictating machines, cash registers, and miscellaneous office machines
74 IV	Visable Record Equipment—book, cabinet, and individual style frames; posting and ledger trays; tub files and cabinets; desk style rotary and V-type files; automatic and floor type rotary files; microform housings; catalog racks; control boards; and visible index binders
74 V	Office Machines—manual typewriters, nonportable and portable
74 VIII	Office Machines—electric erasers, and embossing and stencil-cutting machines
74 XIII A	Word Processing Supplies—magnetic data recording cards
75 I C	Office Supplies—*special use paper*: engineering and draftsman-graph, drawing, tracing, overlay plastic sheets, cardboard and paper embossing; index sheet sets for looseleaf binders; and labels for automatic data processing
75 I D	Office Supplies—blotting paper and supplies
75 II A	Office Supplies—pencils, label marking tapes, chart supplies, desk correspondence sorters, suspended file folders, plastic book jackets, plastic desk trays and sorters, out-of-typewriter correction material, labels, labeling machines, and data binders
75 II B	Office Supplies—looseleaf binders, label tapes, stapling machines, hand labeling machines, water color sets, map tacks, dry transfer sheets, bristol cardboard, pamphlet files, typist copyholders, duplicating stencils, lead pointers, file drawer frames, gummed tape dispensers, pressure-sensitive adhesive tape, and transparent pressure-sensitive index tabs

75 IV A & B	Office Supplies—rubber stamps
75 IV C	Office Supplies—pre-inked rubber stamps
75 V	Office Supplies—*envelopes*: mailing, printed and plain
75 VII	Office Supplies—U. S. Government national credit cards
75 VIII A	Office Supplies—tabulating cards, aperture cards, and copy cards
75 IX	Office Devices—contemporary desk accessories
76 I	Publications—dictionaries, encyclopedias, other reference books and pamphlets, maps, atlases, charts, and globes
76 II	Publications—law, tax, and reporting periodicals
76 III A & B	Publications—medical, trade, text, and technical books; and pamphlets
77 I	Home Entertainment Equipment—phonograph records, 8-track tape cartidges, and cassettes
77 II	Musical Instruments—instruments, amplifiers, accessories, and spare parts
77 III	Home Entertainment Equipment—televisions, radios, phonographs, combination sets, and video cassette recorders
78 I A	Recreational and Athletic Equipment—athletic and sporting equipment
78 I B	Athletic and Recreational Equipment—indoor recreational and gymnasium equipment
78 I C	Athletic and Recreational Equipment—outdoor recreational equipment
79 I A & B	Cleaning Equipment and Supplies—vacuum cleaners, carpet shampooers, floor polishing and scrubbing machines
79 II A	Cleaning Equipment and Supplies—liquid and powdered dishwashing compounds (contractor's standard commercial supplies of detergents, rinse additives, and related supplies) with contractor supplied, installed, and maintained accessory dispensing systems.
80 I A	Paint—tree marking
80 II A	Paint—gloss and semi-gloss latex
81 I A	Packaging and Packing Supplies—cushioning material
81 II A	Packaging and Packing Supplies—steel and nonmetallic strapping
84 II A	Clothing and Furnishings—special purpose clothing
84 II B	Clothing and Furnishings—footwear and special purpose clothing
84 III A	Clothing and Furnishings—men's and young men's
84 III B & C	Clothing and Furnishings—misses', women's, boys', girls', and infants'
84 IV	Jewelry—civilian career service emblems and career service award plaques
84 V A	Clothing and Footware—athletic and recreational
87 IV	Agricultural Supplies—seeds
87 V	Agricultural Supplies—fertilizers and hydrated lime
89 I	Subsistence—nonperishable
89 IV A	Subsistence—freeze-dried foods
93 II	Nonmetallic Fabricated Materials—reflectorized fabric, sheeting, and tape
99 III	Miscellaneous Supplies—cutout letters, numbers, pavement striping tape, vehicle markings, and static ground markers
99 VI A	Trophies and Awards—trophies, plaques, awards, cups, pins, and ribbons
733	Transcripts—stenographic reporting services
733 III	Services—visual arts, graphics, and associated services
739 I A	Services—rental and servicing of portable toilets

739 VI B	Services—rental of measuring and test instruments
739 VII A	Services—*microfilming* surveys, filming, film processing, aperture card mounting, roll to roll duplication, microfiche duplication, film inspection, and security storage
751	Motor Vehicle Rental/Traveler's Pocket Guide—without driver
781 I & II	Professional Film Processing and Videotape Processing Services—motion picture, filmstrip, and slide; videotape duplication
782	Distribution of Audiovisual Materials (Free Loan)—motion picture films, video tapes, cassettes, filmstrips, slides, audio tapes, and related materials
807 I A	Services—clinical laboratory tests (human and/or veterinarian); electrocardiogram analysis service, tissue microslide preparation, (human and/or veterinarian); and rental and service of specialized medical equipment
823	Services—lending library

Most of the schedules carry a large number of individual items under the various categories and subcategories listed. However, you do not need to supply all items listed on a schedule but may be listed for whichever items/services you can offer. You can be on more than one schedule, if you have offerings which fit more than one schedule. However, you cannot be on more than one schedule for the same item or service but must decide which schedule to apply for in those cases where your offering might fit on more than one schedule. For example, you could list rubber stamps on schedule 75 IV A & B, and pre-inked rubber stamps on 75 IV C, but you could not list these items on any other schedule or on the same schedule, since they appear on different schedules. At the same time, you might choose between 71 V D and 71 V E for filing cabinets, but could not list the same filing cabinet on both.

Some of the schedules are mandatory—certain government offices are required to order certain of their supplies from the schedules only—while others may use the schedules or not as they see fit. Lists of these are included in the GSA Program Guide.

The schedules listed here are all national schedules: federal agencies may order from these lists anywhere in the country. The GSA Program Guide carries also a listing of regional schedules issued by regional GSA offices and used only within the areas for which they are issued.

All the items listed in the schedules are items not carried in stock in GSA stores but are "common-use" items. GSA therefore authorizes federal agencies to order these items directly from the contractors listed in the schedules at the terms stipulated in the schedules.

You may note that the schedules number coincides with the numbers under which requirements for such items are listed in the *Commerce Business Daily;* that is, the CBD utilizes the FSC (Federal Stock Code) numbers to classify requirements for which bids are solicited.

How to Apply

Order, from your nearest GSA office, the following forms and publications:

1. GSA Form 1382, *List of Commodities and Services*
2. GSA Program Guide, Stock No. 022-005-0012-0
3. Standard Form 129, *Bidders' Mailing List Application*
4. GSA Form 3038, *Bidders' Mailing List Application Code Sheet*
5. The GSA publication, *Government Business Opportunities*

Read the latter publication, although it will not tell you more than you have already learned (perhaps less, as many find). Then fill out the Standard Form 129 and the GSA Form 3038 (after scanning the Program Guide to determine which schedules you wish to bid for). When the schedules come up for bid, you will receive an Invitation to Bid, which you will submit. In most cases, as long as your prices are in line and your products match the specifications (if any exist for those items), you should have no difficulty negotiating a Basic Ordering Agreement and getting "on the schedule."

This does not mean that you will begin to receive orders automatically, although you may get some spontaneously. It does mean, however, that you may now go out to all government agencies, including those state and local government agencies that qualify (almost all who receive federal funds of any kind qualify) and solicit business, telling them that you are "on the schedule" and supplying your contract number.

You will find it much easier to do business with the government as a result.

A Few of the Departments, Agencies, and Bureaus Encountered in Pursuit of Contracts

Department of Agriculture

Conservation, Research and Education
   Agricultural Research Service
   Cooperative State Research Service
   Extension Service
   Forest Service
   National Agricultural Library
   Soil Conservation Service
Economics, Policy Analysis and Budget
   Budget, Planning and Evaluation
   Economic Management Support Center
   Economic Research Service
   Farmer Cooperative Service
   Statistical Reporting Service
Food and Consumer Services
   Food and Nutrition Service
   Food, Safety and Quality Service
International Affairs and Commodity Programs
   Agricultural Stabilization and Conservation Service
   Federal Crop Insurance Corporation
   Foreign Agricultural Service
Marketing Services
   Agricultural Marketing Service
   Animal and Plant Health Service
   Federal Grain Inspection Service
   Packers and Stockyards Administration
Rural Development
   Farmers Home Administration
   Rural Development Service
   Rural Electrification Administration

Department of Commerce (DOC)

Domestic and International Business Administration
   Bureau of Domestic Commerce

Bureau of East–West Trade
Bureau of International Commerce
Bureau of Resources and Trade Assistance
Economic Development Administration
Maritime Administration
National Fire Prevention and Control Administration
National Oceanic and Atmospheric Administration (NOAA)
Office of the Chief Economist
    Bureau of the Census
    Bureau of Economic Analysis
Office of Minority Business Enterprise (OMBE)
Policy
Science and Technology
    National Bureau of Standards (NBS)
    National Technical Information Service (NTIS)
    Office of Telecommunications
    Patent and Trademark Office
Tourism
    United States Travel Service

Department of Defense (DOD)

Defense Audit Service
Defense Civil Preparedness Agency
Defense Advanced Research Projects Agency
Defense Communications Agency
Defense Contract Audit Agency
Defense Intelligence Agency
Defense Investigative Service
Defense Logistics Agency
Defense Mapping Agency
Defense Nuclear Agency
Defense Security Assistance Agency

Department of the Air Force

Aerospace Defense Command
Air Force Logistics Command
Air Force Systems Command
Air Training Command
Air University
Headquarters Command, USAF
Military Airlift Command
Strategic Air Command
Tactical Air Command

Department of the Army

Military Academy (West Point)
Army Matériel Development and Readiness Command

Department of the Navy

Naval Matériel Command
Bureau of Medicine and Surgery
Military Sealift Command

Bureau of Naval Personnel
Oceanographer of the Navy
Marine Corps

Department of Energy

Federal Energy Regulatory Commission
Energy Information Administration
Economic Regulatory Administration
Office of Energy Research

Department of Health, Education and Welfare

Education Division
  Institute of Museum Services
  National Institute of Education
  Office of Education
Health Care Financing Administration
Human Development Services
  Administration on Aging
  Administration for Children, Youth and Families
  Administration for Handicapped Individuals
  Administration for Native Americans
  Administration for Public Services
Public Health Service
  Alcohol, Drug Abuse, and Mental Health Administration
    National Institute on Alcohol Abuse and Alcoholism
  Center for Disease Control
  Food and Drug Administration
  Bureau of Biologics
  Bureau of Foods
  Bureau of Medical Devices
  Bureau of Veterinary Medicine
  National Center for Toxicological Research
Health Resources Administration
  Bureau of Health Manpower
  Bureau of Health Planning and Resources Development
  National Center for Health Services Research
  National Center for Health Statistics
Health Services Administration
  Bureau of Community Health Services
  Bureau of Medical Services
  Indian Health Service
National Institutes of Health
  Clinical Center
  National Cancer Institute
  National Eye Institute
  National Heart, Lung and Blood Institute
  National Institute of Allergy and Infectious Diseases
  National Institute of Arthritis Metabolism and Infectious Diseases
  National Institute of Child Health and Human Development
  National Institute for Dental Research
  National Institute of Environmental Health Sciences
  National Institute of General Medical Science

National Institute of Neurological and Communicative Disorders and Stroke
National Library of Medicine
Research Grants Division
Research Resources Division
Research Services Division
Social Security Administration

Department of Housing and Urban Development

Government National Mortgage Association
New Community Development Corporation
Federal Insurance Administration
Federal Disaster Assistance Administration

Department of the Interior

Energy and Minerals
  Bureau of Mines
  Geological Survey
  Office of Minerals Policy and Research Analysis
  Mining Enforcement and Safety Administration (MESA)
Fish and Wildlife and Parks
  Bureau of Outdoor Recreation
  National Park Service
  U.S. Fish and Wildlife Service
Indian Affairs
Land and Water Resources
  Bureau of Land Management (BLM)
  Bureau of Reclamation
  Office of Water Research and Technology

Department of Justice

Federal Bureau of Investigation (FBI)
Immigration and Naturalization Service
Drug Enforcement Administration (DEA)
Law Enforcement Assistance Administration (LEAA)
Community Relations Service

Department of Labor

Employment Standards Administration
Employment and Training
  Bureau of Apprenticeship and Training
  U.S. Employment Service (USES)
  Job Corps
Occupational Safety and Health Administration (OSHA)
Bureau of Labor Statistics (BLS)

Department of State

Agency for International Development (AID)

Department of Transportation

Federal Aviation Administration (FAA)
Federal Highway Administration
Federal Railroad Administration (FRA)

National Highway Traffic Safety Administration (NHTSA)
St. Lawrence Seaway Development Corporation
Urban Mass Transportation Administration (UMTA)
U.S. Coast Guard (USCG)

Department of the Treasury

Bureau of Alcohol, Tobacco, and Firearms
Bureau of Engraving and Printing
Bureau of Government Financial Operations
Bureau of the Mint
Bureau of the Public Debt
Federal Law Enforcement Training Center
Internal Revenue Service
Office of Revenue Sharing
U.S. Customs Service
U.S. Secret Service

ACTION

Civil Aeronautics Board

U.S. Civil Service Commission (CSC)
Bureau of Training

Consumer Product Safety Commission (CPSC)

Environmental Protection Agency (EPA)

Federal Communications Commission (FCC)

General Services Administration (GSA)

Automated Data and Telecommunications Service
Federal Supply Service
Public Buildings Service
National Archives and Records Service

Government Printing Office (GPO)

National Academy of Sciences

National Aeronautics and Space Administration (NASA)

National Science Foundation

U.S. Postal Service

Small Business Administration

Veterans Administration

A Typical Work Statement and Instruction (for a Small Contract)

SECTION C

INSTRUCTIONS, CONDITIONS, AND NOTICES TO OFFERORS

a.   Proposals will be typewritten or printed on letter-sized paper and will be legible in the required number of copies. Though legible, neat, orderly, and comprehensive proposals are required, elaborately ornate or excessively costly presentations which feature expensive covers and bindings, superfluous artwork, etc., are not encouraged and are not required.

Proposals shall be presented as briefly and concisely as possible consistent with the desired content and other requirements stipulated in this request for proposal.

    b.   Detailed outline and approach of the proposer's offer.

    c.   Data necessary to support and clarify offer.

    d.   General background, experience, and qualifications of offeror as well as those personnel to be assigned to this work.

    e.   Reference to work of a similar or related military program for Department of Defense or Army Materials and Mechanics Research Center.

    f.   Current availability of equipment and facilities to be used for this work.

    g.   Composition of work group to be assigned to this work; time of each to be allocated to the work and résumés of said personnel.

    h.   List of subcontractor(s) or consultants, if any, which may be required or contemplated by the offeror in this work.

    i.   Include any deviations or exceptions or conditions in regard to the scope of work taken by the offeror.

    j.   All financial information or offer amount breakdowns in support of prices offered for the work shall be, if included in the same document as the technical proposal, a separate, easily removable section thereof. A separate document for prices offered and support thereof may be submitted if preferred.

Note: Proposals which merely offer to perform work in accordance with the technical purchase descriptions, or which fail to present more than cost and delivery data without elaboration, will be deemed nonresponsive and will not be further considered.

SECTION D

EVALUATION AND AWARD FACTORS

    1. The government will select for award that offer from a responsive, responsible offeror which, after considering cost and other factors, represents the lowest price to the government.

    2. Offerors who have government-owned property in their possession are procluded from using such property in connection with the procurement being effected hereby, unless said property is covered by an appropriate contractual instrument requiring fair rental payment to the government and such rental is computed in accordance with existing regulations.

    3. If an offer submitted in response to this solicitation is favorably considered, a preaward survey team may contact your facility to determine your financial and technical ability to perform. Current financial statements and other pertinent data should be available at that time.

The following factors, other than price, not necessarily in the order stated, will be the basis for evaluating technical proposals:

    a. Demonstrate technical competence in rubber technology.

    b. Outline and approach to accomplish the work and understanding of the requirements of the work.

    c. Past experience in similar commercial or government projects.

    d. Adequacy of organization and personnel.

Factor a will carry twice the weight of factor b.

Factor b will carry one-half ($1/2$) the weight of factor a.

Factor c will carry approximately one-third ($1/3$) the weight of factor a.

Factor d will carry one-fifth ($1/5$) the weight of factor a.

Basis of Award

The government may award a contract based on initial offers received without discussion of such offers. Accordingly each initial offer should be submitted on the most favorable terms from a price and technical standpoint which the offeror can submit to the government.

SECTION F

WORK DESCRIPTION

Part II—Schedule

F-1. The contractor shall perform the following work requirements:

F-1.1. Beginning with the effective date of contract and continuing for ten (10) months, the contractor as an independent contractor, not as as an agent of the government, shall furnish personnel, materials, equipment, and facilities necessary to update MIL-HDBK-149A and prepare a final draft to be used for "review-and-comments" phase followed by all necessary corrections or other changes either technical or editorial.

F-2. MIL-HDBK-149A shall be revised in order to reflect the current state of the art. The format for the specification shall be single-column unjustified. In addition to updating and editing the present edition, a final-draft camera-ready copy (orginal and two copies) for use in printing.

F-2.1. The preliminary draft text will be double-spaced to permit writing comments on each page, both between the lines and in the margins. All photographs will be submitted on $8 \times 10 \frac{1}{2}$ glossy prints (three each). All tables and line drawings will be drafts only, since they may be subject to considerable change. Copyright releases must be furnished. The preliminary draft shall be prepared in seven (7) months, then the government shall review for two (2) months and return to the contractor for correction. The final camera-ready copies shall be delivered in one (1) month from the date of return of the preliminary draft by the government.

SECTION H

DELIVERIES OR PERFORMANCE

1. Time of Delivery (1974 Apr)

(a) Delivery is desired by the government in accordance with the following schedule:

Item No.	Quantity	Time—Within the number of days stated below after the date of contract.
0001	1 Job	270 days
___	___	___
___	___	___

REQUIRED DELIVERY SCHEDULE

Item No.	Quantity	Time—Within the number of days stated below after the date of contract.
0001	1 Job	330 days
___	___	___
___	___	___

If the offeror is unable to meet the required delivery schedule, he may, without prejudice to the evaluation of his offer, set forth his proposed delivery schedule below.

If the offeror does not propose a different delivery schedule, the government's DESIRED delivery schedule shall apply.

OFFEROR'S PROPOSED DELIVERY SCHEDULE

(To Be Completed by Offeror)

Item No.   Quantity   Time—Within the number of days stated
below after the date of contract.

—————   —————   —————

—————   —————   —————

—————   —————   —————

2. Performance of required services under this contract shall be at the contractor's plant, located at ———
3. Period of performance of required services under this contract shall be as set forth below:

———days after date of award of contract.

Date of completion of this contract shall be —————.

Note: Above information shall be completed at time of award.

Proposal Checklist

1. Theme or Main Message. Is it introduced early? Maintained throughout the proposal? Clear and unequivocal? Responsive to customer's desires? Consistent?

2. Approach and Arguments. Clearly defined? "Proven"? Fresh and attention-getting without being radically new?

3. Editorial and Style. Is writing crystal clear? Unambiguous? Direct, to the point? Smooth flowing, with logical progression of ideas?

4. Responsiveness. Have you covered every point, "responded" to every specification? Used a response matrix? Addressed customer desires in all cases? (Especially for evaluation criteria.)

5. Proposed Program. Is program specific, detailed? Follow technical discussion? All deliverables, major tasks/functions clearly identified? Schedules stated? Clear, logical project organization?

6. Graphics. Have you used charts, illustrations effectively? Is proposed project flow-charted? Easy to read, to understand?

7. Résumés. Have they been tailored to requirements? Are they the best you have to offer? Are they right for the job? For the assigned functions?

8. Proposed Management. Is a good management plan presented? Good liaison with customer? Quality control? Is responsiveness to customer desires ensured? Is project importance to proposer shown?

9. Proposer's Credentials. Have you selected the best possible past projects to illustrate qualifications? Demonstrated relevance to proposed project? Described all relevant facilities, resources?

10. Costs. Consistent with proposed program, man loading, tasks, end products? Are all costs accounted for?

11. Transmittal Letter. Does it reflect theme, summarily? Sum up your credentials, your approach, your predicted (promised) results?

Glossary

advertised bid, advertised procurement: Procurement requiring public opening of bids, usually requires price quotes only; procured under IFB.

AEC: Atomic Energy Commission.

best and final offer: Invitation often extended to finalists in negotiated procurement to review and adjust prices before final decision on award.

bid set: Package of information and forms required to make bid; same as solicitation package.

bidders' conference: Conference held in advance of certain awards to provide more information and to answer questions.

BOA: Basic Ordering Agreement; contract for set rates, with quantity of work to be done indefinite.

CBD: Commerce Business Daily.

CPAF: Cost plus award fee; type of contract often used by NASA.

CPFF: Cost plus fixed fee; type of contract often used when costs are difficult to estimate in advance.

CSC: Civil Service Commission.

DCAA: Defense Contract Audit Agency; auditors for government, often called upon to audit contractors' books on large procurements.

DOL: Department of Labor.

DOT: Department of Transportation.

end product: Resultant item to be delivered, as a result of a contract.

ERDA: Energy Research and Development Administration.

evaluation criteria: The stated factors for evaluating a proposal.

FAA: Federal Aviation Administration; part of DOT.

FDA: Food and Drug Administration.

FEA: Federal Energy Administration.

FP: Fixed price (contract).

FRA: Federal Railroad Administration (part of DOT).

GSA: General Services Administration.

GSA Schedule: Directory listing firms and individuals holding BOAs with GSA for graphic arts services and related writing.

HEW: Health, Education and Welfare (Department of).

HSA: Health Services Administration.

HUD: Housing and Urban Development (Department of).

IFB: Information for Bid; see *advertised bid*.

indefinite quantity: See *BOA*.

labor–hour contract: Type of BOA, listing labor rates per hour.

LEAA: Law Enforcement Assistance Administration (part of Justice Department).

NASA: National Aviation and Aeronautics Administration.

negotiated procurement: Usually requiring a proposal, not necessarily awarded to low bidder, often involving negotiations before award made; usually solicited by RFP; see *RFP*.

NHTSA: National Highway Traffic Safety Administration (part of DOT).

NIDA: National Institute of Drug Abuse (part of HEW).

NIH: National Institutes of Health (part of HEW).

NIMH: National Institutes of Mental Health (part of HEW).

NLM: National Library of Medicine (part of HEW).

NOL: Naval Ordnance Laboratory.

nonresponsive: Characteristic of proposal or performance indicating bidder/contractor not responding to specified need of government; grounds for disqualification of bid, cancellation of contract.

NRL: Naval Research Laboratory.

OE: Office of Education (part of HEW).

OSHA: Occupational Safety and Health Administration (part of DOL).

PHS: Public Health Service (part of HEW).

preaward survey: Visit to bidder's facility, with inspection to verify ability to do job before awarding contract.

proposal: Response to RFP, describing what bidder proposes to do, how he will do it, what he estimates cost to be, what his qualifications are to do the job, why he should have contract.

purchase order: Shortcut method for buying goods or services, up to $10,000.

RFP: Request for Proposal; see *Proposal*.

RFQ: Request for Quotation; usually requires price only, not binding as a bid, but often used in place of RFP for small contract procurements.

SOW: Statement of Work, which is normally part of any solicitation package.

Standard Form 33: Used as first sheet and contracting form for most procurements.

Standard Form 60: Used to estimate costs for nondefense agencies.

Standard Form 129: Used to apply for inclusion on bidders' lists.

Standard Form 633: Same as Standard Form 60, used by defense agencies.

task order: Method for ordering work under a BOA.

T & M: Time and Material, a contract form somewhat along the lines of a BOA.

USAF: U.S. Air Force.

USCG: U.S. Coast Guard.

USDA: U.S. Department of Agriculture.

USPS: U.S. Postal Service.

Index

ACTION, 16
Agencies, U.S. Government, 13-25, 273-277
Departments, structures, and missions,
  Agriculture (USDA), 17
  Commerce, (DOC), 17-18
  Defense (DOD), 18
  Energy (DOE), 21-22
  Housing and Urban Development (HUD), 19
  Interior (DOI), 19-20
  Justice (DOJ), 20
  Labor (DOL), 20
  State, 20
  Transportation (DOT), 21
  Treasury, 21
guide to, *United States Government Manual*, 15
list of, 15-17, 273-277
location of, federal regions, 14
organizational units, 14-15
other agencies, structures, and missions
  Consumer Product Safety Commission (CPSC), 22, 25
  Economic Development Administration (EDA), 25
  Environmental Protection Agency (EPA), 22, 25
  General Services Administration (GSA), 22
  National Aeronautics and Space Administration (NASA), 23
  National Science Foundation (NSF), 23

Agencies, U.S. Government (*cont'd*)
  other agencies, structures, and missions (*cont'd*)
    Occupational Safety and Health Administration (OSHA), 25
    Postal Service (USPS), 23-24
    Small Business Administration (SBA), 23
Agency for International Development (AID), 20
Agriculture, Department of, 15, 17, 52
Air Force, U.S. (USAF), 15, 28, 52, 92
American Red Cross (ARC), 16, 17
AMTRAK, 17
Appalachian Regional Commission (ARC), 17
Architects and engineers, 249-251
  public advisory panels, 249
  special procedures, Standard Forms 254 and 255, 249
Argument, technical. *See* Technical argument
Armed Services Procurement Regulations (ASPR), 27. *See also* Procurement, government
Army, U.S. (USA), 11, 15, 24, 52, 134
Apollo, 29
Automated Data and Telecommunications Service (ADTS), 22

Ballistic Missile Early Warning System (BMEWS), 28
Best and final, 148. *See also* Negotiations
Bidders lists, application for, 46-48
Bid rooms, 49

Bid opportunities, learning of, 49
Bids,
    disqualification of, causes for, 69-70
    how to prepare and submit, 69-82
Brookings Institution, 4
Budget, federal, 4
Bureau of Indian Affairs (BIA), 20
Bureau of Labor Statistics (BLS), 20
Bureau of Land Management (BLM), 20

Cash flow, 162-163. *See also* Costs and
    costing
Center for Disease Control (CDC), 19
Changes, 67, 68. *See also* Costs and
    costing
Chart, organization, 142-143
Checklist, proposal, 280
Civil Aeronautics Board (CAB), 16
Civil Service Commission (CSC), 17
Coal Research, Office of, 20
Coast Guard, U.S. (USCG), 15, 20, 21
Commerce Business Daily (CBD), 8, 9,
    35-46, 52, 60
    cost of, 35
    goods and services listed in, 39-41
    how to order, 260
    how to read, 37
    how to use, 41-44
    illustration of, 36
Commerce, Department of (DOC), 4, 8,
    15, 17, 18, 25, 35, 36, 52, 258
    aids to business, 55, 57-60
Competition in procurement, 35
Congress, U.S., 13, 16, 24, 26, 52
Consultants, use of, 166
Consumer Product Safety Commission
    (CPSC), 16, 22, 25, 47
Contracts
    modifications and amendments to,
        176-177
    types of
        basic ordering agreement, 63
        cost plus fixed fee, 63
        fixed price, 61
        time and material, 63
Costs and costing, 146-168
    effect on evaluation, 147
    estimating, 148
    forms, government
        DD 633, 157-159
        SF 60, 158-159
    supporting in technical proposal,
        174-177

costs and costing (*cont'd*)
    types of costs
        cash flow, 162-163
        changes, 167-168
        direct and indirect, 149-151
        expense pools, 159-162
        G & A, 151-165
        overhead, 151-166
Cost proposal. *See also* Costs and
        costing
    separating from technical proposal,
        174
    supporting technical program,
        174-177
Customs Bureau, 21

Debriefing, 11
Defense, Department of (DOD), 15,
        18, 19, 52, 92, 155
    small business program of, 55
Departments, agencies, and bureaus,
        list of, 273-277
District of Columbia (DC), 16
Defense Supply Agency (DSA), 45, 52
Drug Enforcement Administration
        (DEA), 19, 20

Economic Development Administra-
        tion (EDA), 17, 18, 25, 55, 58, 59
Energy, Department of, 15, 20, 21,
        22, 29, 33, 47, 52, 53, 99. *See
        also* Energy Research and De-
        velopment Administration;
        Federal Energy Administration
Energy Research and Development
        Administration, 21, 33. *See also*
        Energy, Department of
Engineers, Corps of (C/E), 14, 52, 133,
        137
Environmental Protection Agency
        (EPA), 16, 17, 18, 22, 25, 30,
        52, 53
Equal Employment Opportunity
        Commission (EEOC), 16
Evaluation, proposals. *See* Proposal
        evaluation
Executive summary, the, 227-229

Farm Credit Administration (FCA),
        16
Federal Acquisition Regulations
        (FAR), 27

Federal Aviation Administration
(FAA), 15, 20
Federal Bureau of Investigation
(FBI), 20
Federal Communications Commission
(FCC), 16
Federal Energy Administration (FEA),
21. *See also* Energy, Department
of
Federal Highway Administration
(FHA), 21
Federal Power Commission (FPC),
21, 22
Federal Procurement Regulations
(FPR), 27. *See also* Procure-
ment, government
Federal Railroad Administration (FRA), 21
Federal regions, 13, 14
Federal Register, The, 49
Federal stock numbers, 45
Federal Supply schedules
general information, 264-265
how to apply for, 272-273
list of, 265-272
Federal Supply Service (FSS), 22, 31, 48
Federal Trade Commission (FTC), 16
Fish and Wildlife Service, U.S., 28
Flowcharts, 130-135
example of, 131
how to develop, 130-133
types of, 133-135
Food and Drug Administration (FDA),
15, 19
Foreign import damage. *See also* Labor,
Department of
EDA program for, 58
Forest Service, U.S. (FS), 17
Formats, proposal. *See* Proposal formats
and packaging
Forms, government. *See also* Costs and
costing
illustration of, 65
SF 33, 64-65, 66, 69

G & A, 27-28. *See also* Costs and
costing
General Accounting Office (GAO), 11,
16, 32, 85
General Services Administration (GSA),
12, 16, 17, 22, 31, 45, 51, 52, 60,
257, 258
business service centers of, 56
regional offices of, 260

Glossary of terms, 281-282
Goddard Space Flight Center (GSFC),
22
Government markets. *See* Markets, U.S.
Government
Government Printing Office (GPO), 16,
31, 32. *See also* Markets, U.S.
Government, for printing
offices of, 263

Health, Education and Welfare (HEW),
Department of, 15, 19, 29, 30,
51-52
Health Resources Administration
(HRA), 19
Health Services Administration (HSA),
19
Housing and Urban Development
(HUD), Department of, 15, 19, 32

Illustrations, use of, 236. *See also*
Proposal formats and packaging
Information Agency, U.S. (USIA), 17
Information for Bid (IFB), 37-39,
69-70
forms for, 64-65
rules for, 69-70
Innovations, proposed, 186-187
Interior, Department of (DOI), 16, 19,
52
Internal Revenue Service (IRS), 21
Interstate Commerce Commission
(ICC), 16

Job Corps, 20
Justice, Department of (DOJ), 16, 19,
20

Labor, Department of (DOL), 16, 20,
26, 30, 51, 58, 215
role in foreign import damage, 58
Law Enforcement Assistance Administration (LEAA), 19, 20
Library of Congress, 16

Management and Budget, Office of
(OMB), 14, 16
Marine Corps, U.S. (USMC), 18, 21
Maritime Commission, U. S., 16, 17
Markets, U.S. Government
analysis of, 28-34
for commodities and supply con-
tracts, 31

Markets, U.S. Government (*cont'd*)
  for custom hardware, 29
  for custom services, 29-30
  facts, general, 10
  help in selling to, 54-60
  for management services, 33-34
  overview of, 3-5
  for printing, 31-32
  prospecting in, 35-53
Milestone chart, example of, 136-137
Mining Enforcement and Safety Administration (MESA), 20

National Academy of Sciences (NAS), 17
National Aeronautics and Space Administration (NASA), 11, 16, 17, 23, 27, 30, 33, 51, 52, 85, 91, 103, 116, 253
  aid for minority enterprise, 56, 58
National Archives and Records Service (ARS), 22
National Cancer Institute (NCI), 19, 47
National Heart and Lung Institute (NHLI), 19
National Highway Traffic Safety Administration (NHTSA), 21
National Institute of Education (NIE), 19
National Institutes of Health (NIH), 15, 19
National Library of Medicine (NLM), 19
Naval Academy, U.S., 33
Navy, U.S. (USN), 15, 18, 28, 29, 52, 69, 92
  aid for minority enterprise, 58
Negotiations, 252-256
  best and final offers, 252
  competitive range, 252
  importance of costs in, 254-255
  meaning of "negotiation," 252
  six possible positions, 254
  who should participate, 256

Occupational Safety and Health Administration (OSHA), 6, 15, 20, 25, 51
Oceanic and Atmospheric Administration, National (NOAA), 17
Office of Economic Opportunity (OEO), 16, 31, 53
Office of Education (OE), 19, 33
Office of Federal Procurement Policy (OFPP), 27

Office of Management and Budget (OMB), 4, 16
Office of Minority Business Enterprise (OMBE), 17, 18, 55, 57, 258
Office of Oil and Gas, 20
Overhead. *See* Costs and costing

Patent Office, 17
Pension Benefit Guaranty Corporation (PBGC), 31
Persuasive writing. *See* Writing, persuasive; Proposalmanship
Postal Service Training and Development Institute (PST&DI), 6, 53
Postal Service, U.S. (USPS), 5, 17, 23-24, 31, 52, 53, 60, 76, 94, 204. *See also* Postal Service Training and Development Institute
Pricing. *See also* Costs and costing
  danger of pricing too low, 171-174
  handling the hard-to-price requirement, 177-179
Procurement, government. *See also* Federal Supply schedules; Federal Supply Service; Markets, U.S. Government
  centralized, 60
  mechanisms of, 61-68
  regulations, 27
Production, proposal. *See* Proposal production
Progress payments, 61
Project, proposed
  management, 141
  management control, 141
  organization, 142-148
Proposal, cost. *See* Cost proposal
Proposal evaluation
  best and final, 86-87
  criteria for, 83
Proposal formats and packaging, 218-253
  appendices and exhibits, 239-240
  basic considerations, 220
  credibility, 238-239
  executive summary, 227-230
  letter of transmittal, 241-243
  miscellaneous format matters, 235
  narrative hooks, 225
  outline, suggested
    discussion, 221-222
    experience and qualifications, 223
    front matter, 221

Proposal formats and packaging (*cont'd*)
  outline, suggested (*cont'd*)
    highlights, 224
    introduction, 221
    proposed program, 222
    philosophy, 237
    response matrix, 231-233
    résumés, 233-234
    title page, 230
    titling illustrations, 236
Proposalmanship, 91-114. *See also* Writing, persuasive
  meaning of, 82
  strategies in, 92
  strategies, evolution of, 94-138
    detail as a strategy, 137-138
    graphics method for, 103-110
    intelligence-gathering for, 97-98
    RFP analysis, 98, 101
    storyboarding method for, 111-114
    types of strategy, 98-100
Proposal intelligence-gathering, methods for
  Freedom of Information Act, using, 116
  miscellaneous methods, 120-123
  at preproposal conference, 119-120
  through RFP analysis, 117-119
Proposal production, 244-248
  composition and artwork, 244-245
  duplicating, 245-246
  handling oversized drawings, 245-246
Proposal, technical. *See* Technical proposal
Proposal, unsolicited, 49
Proposal writing. *See* Proposalmanship
Proprietaries, selling to government agencies, 45
Proprietary information, safeguarding, 179-180
Protests, 11, 84-85
  Fairchild *v* GE case, 11, 85
  role of GAO, 85
Public Buildings Service (PBS), 22
Public Health Service (PHS), 15, 19, 53

RCA, 28, 29
Request for Proposal (RFP), 37, 39, 71-74, 114-145. *See also* Proposalmanship
  advantages of vague RFP, 114-115
  form for, 64-65
  reasons for issuing, 71-74
  vague versus detailed, 114

Request for Quotation (RFQ), 38-39
Research & Development (R&D)
  general, 28, 29
  solicitations for, 67, 72
  sources sought, 42-44
  targets for, 52
Résumés, 140-145, 233-234. *See also* Proposalmanship; Writing, persuasive

Small Business Act, 11, 25, 59
Small Business Administration (SBA), 16, 22-23, 25, 32, 33, 54-57, 59, 261-263
  offices of, 261-263
  programs of, 54-55, 57, 59
Small purchases, government, 4, 50
Smithsonian Institution, 16
Social and Rehabilitation Service (SRS), 19
Social Security Administration (SSA), 19
Solicitations, types, 61-69
  Information for Bid (IFB), 61, 62, 64, 66, 69
  Request for Proposal (RFP), 61, 62, 64, 66, 70-71
  Request for Quotation (RFQ), 61, 66, 67
Sports Fisheries and Wildlife, Bureau of, 20
Standards, National Bureau of (NBS), 17
State, Department of, 16, 20, 258
Strategies, technical/program, 124-138. *See also* Proposalmanship; Writing, persuasive
  brainstorming for ideas, 130
  detail as strategy, 137-138
  developing program strategies, 127-130
  logical argument, 126-127
  the unique selling point, 125-126

Technical argument, 185-186. *See also* Writing, persuasive
Technical Information Service, National (NTIS), 17
Technical proposal. *See also* Proposalmanship; Writing, persuasive
  as an offer, 237
  as a sales presentation, 182, 191-193
  separating from cost proposal, 174
  unsolicited, 49
Transportation, Department of (DOT), 15, 16, 20, 52
Treasury, Department of, 16, 20, 21

United States Government Manual, 15
Unsolicited proposal, 49
Urban Mass Transportation Administra-
tion, 21
Useful publications, other, 259-260

Veterans Administration (VA), 17

Water Resources Research, Office of, 20

Work Statement. *See also* Proposalmanship
typical, 277-280
Writing, persuasive. *See also* Proposalmanship
achieving credibility, 238-240
art of, 182-185
communication in, 188-191, 198-201
good and bad writing, 205-217
outlining and planning, 212-213